ESCAPE
FROM
DANNEMORA

Michael Benson

ESCAPE FROM DANNEMORA

Richard Matt,

David Sweat,

and the

Great Adirondack

Manhunt

ForeEdge

ForeEdge

An imprint of University Press of New England

www.upne.com

© 2017 Michael Benson

All rights reserved

Manufactured in the United States of America

Designed by Mindy Basinger Hill

Typeset in Minion Pro

For permission to reproduce any of the material
in this book, contact Permissions, University Press
of New England, One Court Street, Suite 250,
Lebanon NH 03766; or visit www.upne.com

Paperback ISBN: 978-1-61168-976-1

Ebook ISBN: 978-1-5126-0044-5

Library of Congress Cataloging-in-Publication data
available upon request

5   4   3   2   1

To the loving memory of

Rita Alice Gertrude Treu Benson

1932–2015

CONTENTS

Illustrations follow page 118

AUTHOR'S NOTE

Although this is a true story, some names and locations have been changed to protect the privacy of the innocent. When possible, the spoken word has been quoted verbatim. However, when that is not possible, conversations have been reconstructed as closely as possible to reality based on the recollections of those who spoke and heard the words. In places there has been a slight editing of spoken words, but only to improve readability. The denotations and connotations of the words remain unaltered. In some cases, witnesses are credited with verbal quotes that in reality only occurred in written form. Some characters may be composites.

ESCAPE FROM DANNEMORA

UP
NORTH

Claustrophobia had nothing to do with it. If you were tunneling into the side of a mountain, or deep into the earth in search of ore, that might feel cramped. But this was different. It wasn't tunneling in. It was tunneling *out*. And once you were out of your cell, out the hole in the corner near the floor, onto the six-story catwalk on the other side, and into the musty maze of institutional infrastructure—a three-dimensional blueprint of access routes and rat runs—you could feel it: the flicking lick of incipient freedom.

About three minutes in you had to shimmy down, popping out in the prison's underground tunnel system. Ha! The beast had dug her own tunnels. How else could the maintenance guys fix a broken pipe? One wrung of the ladder after another, just another hundred feet of slithering through the pipe till you could walk again.

Out of A Block—they called it "Honor Block," another joke—and under the laundry facility, it was like a military op; the key was to control your breathing, nice and steady, and focus on the game plan. Walking like Quasimodo now, hunched over, and then squeezing through a hole to the system of a neighboring cellblock.

You didn't want to go out of your way to make a racket, of course, but you didn't have to stay quiet. Siberia was never quiet. Time was an all-quiet command at 10:00 p.m. that made you put on your headphones. If you disobeyed, guards would go into the catwalks, turn off your power. Inmates complained, and the administration took the prisoners' side, nice, and took the keys to the catwalks away from the guards. Now the air was alive with a constant syncopation of scattered and truncated sounds, human and mechanical, natural and artificial, and the bulk of the clamor was vague and distant, until the brain interpreted it all as crying.

Every inmate in A Block, and between A Block and the Wall, had heard the poltergeists banging tin drums up and down the heating system, dragging the heavy chains of their sins through the underworld like the ghost of Jacob

Marley. So none now gave a thought to the soft and unidentified whimper of slinking men working somewhere in the distance below with little light or air.

If the guys who designed the prison had run the pipe two feet deeper, you might've never known it was there. But it was just under the surface, so that it caused a goddamn speed bump in the rec yard.

It had taken so long to cut these final two holes, one to get into the heating pipe, one to get out. More slithering, the tightest squeeze yet. Your partner had to lose forty pounds in order to pull off this part, and still it was a tight squeeze. In the pipe and then out—now you're outside the prison wall and into the sewer, up through the sewer grade—then, Atlas lifting the world, the clean and jerk of the final manhole cover, and finally the emergence. You are both sweat-soaked and sooty, now officially escapees, experiencing three, four beats of solid exhilaration, the surreal enveloping caress of being somewhere else, outside. You were outside. The air smelled of nothing, just crisp and fresh.

Now it was just drive all night, first stop West Virginia!

Then it struck you like a sobering slap to the forehead. Where was the bitch with the car? With the weapons? With the change of clothes? With, you know, the rest of the escape? At first you thought maybe we're early, ducked back into the hole for a few minutes. Five minutes. Ten minutes. You did your best to chill out your partner who was disturbingly quick to panic. Poked your head back up. She wasn't there. The weapons and clothes weren't there. Maybe she just chickened out, maybe she ratted, and maybe you should start thinking of plan B. Then you remembered holy shit there was no plan B. So you made something up on the spot. WTF. You weren't going to turn around and go back. Move at night; get to Mexico. Just head south. You couldn't miss it. There was a lot of room for improvisation down the road, but now, standing in the terror and tremor of freedom, there was only one thing for you to do. You ran, through the backyards of the village homes, and as soon as possible toward the trees, into the woods. Assuming that woman kept her yap corked, you still had hours before anyone would know you were gone.

You were smart enough to know that there would be no one out there to help. Your crimes—the crimes that put you in prison in the first place—lacked the romance that might have earned you a modicum of sympathy. If you'd been bank robbers, there would have been someone somewhere rooting for you. But, as it was, you were just a pair of dirtbags, pure and simple. A hundred years ago you'd have been put down like animals. No one was on your side.

When folks think of New York, their first thought is of the City, with its bustle and cloud-tickling skyline. Those who've driven the New York State Thruway or taken Amtrak from New York City to Chicago know a New York of wide rivers, rounded and wooded hills, while bus travelers see the state's crystal and Finger Lakes, and diminutive villages of white houses with Kelly Green shutters. Those who have coursed the state's Southern Tier may recall Canisteo's living sign, the town's name inscribed in the earth with trees. Take a vacation. Taste some wine. The cliffs and falls of Letchworth Park are awesome. In the west, the piston power of Niagara Falls is still a favorite for honeymooners.

But comparatively few know that New York also includes a vast area of wilderness commonly referred to by its rare and scattered residents as "Up North." The Adirondack Mountain area, where bears outnumber people, includes everything from Albany to the Canadian border, a practically untouched forest larger in acreage than any in the United States.

More than 132,000 people are residents of the designated "foreverwild," most of them clustered into about a hundred towns, villages, and hamlets. The area has maintained its virtue largely due to governmental action. In 1885, the state legislature passed the Forest Preserve Act, ensuring that the huge Adirondack Preserve area "shall be forever kept as wild forest lands."

In 1892, new legislation created Adirondack Park "to be forever reserved for the use of all the people." The new law weakened the old one in some ways, however. The Forest Commission could now sell land anywhere in the Adirondacks and lease land to private individuals for camps and cottages. The law was passed in an effort to stem water and lumber consumption. With its passing, the whole region, six million acres of it, was now a park. The designated area had six million acres, three thousand lakes, and one hundred mountains taller than five thousand feet high. It was a little bit smaller than the state of Vermont, the largest publicly protected area in the lower forty-eight, bigger than Yellowstone, Grand Canyon, Everglades, and Glacier combined.[1]

And the commission did sell and lease the land, until half of the park was constitutionally protected, while the other half was private land. Private yes but hardly an industrial city; development on the privately owned or leased land was restricted to minimize the impact on nature.

There were two thousand miles of hiking trails and twelve hundred miles of river. It was impossible to determine the number of visitors the park received annually because there was no admission fee, no gates, and no method of counting.

And so, a long time ago, because of that massive expanse of rough terrain, unchallenged by the parasitic development of Man, the Adirondack area was correctly determined to be an excellent place to build a maximum-security prison.[2]

During the late spring and early summer of 2015 there came in the North Country of New York State twenty-three dreary, drizzly, riveting days. As Henry David Thoreau said, "Most men lead lives of quiet desperation"—well, here was the exception. Here was the story of two men whose desperation was noisy as hell, and it might've gotten noisier were it not for the vigilance of stalwart peacekeepers.

It had been somewhere in the neighborhood of 150 years since an inmate had *successfully* escaped from Dannemora. They had gotten away from work farms and chain gangs, and they'd gotten out of the prison proper as well. But since the days when the prison was surrounded by a fence made of wood, all escapees were either captured and brought back, or died. Some simply vanished, and their death was assumed.[3]

It was enough to discourage a fellow from trying, but these guys were different. They were smarter than the average inmates, especially when together. Their skills were complementary, and they focused on escape.

The staff believed that escape from Dannemora was impossible, a belief that led to complacency, creating a culture that could be exploited. And if the loudly desperate men knew anything, they knew how to shamelessly exploit.

They'd coursed a twenty-minute claustrophobic labyrinth of corridors and tunnels until they emerged into freedom on the outside. Now they were killers on the loose, deadly and desperate: it was the biggest domestic news story of 2015. From the cultural indicators of its establishment wing to the neophyte digerati along its fringe, the fifth estate wasn't an industry known for attention span. Still, the Dannemora story had staying power.

It was simple: you couldn't match the balls on these guys. After months of planning and noisily cutting away barriers, on June 6, two convicted murderers crawled their way out of a maximum-security prison and—in a manhunt worthy of Bonnie and Clyde—eluded police for three weeks.

It was a page-turner of a story, because all of the pieces were in motion and no one knew how it would end. But there would probably be blood. It would turn out to be perhaps the most newsworthy thing ever to occur in the North Country, certainly the biggest story since the 1980 Winter Olympics were held in Lake Placid. The *Boston Globe* called it "a bold escape for the ages." It also shone a bright light into the dark basement of the correctional system, illuminating some things prison officials would rather keep in the dark. The story that unfolded was one of adventure, psychology, sex, depravity, sociopathy, and brutality.

The trouble was discovered at 5:17 a.m., June 6. Corrections Officer Ronald Blair was conducting the morning standing count, when he came to cell 23. The light in the cell was off.

"Hey, get up," Blair said.

No movement.

"Come on, get your ass up."

Nothing.

Blair reached in, grabbed the bed, and shook it. He grabbed the sheet and then he saw. There was no one in the bed. It was a dummy fashioned from old clothes. Blair ran over to cell 22. Same thing. He felt as if he was going to throw up. He took off on a full run and almost fell down the steps to report his finding.

No alarm sounded, no siren. There had been an alarm system at CCF years back, with a speaker outside the big wall to alert the citizens of Dannemora. But no one knew if it still worked and, if it did, if it would be heeded. Fear was, it had been so long since the alarm had gone off that no one would know what it signified.

At 6:06 a.m., June 6, state police sent out word that the morning head count at the Dannemora prison had come up two short. "Unaccounted for" quickly became "confirmed escaped." That put into motion an annually practiced protocol. Notifications went out. Perimeters were put in place.

The initial BOLO (be on the lookout) sent chills through the veins of some members of New York State law enforcement, a shivery, "Oh, no, no, no." The two convicted murderers that escaped from the Clinton Correctional Facility (CCF) in Dannemora were a couple of bad, bad men named Richard Matt and David Sweat.

Only a few hours after the CCF morning head count came up two shy, Clinton County district attorney Andrew Wylie was in his car on his way to a youth soccer tournament in Burlington, Vermont. As he told Cara Chapman of the *Press-Republican*, the weather was perfect, a sunny late spring day, a day that teased of summer pleasures to come.

Wylie had been the Clinton County DA since December 30, 2005. Before that he was a criminal defense lawyer in the county for seventeen years, working in the law offices of his father Robert P. Wylie. He belonged to all the right clubs and organizations, had married Natalie Brassard Wylie, an elementary school teacher at Seton Academy, and they had five children. Today he loved life and had soccer on his mind when he received a text from state police captain Robert LaFountain.

"Please call me."

Oh-oh. Wylie groaned, pulled over, and made the call.

Two prisoners escaped, a cop killer and a mutilation murderer. Nice.

"OK, so where are they?" Wylie said.

"We don't know."

"What do you mean you don't know?"

LaFountain said, "We think they went out through an exit at the backs of their cells, went down into a tunnel system through a steam pipe and exiting out a manhole. We don't know if they are still in the vicinity or if they grabbed a car and are miles away."

Wylie finished the trip to Burlington, made sure his soccer team was okay without him, and then returned to Clinton County, which was already in full-fledged crisis mode.[4]

Clinton County sheriff David Favro had seen the weather report. It was supposed to get rainy and stay rainy for weeks. But this Saturday was scheduled to be nice, the perfect day for a "workbee." His sons were coming over.

Friends were stopping by. Attendance was expected to be good considering that the "work" that needed to "bee" done was the grueling installation of a stone patio—360 sixteen-by-sixteen blocks.

So when Sheriff Favro received the first phone call, two prisoners missing from morning bed check, he was almost rooting for an opportunity to do police work rather than the manual labor waiting at home.

"My first reaction was that it was impossible for a prisoner to get past the walls. The missing prisoners, I believed, were still inside the walls somewhere, hiding in one of a million places. They just hadn't found them yet."

Then came the second call. They'd found the place where the wall had been breeched. The killers were back in society. That was it; the patio would have to be built without him.

Sheriff Favro called his management people and mobilized his personnel. He listened to the descriptions of the escapees:

Richard William Matt was a white male. Six foot, 210, black hair, hazel eyes, a tattoo on his back that read "Mexico Forever," a heart on his chest and left shoulder, and a Marine Corps insignia on his right shoulder; date of birth June 25, 1966.

David Paul Sweat was white, five ten, 165, brown and green, date of birth June 14, 1980. Right-hand fingers tattoo: "IFB," left-arm tattoo: "REBEL."

One was a cop killer; the other, a torturer and psychopath. Not an atom of conscience between them. And now they were on the run. The sensationalized news went out, in screaming headlines and from shouting heads on high-definition flat screens, frightening everyone everywhere, but nowhere more intensely than those within a thirty-mile circumference of Dannemora, New York.[5]

Retired North Tonawanda chief of detectives Glenn D. Gardner was in the car when he got the news. His girlfriend was driving, and they were on a North Tonawanda street heading home after a shop at the farmer's market. Gardner's cell phone rang, and it was a cop, informing him that his "ol' buddy" Rick Matt had busted out of jail, along with another guy.

Gardner felt his heart pound. He thought of Matt's eyes. Matt didn't have eyes like other men. They were hard, cold, black, and evil, eyes of the devil.[6]

Gardner was the one who had found a key clue that put Matt in prison, and he'd testified for eleven hours at Matt's trial. Matt had once tried to put a hit on Gardner, offered to pay two soon-to-be-released jail mates to bump him off. Luckily for Gardner, the "hit men" chose to rat out Matt rather than follow through with the plot.

Gardner told his girlfriend the news, and "she panicked. So I put her and her daughter in a hotel for a few days, and even then they couldn't sleep."

How could they let Richard Matt escape? Gardner asked himself that question within seconds of hearing the news, and he hasn't stopped asking it yet.[7]

Louis Haremski, one of the special prosecutors in Erie County who had helped put Richard Matt away—presumably forever—had retired and become a furniture builder with his son. They were working on a project when Haremski received a phone call from a state trooper. Richard Matt was out and on the run.[8]

"I was concerned but not worried," Haremski recalled. "I asked the trooper if this was a courtesy call or if they were going to offer protection to my family and me. He said, no, just a courtesy call. I knew that Matt had a list of people he didn't like, and although I might have been on it, I was pretty sure I wasn't near the top."

Haremski was offered a shotgun and a rifle by friends in order to protect himself, but no one wanted to part with a handgun.

Journalist Brian Mann, who would go on to write extensively about the escape, later remembered that first inkling that something was terribly wrong. It had been a perfect-weather weekend, but now there was to be a press conference. Anthony Annucci, acting commissioner of the state correctional system, was scheduled to speak. It hadn't started yet, but there was something *gravitational* about the cops already in the room. Feet moved heavily. Shoulders slumped. Chins hung. Body language was *heavy*.

Something had gone wrong at Dannemora. When Annucci began his statement, Mann was deeply affected by "how devastated" he sounded as he bluntly doled out the terrible news.

At the press conference, Major Charles Guess was asked for his theory on Matt and Sweat's whereabouts. New York State Police Major Charles Guess, commander of Troop B, didn't comfort anyone when he said, "They could be literally anywhere," and "just about every cabin or outbuilding in the North

Country has one or more shotguns or weapons. We are operating under the belief that these men are armed. They're extremely cunning. Why wouldn't they try to arm themselves?"

Annucci concluded the conference with a warning, simple yet terrifying: "Lock your doors." Tabloid reporters' eyes lit up. The killers could be under anyone's bed. How many newspapers was *that* going to sell?

The locals did as they were told. You couldn't overestimate the danger. This wasn't just a burglar wandering around, or a panty-sniffing breaking-and-entering man. This was much worse, like having two monsters walking through the woods, Frankenstein and the Wolf Man teaming up.

In the village of Dannemora, the fear was slow to sink in. The news was spreading, but it was a Saturday and folks were going about their business. The Smith Street little league baseball games went on as scheduled. If you lived in the prison area you had to go out, live your life, but before long there were reminders everywhere of the crisis: sorry, road closed; sorry, that neighborhood is quarantined; sorry, can't go past the police tape. It felt to the innocent and civilized motorists of the North as if every road were sealed, and that was a good feeling. Safe. You couldn't get from here to there without scrutiny from the law.[9]

The Clinton County DA said long-term preparation and planning were necessary for the escapees to pull it off. They hadn't planned it on the fourth and escaped on the fifth. This was a piece of work, demonstrating both cunning and tenacity. These guys were smart, industrious, and thoroughly dangerous.

One person most deeply affected by the news of the escape was Philip Tarsia, the seventy-eight-year-old father of the man that David Sweat murdered. Another was William Rickerson Jr., whose dad had been gruesomely murdered by the fiend Richard Matt. Rickerson had a measured response that betrayed none of his anxiety. He said, "I'm going to let the officials do what they're going to do and handle the situation." But he said it with hands clenched into white-knuckled fists.

Tarsia said, "The news is devastating. They said he had life without parole, and then this happens, so it doesn't mean much for the system, right?" Tarsia's son was murdered on the Fourth of July, 2002, so this time of year was the toughest for the family. "When we have our parties and stuff, he was there. That's where it's all brought back," Tarsia told *People* magazine. "The Fourth of July, we have it at the park every year, so it's a memory." He added that he was trying not to think about the prison break. "To think about it just brings up the worst things."[10]

It had been four in the morning of Independence Day when Broome County sheriff's deputy Kevin J. Tarsia was shot in the line of duty. Three men were arrested, and now one of them was free, walking where he didn't belong, among the civilized and innocent. Among *us*.

ONE
LITTLE
SIBERIA

They call it Little Siberia because of the long, frigid winters, and the surrounding wilderness. Back in winters of old, deliveries were made by horse-drawn sledges. The climate, wilderness, and isolation are natural deterrents to escape from Dannemora. The location was just as important as that concrete wall. The few who had made it out, and more on them later, have found themselves in the thick forests of the rolling Dannemora hills. Good luck.[1]

But its true name is the Clinton Correctional Facility, formerly Clinton Prison, because it's in Clinton County, New York. It is a maximum-security state prison—and old, one of the oldest, built in 1844 as an "outpost prison."[2]

According to Andrea Guynup of *All Points North* (a magazine dedicated to the North Country), the prison's location was considered prime because it was in a valley, close to iron mines and near the hills of Lyon Mountain.[3]

The first inmates lived in shacks heated by wood in the winter and were chained together and forced to construct the prison. As it turned out, doing construction work while wearing chains is a difficult task, even for the fittest prisoner. After a while the chains were removed to hasten construction.

In the beginning, iron mining was the main operation of the prison. There were three main mines within the prison walls with inmates (of course) doing the digging. Not only did the prison make labor at the mines very cheap, but also the operation was state of the art.

The mines were all within the stockade, and the iron ore was sent to the mills via a tram designed by inventor Ransom Cook, after whom Dannemora's main street is named. The iron ore was mechanically elevated, crushed, winnowed, and separated, all with equipment designed by Cook. (The "Fairbanks Mine" was at the current site of the corner of Fairbanks Avenue and North Emmons Street, where remnants of the old stockade can still be seen.)

Mining dwindled, iron value depreciated, and by 1877 the mines were closed. To provide employment for the inmates, they were assigned daily maintenance and repairs. Some made shoes or sewed uniforms to send to other state institutions. Shirts, sheets, and household goods were produced under sweathouse conditions, causing no doubt close conditions as each prisoner was only allowed one bath per fortnight.

Many inmates were put on road detail—or on a detail building roadbeds for the railroad. That always led to a few escapes.

Until December 14, 1854, the town of Dannemora was known as Beekmantown, made up of untamed, mountainous land with a sandy soil covered with trees. Then, as now, the only village was in the southeast corner of the township and existed almost exclusively to serve the prison. The 1860 edition of *French's Gazetteer of the State of New York* reported, "The prison was located here in 1845 for the purpose of employing convicts in the mining and manufacture of iron, so that their labor would not come so directly in competition with the other mechanical trades." That article went on to say that the state legislature had only recently declared it permissible to use convict labor in the mining and smelting of iron ore.

Long before a Clinton inmate died in the electric chair, prisoners died in mining accidents. Iron had been a primary concern of the region since it was discovered there in 1831. The name Dannemora came from an iron-ore mine in Sweden worked by Danish men. *Danne* comes from Danish, or Danes; and *Mora*, a Swedish "fenny spruce," that is, a strong and tough spruce tree. Less than seven years spanned the arrival of the village's first settler, Thomas Hooker, in 1838, and the birth of the prison.

The grand opening of Clinton Prison on June 3, 1845, began with a surreal parade, not of bands and clowns, floats and balloons, but of defeated men in lockstep dressed in zebra-stripe uniforms. As villagers gazed upon the spectacle with open mouths, the incoming prisoners were marched up and down hills for the seventeen miles from Plattsburgh to the prison's front gate.

The prison was only weeks old when two inmates serving time for burglary climbed the stockade wall and disappeared into the dense nearby woods. The inmates apparently forgot their compass as they, while attempting to flee into Canada, inadvertently doubled back and were captured two days later only a few hundred yards from where they'd escaped.

In 1874, inmate John Filkins escaped. His method of exit remains unclear. When a skeleton was discovered in the prison sewer system in 1875, it was assumed to be Filkins, but that same year a witness in Canada claimed to have seen and talked with Filkins.[4]

The original prison was a cluster of wooden structures surrounded by a twenty-foot-high wooden fence. Irregularly spaced around the circuit were nine tiny houses on tall stilts above the fence, each with a small, one-man balcony. Each house was reached via stairs that came up through a trap door in the floor. The discouraging factor was the staff posted on each balcony with a repeating rifle.

As is true in almost all "civilized" prisons, well-behaved prisoners were rewarded (how else to get them to behave?), and very good long-term prisoners were rewarded greatly. In the nineteenth century, there were shanties at ground level, adjacent to the guard towers just inside the wall. One old-timer had been there for so long, and had been so good, that he was given his own shanty in which to live.

Though that first fence was made of wood, it was well built, the pickets pressed together so tightly that you couldn't fit a pin between them. The fence enclosed the prison, creating what was perhaps a mile-long circuit. The fence failed to intimidate most inmates and encouraged some.

It wasn't a physical issue. There were ways to get over the fence. There were mature trees growing in the recreation yard, tall enough for escapees to climb, jump over the fence, and skedaddle into the woods. Dozens escaped,[5] an uncounted number never to be seen again. Unless the escaped men were spotted by reliable witnesses, they were assumed to have fallen victim to the elements.

Back then, when a prisoner escaped, the alarm was sounded by firing a cannon. In 1860, James "The Gay Deceiver" Whiting used disguise to escape. He acquired a set of civvies and walked out the front gate. Whiting remained free for close to a year and made it as far as Philadelphia where he was arrested for selling bogus jewels at real jewels prices and a cop recognized his mug shot.[6]

As the number of prisoners grew, the prison had to grow to accommodate them. After forty years of brutal weather, the fence showed signs of rot, and folks on the outside were complaining that it offered them inadequate protection from the animals inside. The fence was replaced in stages from 1884 to 1887 by a forty-foot-high stone fence, with all of the stones cut from Lyon Mountain behind the prison. To pay for the new wall, New York State appropriated $20,000. When the money ran out, they stopped building, and for years the new wall did not go all the way around. There was still some stockade wooden fencing on the backside, the side furthest from Cook Street.

In 1890, fire destroyed the prison's main building, a three-story structure that contained the mess hall, offices, guardroom, and kitchen. (Dannemora didn't get its own fire department until 1894.) But that loss was more than offset by much new construction, a state shop, a hospital, a fifty-by-one-hundred-foot bathhouse, a factory building, and a new mess hall.

Prisoners were lockstepped to the bathhouse in groups of fifty, each prisoner bathing once every two weeks.

A prisoner named Peter James, incarcerated for murder during a robbery, busted out of Dannemora in 1903. James's prison job was maintaining a basement engine for the prison tin shop. Working only a few minutes each day to avoid detection, he worked for years, chipping away at an escape route, using smuggled pieces of tin as his tool. Other inmates knew about and supported his efforts, and a system was rigged so a bell at the end of a string would ring if guards were approaching. His tunnel grew to be twenty feet long and connected to the sewer system. He and three other inmates escaped through a manhole in a field outside the prison and remained free for five days before being captured four miles from the Canadian border.[7]

Some prisoners avoided the problem of getting over or under the prison wall entirely by making their run for it while already on the outside. That was possible for prisoners, such as George Leggins of Coxsackie, who escaped while assigned to a farm crew tending to cows, chickens, and pigs. At age twenty-eight and serving eighteen months for grand larceny, Leggins escaped from the farm on July 31, 1915, while wearing his prison uniform (gray pants and striped shirt). Dogs tracked Leggins as far as Chazy Lake where it was incorrectly presumed he had drowned. He was briefly recaptured in Coxsackie on November 19, 1915, but broke out of the Coxsackie jail that same day, remained free for four days, was recaptured, and was returned to Dannemora, where he remained.[8] At the time, the *Plattsburgh Sentinel* reported, "Warden Trombly was notified of the second capture of the prisoner and he asked the Albany chief of police to guard the man carefully and that he would send an officer from the prison after him on the first available train. The Albany police chief informed the warden that there was not a chance of Leggins making another getaway and he would again sleep in a cell in Clinton prison that night."

Almost seventy prisoners escaped from Dannemora between 1914 and 1922, the great majority of them from road gangs and work farms, but twelve got loose from within the walls, exiting via the hospital, chapel, and boiler room. Almost everyone was caught. Those that weren't were presumed dead of exposure trying to survive in the angry wild.

And right there, that was the reason for complacency at Clinton Correctional Facility (CCF). If the wall didn't get 'em, the wilderness would. The rugged terrain was to Clinton what the choppy waters of San Francisco Bay were for Alcatraz Island.[9]

Dannemora was the hardest place in the state to do time during World War I and the Great Depression.[10] According to notoriety, the primary reasons were the frequency and severity of the beatings. This may still be true today, but the prison's reputation was particularly violent from 1900 to 1930.

In Dannemora, the stone wall was resurfaced and built up with concrete between 1933 and 1935, an effort that began the "big house" era, when the prison population drastically increased. (CCF's A Block, which will be a focus of this story, was built during that same construction period.) The prison was originally designed to hold five hundred, but the inmate population grew to 2,700.

During the early days of the prison, when transportation remained primitive, employees were required to live in the village of Dannemora to make sure all hands were only minutes away in case there was "a problem."

The Dannemora prison has long been the go-to facility for prisoners with medical problems, either physical or mental. First the physical: In the nineteenth century, one of the most common and serious physical ailments was the contagious lung disease tuberculosis, and Dannemora's fresh mountain air was thought to be kind to TB sufferers. Outside prisoners that contracted TB were transferred up north, an influx that continued for generations until it eventually—in 1941— necessitated an in-prison hospital with beds for two hundred inmates. It served as a general doctor's office and TB hospital. Now the mental: On May 4, 1899, Governor Theodore Roosevelt signed an act that brought about the Dannemora State Hospital to "confine and care for" insane convicts. The state hospital, which was outside the big fence but had its own barriers, was not phased out until 1972. It spent three years as the

Adirondack Correctional Treatment and Evaluation Center. Since 1975, the building had been the Clinton Annex—a medium-security facility.

Frank Dimatteo, publisher of *Mob Candy* and author of *President Street Boys*, never did time in Dannemora, but he did regularly come to visit his godfather Robert "Bobby Darrow" Bongiovi who was serving a life sentence for murder. Frank said, "The Dannemora prison was a hellhole. It looked like a fort, had to be the worst prison in the state. How anyone could serve time there is a miracle."[11]

In the village, almost everybody worked inside, but not everybody. A few worked outside the walls, and there was very little turnover among their ranks. Bob Breyette of Bob's Barber Shop on Cook Street has been cutting hair in that same spot for fifty years.[12]

Dannemora was, and is, a company town. "At one time, just about everyone who lived in the village worked inside the prison walls," said Walter "Pete" Light, who for thirty-one years was a corrections officer. He retired in 1999 and became the CCF historian.

For many Dannemora families, becoming a CCF employee has become a family tradition. Employees today are the sons and daughters, grandsons and granddaughters, of CCF employees.

Outsiders might have the notion that prisoners were inside and civilians outside, but that distinction was blurred—and always had been. Not only did most villagers work inside the walls, but also seeing prisoners on the outside wasn't unusual either. Dannemora Village children got used to seeing prisoners, even as they walked to school. Inmates drove tractors. They cleaned up at the skating rink. Prisoners looked lazy. Nearby guards looked bored. For a resident, prisoners were part of the scenery.

As one might expect, the publically acknowledged methods of disciplining prisoners have grown more humane over the years. (What goes on behind doors in private perhaps not as much.) During the nineteenth century, there were no bathing facilities for prisoners, who wore striped uniforms at all times, were forced to walk in lockstep,[13] and were required to remain silent. Into the twentieth century, when prison life was *supposed* to be brutal, it was okay for guards to tie unruly prisoners to the floor and beat them with leather paddles.

In 1892, one of New York State's first electric chairs was installed at Clinton, in the basement of the Administration Building. The first prisoner to take the longest walk was convicted murderer Joseph "Cal" Wood, who fried on August 2.[14]

Even as many formerly common disciplinary techniques were considered cruel and unusual over the first decades of the twentieth century, a notable exception was the electric chair, which was seen as a civilized high-tech alternative to the gallows.

Edwin F. Davis, who was also the executioner, built the chair in Auburn Prison near Syracuse, New York. Twenty-six inmates were executed by Dannemora's version of Ol' Sparky. All were dispatched to the prison cemetery for burial.

The chair's biggest day came on October 1, 1903, when three brothers—Willis, Burton, and Fred Van Wormer, convicted of killing their uncle on Christmas Eve 1901—were sizzled in a single day.

The final prisoner to be electrocuted at Dannemora was Fred Poulin, on February 12, 1913. After that, new state legislation required that all prisoners sentenced to death be sent to (or transferred to) Sing Sing. Capital punishment in New York State was outlawed all together in 1965. Today the most severe punishment an inmate must endure in New York State is solitary confinement.

In late 1927, a wooden box addressed to the prison's industrial department, with the return address of warden Harry M. Kaiser, was intercepted following a tip from a snitch. The box was found to contain six automatic pistols, four hundred rounds of ammunition, three bottles of liquor, and maps. Later, a second box with six more guns was intercepted. The plot was linked to a prisoner named Leon Kramer, a member of the "Whitemore Gang" of jewelry thieves.[15]

On the morning of July 22, 1929, a riot occurred within the Dannemora walls that exposed the prison's brutal conditions and led to prison reform. Trouble started after breakfast in the mess hall. An agitated pack of prisoners attacked guards with clubs and stones. A guard atop the wall shot a club-wielding prisoner, and a full-fledged riot ensued. An army of 1,300 prisoners set fire to the powerhouse and smashed the dynamo, an early form of electrical generator that produced direct current. They fed the fires with wood shavings from the carpenter shop. According to a contemporary report, the rioters "stormed the walls" despite "withering gunfire."[16] State police from Malone and Plattsburgh came to help, wearing bulletproof vests and carrying rifles. Game wardens and border patrol officers assisted. Firemen had to scale the walls and shoot water down onto the fires. Men from the village were recruited to man the top of the wall with their rifles. As black smoke billowed up from inside the prison, curious villagers leaned ladders against the Cook Street wall and climbed them so they could watch the action.

The riot continued into the afternoon, with guards feeling increasingly outgunned and outmanned. To turn the tide, state troopers were called in, and then the Twenty-Sixth Infantry, which arrived with grenades, tear gas, machine guns, and shotguns. But as it turned out the infantry was not needed. The threat of the infantry was enough—this, combined with a case of mistaken identity. Trying to get a bird's-eye view of the action, photojournalists chartered a plane to fly repeatedly over the prison so they could take pictures. The plane frightened the rioters, who feared it was a bomber, and the uprising quieted.

Many prisoners surrendered without any more fight, while about a hundred inmates barricaded themselves in the tailor shop.

Considering the extent of the staff firepower, it's amazing that the carnage wasn't worse. Three inmates died, twenty prisoners were wounded, several corrections officers were injured, and two buildings were destroyed, causing $200,000 in damage.

The fires were so severe that three fire departments from three neighboring towns were called in to douse them. The fierce firefighting battle went on for so long that it drained the prison's reservoir.

Later that year, a pump house was built on windblown and choppy Chazy Lake, running four miles north to south in the valley between Lyon and Ellenburg Mountains. To supply water to the prison and hospital, large pipes were laid that went over a mountain to supply the new, larger reservoirs that were built behind the prison.

On October 2, 1929, twenty-one-year-old Nick Mastro (real name: Bruno Montorio) of Schenectady was shot and killed as he tried to escape from Clinton. He'd been serving a twenty-one-year sentence for robbery and assault.[17] Mastro, while on a recreation break, climbed an electric light pole and had reached the top of the prison wall. A guard named Jeremiah Callahan rushed to meet him armed only with his billy club. As the two struggled atop the wall, a second guard named Thomas Brantigan ran from the principal keeper's office and shot Mastro in the hip. Mastro fell from atop the wall. Callahan ran back to his guardhouse and grabbed his submachine gun. Mastro tried to attack him once again; Callahan pulled the trigger and shot the prisoner dead.[18]

Prison reforms put an end to major uprisings in Dannemora, but smaller so-called mini-riots were still an occasional problem, one in 1987 and, more significantly, one just a few weeks before Richard Matt and David Sweat escaped.[19]

CCF is so large and the village of Dannemora so small (population 3,936 as of 2016,[20] but 75 percent of them are inmates) that from an aerial view it looks about half and half. The prison is such an integral part of the village that the main thoroughfare, Cook Street, runs hard against the prison's imposing southern wall.

It is that main street, with shingled storefronts on one side and an imposing wall on the other, that makes the village unique—a downright weird juxtaposition of American Dream and Nightmare.

Ross Douthat wrote in the *New York Times*, "To residents, that wall means money, jobs, security. But driving through, it doesn't feel like something people should get used to—this prison at the end of America, huge and crowded, yet invisible to most of us."[21]

Without the prison, Dannemora might be confused for a farming community. The church on Clark Street—only one block from where the escapees popped up—has a congregation of forty-one.

It is a village light on amenities. There are three stores: dollar, general, and liquor. And there are two restaurants: Chinese and pizzeria, the latter only open at night. If a resident wanted to, say, participate in a Fourth of July celebration, he or she had to drive thirty-five miles to Lake Champlain. At one time there were five hotels, kept in business by loved ones visiting inmates. Now there are none, all put out of business by larger chain hotels in Plattsburgh.

Tanya Stewart, who worked at the local Mobil station convenience store, said that the village would quickly empty and become a ghost town if the prison were closed. "Dannemora would cease to exist," she said.[22]

Like many village dwellers, it was the simple things that kept Dannemorans happy. Lisa Benson, commander and bartender at the local American Legion Hall, called the region slower but beautiful. There were long winters when she considered moving to Florida, but they told her about the humidity, the tree frogs that made you sick, and big cockroaches that fell from the trees, so she was staying up north.[23]

Many notorious criminals had done time in misery within those forty-foot walls. These included Charles "Lucky" Luciano, the Sicilian-born mobster, considered by many to be the father of modern organized crime in America. It was Luciano who thought big and melded crime families across the nation into a powerful syndicate. Luciano went to Dannemora following convictions on dozens of counts of "compulsory prostitution." He stayed for ten years before being deported to Italy prior to World War II.

On March 25, 1990, eighty-seven lives were extinguished by an arson fire at the Happy Land Social Club in the West Farms section of the Bronx.[24] The killer turned out to be a Julio Gonzalez, a jilted lover, who got back at his girlfriend with weapons of mass destruction: a gallon of gas and a match. He torched a packed social club—a firetrap, a joint with one exit, and an exit that was blocked with fire—and everyone inside died. He was sentenced on September 19, 1991, to a total of 4,350 years and sent to suffer in Dannemora.

In the Hamptons, a rich vacation paradise on Long Island, Wall Street financier Ted Ammon was bludgeoned to death in the autumn of 2001 by Daniel Pelosi, an electrician who was working on the Ammon townhouse and having an affair with Pelosi's wife, Generosa (whom Pelosi married in 2002, a year before she died of breast cancer). He was convicted of second-degree murder in 2004 and sent to CCF.[25]

Joel Rifkin of East Meadow, Long Island, killed seventeen prostitutes between 1989 and 1993. His reign of terror ended on June 28, 1993, when New York State troopers spotted Rifkin driving a pickup truck with no rear license plate. After a car chase, the troopers pulled back a tarpaulin in the trunk bed and discovered the naked and decomposing body of a woman. Rifkin was convicted of killing nine but confessed to killing eighteen. He was sentenced to 203 years to life inside the Dannemora walls.

Robert Chambers, young and handsome "Preppy Killer," was convicted of murdering eighteen-year-old Jennifer Levin on August 26, 1986, despite his claim that the Central Park murder came about because of his date's penchant for "rough sex." He was sentenced to fifteen years in prison and served all of it because of his numerous infractions of the rules. He was released but quickly returned following a drug arrest.

Joel Steinberg was a disbarred New York State criminal defense attorney turned child-abuse murderer. He was convicted of manslaughter in connection with the death of a six-year-old girl. Steinberg and his hideously abused live-in partner, Hedda Nussbaum, claimed the victim was their adopted daughter, but investigation revealed no adoption had ever taken place.[26] He was sent to Dannemora for seventeen years.[27]

And Marlon Legere, the Trinidad-born cop killer convicted of killing NYPD detectives Robert Parker and Patrick Rafferty on September 10, 2004. He'd twice done time for sexual assault and was involved in drugs when his mom dropped a dime on him, resulting in the homicidal encounter.

Perhaps the inmate whose story most resembled that of Matt and Sweat was Ralph "Bucky" Phillips, who escaped from the Erie County Holding Center in April 2006 using a can opener. His escape started a long and intense manhunt, unequaled in New York State until June 2015. On June 10, 2006, Phillips shot and seriously wounded state trooper Sean Brown with a .38 handgun at a red light ten miles north of Elmira, New York. On August 31, Phillips used a high-powered rifle to shoot troopers Donald Baker and Joseph Longobardo who were staking out the house of one of Phillips's family members in Chautauqua County.[28] Longobardo died from his wound. By this time the reward for information leading to the capture of Phillips was up to close to $500,000. Phillips was taken by Pennsylvania State Police in Warren County without gunfire. Phillips was sent to Dannemora, where he is serving life without parole (LWP).

Some guys committed notorious crimes to get to Dannemora, and some committed their dastardly acts after they were released from Little Siberia. In this second category was Robert Garrow, who served time for rape at CCF during the 1960s and went on to become a serial killer, perhaps responsible for as many as twenty-seven murders, some of them killed during a 1973 spree that took Garrow from Syracuse to the Adirondacks. He was shot, wounded, and recaptured in Essex County and was eventually convicted of four murders and sentenced to twenty-five years, four of which he spent at CCF before transferring to Fishkill. He escaped from Fishkill in 1978 and was free for three days before he died in a police shootout.

Axe-wielding Christopher Porco murdered his father and tried to kill his mother in 2004. He is serving fifty years to life in Dannemora.

Some of CCF's most famous residents only made a (comparatively) brief appearance. Tupac Shakur spent nine months in Dannemora after a 1995 sex-abuse rap.

The Beat Poets were a group that included author Jack Kerouac and poet Allen Ginsberg. Another one of the Beats was Gregory Corso, who'd been sent to Dannemora for three years when he was a teenager.[29] His crime: he'd stolen a suit.

Dannemora is usually a symbol of justice done but has been the site of great injustice as well. On September 7, 1988, wealthy Seymour and Arlene Tankleff were murdered in their luxurious Belle Terre home on Long Island. Law enforcement was unusually tunnel-visioned, and seventeen-year-old son Marty was the only suspect. After many hours of sleep deprivation and intense interrogation, Marty confessed. He was arrested and in 1990 tried and convicted of killing his parents—charges that, when well rested, he vehemently denied. Tankleff spent seventeen years in prison, many of them in Dannemora, before a reinvestigation determined that there had been insufficient evidence to convict him in the first place.

The adventures of Matt and Sweat in the Adirondack woods was not the first time that a newsworthy manhunt took place in that wilderness. During the late summer of 1881 an Adirondack guide (or someone impersonating an Adirondack guide, depending on whom you believe) named Charles Parker became a rapist by forcing himself on the woman he was guiding through no-man's land. Following his arrest he somehow slipped his cuffs and disappeared into the backwoods. Parker remained free for three days until he had the misfortune of encountering master boat-builder Warren Cole of Long Lake. Cole singlehandedly shot, wounded, and apprehended Parker.[30]

Another manhunt was for life-long criminal Alvin "Sam" Pasco in the spring of 1918. A third was for Major James Call, a cop killer, in 1954. Both got their man.[31]

Dannemora has its own church, the Church of St. Dismas, the Good Thief, built on a 1.1-acre footprint, by prisoners between 1939 and 1941. It was a neo-Gothic stone chapel, designed by Frederick Vernon Murphy and Thomas Lorcroft, and the first denominational church (Roman Catholic) built within prison walls. It was made of fieldstones salvaged from some of the prison's original buildings, dating back to the mid-nineteenth century, including the prison's first cellblock. The roof was of slate gable, and its spire peaked at 106 feet up. But perhaps its most impressive feature is its huge oak doors with metal, medieval-style strapwork. Inmates created the paintings and stained glass and built the pews that were constructed of Appalachian red oak donated by former inmate Lucky Luciano. The altar reportedly dated back to 1521 and was brought to the New World by Ferdinand Magellan from the Philippines. The wooden panels framing the crucifix were said to have come from Magellan's ship. The priceless relics were donated to the prison by a "wealthy New York woman." In 1991, the Church of St. Dismas was named to the National Register of Historic Places.

There are some things about Dannemora that have not changed in the last 170 years, and one is the view. Beyond the walls, the hills and trees are still an artist's palette of ever-changing hue, morphing from lime to ochre and russet depending on the time of day, the weather, and the season.

TWO
A CHEMICAL REACTION

During the weeks, months, and even years before the great escape, correction officers attended labor-management meetings and expressed concern about security weaknesses at the prison. The predominant complaint was that officers were not allowed to frisk and search employees upon entering the prison. Specific concerns were raised before Superintendent Steven Racette about security weaknesses in the prison tailor shop. At one meeting, held in September 2014, officers told Deputy Superintendent Donald Quinn that there was confusion at the main gate regarding frisking employees and which items could be carried in. The rules were vague. When it was unclear, officers sought a clarification, which sometimes never came. At another meeting between administrators and members of the union, the New York State Correctional Officers and Police Benevolent Association (NYSCOPBA), held on June 17, 2014, officers pointed out that civilian employees were allowed to enter the prison tailor shop as early as 6:00 a.m., which was ninety minutes before correction officers were posted there.

Security staff numbered 1,005, and seven hundred additional prisoners lived in the prison's annex, which was two hundred yards outside the southwest corner of the Wall. On June 5, 2015, the prisoner population of Clinton Correctional Facility (CCF) was 2,687.[1] On June 6 that number was down to 2,685.

To get Sweat's former neighbor to move, Matt bribed him with $100 in cigarettes and two handmade porno books. From January 24, 2015, on, Matt and Sweat were in cells A6-22 and A6-23.

Hindsight was always twenty-twenty, but the truth was, there *were* prison guards who before the fact didn't like Richard Matt and David Sweat in adjoining cells. Why let these two assholes put their heads together? Prisoners with escape skills needed to be separated, a lesson Hitler learned the hard way during World War II with Colditz Castle.[2]

Prison was filled with men who had done desperate things, but even within the highest walls, a majority of the men have consciences, a spot of real humanity inside, even if it's been battered and bruised by life. These two, however, Matt and Sweat, if they had souls to begin with, they had been calloused over early on. Both had suffered brutal childhoods and learned little of happiness and hope.

Plus, they had complementary skills. One had demonstrated his ability to escape. The other had an engineer's ability to read blueprints, upside down, from across the room. Both had little to lose. Both had spent the majority of their adult years behind bars. Matt, as an adult, had only been free for four and a half years. This was despite the fact that he had a history of escaping.

Since his initial incarceration at age seventeen, Sweat had known even less freedom: a pitiful three years on the outside.

By the time Sweat arrived in Dannemora, he had a well-earned reputation as a planner. As he was busted for the arms robbery that led to his murder charge, police discovered him to have maps, sketches, and lists of things to do in connection with the crime. He documented a 1996 burglary plot—and he had a "to do" list in 1997 in his Broome County jail cell.

Now, in Dannemora, the belief was that Sweat was never going to see the outside again, LWP, life without parole, they call it. Matt was serving twenty five to life.

It was like a chemical reaction, a bubbling up from the depths-of-hell alchemy. The instant Matt and Sweat saw one another they knew. They were a team with a manifest destiny: replacing leaden bars with golden freedom. As Sweat later admitted, almost immediately they began to have serious discussions.

How the hell do we get out of here? Let's do it because it's hard. Let's stand beside Alfie Hinds in the Prison Escape Hall of Fame.[3]

They became friends during their interactions outside their cells at first. In Honor Block there were 192 cells, 174 of them occupied; the others were used as showers, toilets, and utility closets. The prisoners were allowed to be out of their cells for most of the day. Each day they had recreation on a lower level where there was a TV and facilities for cooking.

Sweat convinced the guy in the cell next to Matt to swap cells with him. Always seeking to keep prisoners happy, administration allowed it, and that was how Matt and Sweat became next-cell neighbors: A Block, cells 22 and 23.

Before long, Sweat was cutting a hole in the wall of his cell. During the next weeks and months he would feel like a rubber-gloved doctor carefully fingering an alien skull, looking for soft spots. He found his way inside the beast and felt around for places where he might break on through to the other side. Sweat chipped away at the prison's outer wall for a while before realizing it was easier to gain access to the eighteen-inch diameter pipe that went through that wall.

On the morning of June 6, investigators knew very little about what had occurred. They didn't know how long the escape was planned, who was in on it, or where the escapees got the tools they needed to pull it off.

Although the escape plan may have been in the works for many months, the labor could not have started until May 2015, it was assumed, after the prison's heating system was turned off for the summer.

Most of the labor must have been done by Sweat, it was assumed. He was younger and in far better condition. Matt had to cut the hole in his own cell, however. It took him longer than it had Sweat, and his work was noticeably sloppier. The first step would have been to slice through a ⅜-inch-thick steel wall around the ten-by-ten-inch air vents at the head of their cots, enlarging the openings so that they could crawl through. The men had to scratch at a single spot in the wall until a hole was formed and then insert a hacksaw blade and saw. Most of the in-cell work must have been done when the other inmates were in the mess hall or engaged in recreation. Recreation time would have been best as the noise from card games and the slamming of dominoes would help cover up the noise of cutting metal. The men could take turns, one looking out while the other worked. Metal shavings could be flushed down the toilet.

The escape, investigators erroneously assumed, required power tools. Two convicts in a maximum-security prison had used power tools in their cells and no one had noticed. You had to understand Dannemora to get it. Inside the walls, idle hands were the tools of the devil, and CCF had a time-honored tradition of keeping the prisoners happy by keeping those potentially dangerous hands busy, something of the prisoner's own design.

Tools and puttering around with little projects had been woven into the prison's culture.

Forget for a moment about how the inmates acquired the tools. To an outsider anyway, it seemed absurd. How was it that no one had heard those tools in use? A power drill at 5:00 a.m.? It should have disturbed someone—but no one heard a thing.

This struck the authorities as ludicrous. Other prisoners and prison personnel alike must have known what was going on, and yet all kept mum. How could that be? Were the lunatics running the asylum? The absurdity led Governor Andrew Cuomo to quip to a pool of assembled reporters, "They must all be heavy sleepers."

Law enforcement understood some of the psychology: what happens in Clinton stays in Clinton. Snitches get stitches. But would the staff carry it this far?

It is impossible to know just how many hours Sweat spent before the escape, exploring the catacombs of the prison, thinking in three dimensions, and determining the shortest path to the outside—all seemingly without worry that his absence from his cell would be discovered. The hole he'd cut in the back of his cell was concealed by a grate that he replaced after exiting or entering his cell. For all intents and purposes, Sweat's cell had a backdoor and had for a long time before the escape. Everyone concerned believed that he'd had to cut holes along the way, a hole through a thick brick wall, a hole to crawl inside a metal steam pipe, and another at the other end of the pipe so they could get out.

Sweat demonstrated incredible tenacity. How many dead-ends did he hit? How much trial and error was there? Psychologically, Sweat's nightly journey outside his cell into the belly of the beast must've empowered him, had his adrenaline squirting. It made him feel already *partially free*, a rogue prisoner moving unshackled in parts of the prison where there were no guards, where the hellish sights and sounds of a maximum-security facility seemed far away.

Escaping, Sweat would later say, was not a task for the impatient, for the weak. It took an iron constitution and what the *New York Times* called "a MacGyver-like sense of ingenuity."[4]

As soon as the evening head count was completed, the escapees had sculpted a pile of clothes on their beds, so it looked from outside as if they were asleep in their cots, under the covers, wearing a hoodie.

Although there were seven hours between the night and morning head count, there were supposed to be bed checks every two hours, and both escapees passed the bed-checks test all night long. Like the all-quiet command, effective bed checks had gone away. It used to be that bed checks were done with a flashlight, and prisoners complained about the light in their eyes when they were trying to sleep—so, no more flashlights. It used to be that a bed check wasn't considered positive until the guard could see the prisoner's head, but prisoners complained that their incarcerated noggins got cold, so they were allowed to cover their heads with blankets or pillows.

With the new rules, Sweat had been getting past the bed checks for months. Nobody was looking for skin, poking to verify. When procedure was followed at all, it was cursory, a quick glance and that was it. There's a man-shaped lump on the cot. Check.

Prison officials had arrogantly believed that getting out was impossible. That had been the feeling for years. If there was a way out from the fourth floor of the honor block, they further believed, prisoners had no way of figuring out what it was. But that kind of thinking underestimated the intelligence of David Sweat and the patience of men doing nothing but time.

Small pieces of intelligence had needed to be pieced together to envision the route to freedom: First of all, the prisoners would need to know that there were spaces between walls large enough for men to move around in, spaces *designed* for men to move around, to make maintenance and repair of the prison's internal systems convenient for workers. In Sweat and Matt's case, they knew that one of these spaces ran adjacent to the backs of their cells.

Officials would later learn that, not only had the prisoners heard men working on the other side of their cell wall during recent renovations, but also a prison guard had actually given Matt a small tour of the space, so he knew the location of the electric box, of the ladder. Even without that knowledge, investigators could easily conclude that, before the escapees created square holes in the air vents at the backs of their cells, they would have needed to know that an inviting and unobserved space existed on the other side, one that offered a potential route to the outside. That space contained a metallic catwalk, large enough for a man to stand, and it followed a steam pipe to where there was a metal ladder mounted on the wall that led from the fourth floor six stories down, *all the way down*, to the cellblock's subbasement.

He would need to know that the ladder would lead to a main heating pipe, one that went through a two-foot-thick brick wall, and that the pipe led to another ladder, leading up to street level, on the outside now, to a manhole four hundred feet beyond the prison walls at the intersection of Bouck (pronounced Buck) and Barker streets in the peaceful village of Dannemora.

He would need to know that that those pipes were large enough to accommodate a grown man. (The escapees must've known the precise size of the pipes beforehand as Matt went on a diet for months in order to fit.) They would need to know that they could punch man-sized holes in that steam pipe. Once that knowledge was attained, it was just a matter of creating entrances and exits for the pipes, smashing a hole through a two-foot-thick basement-level brick wall that blocked the path, and cutting a chain and bolt lock that held the exit manhole in place.

It was presumed that power tools were necessary to create the required holes. Where had those come from? This was unknown—although one of the first things investigators did was interview contractors who'd been working within the building, searching for accomplices. The power tools would have needed power, which must have been acquired by opening the electrical box in the catwalk behind their cells and running wires all the way to the worksite. That's a lot of extension cord! Where had that come from?

The escape had necessitated a genius level of planning combined with hours of agonizing labor. Re-creating the escape in their minds, investigators were most puzzled by how the men had cut the exit hole in the pipe. Making a hole to get into the pipe was one thing, but the exit hole would have needed to be cut while stretched out inside the pipe—quite a feat.

So, now those arrogant prison officials knew that escape was not impossible at all. It was unlikely, sure, but that wasn't good enough. It was like the prison version of Murphy's Law: if it can be done, it will be done. As investigators first traced the escape route they came across items that caused loathing to rise within them like bile. Sweat and Matt had placed notes. One was an explanation reading, "You left me no choice but to grow old & die in here. I had to do something. 6-5-15." Another was written on a painting of actor James Gandolfini (best known for his TV role as Tony Soprano) that said "Time to go, Kid!" Another note, placed deeper into the escape route, was a Post-it with the greeting "Have a nice day!" Accompanying the message was—for reasons unknown, maybe just because they were assholes—a drawing depicting an offensive caricature of a bucktoothed Asian face.

The media exploded into alpha-story mode. Newspaper reporters demanded the wood.[5] Web news was teased and tweeted. Memes went viral. Journalists disseminated the who, what, when, and why—but not so much the where. There was no where.

Local reporters sought out old-time Dannemora prison workers for com- ment—guys like John Egan, who began shoveling coal onto a conveyor sys- tem that fed massive boilers in the CCF boiler room in 1947.[6] Egan's father was a prison employee before him, the head of maintenance. Egan said he was flabbergasted and saddened by the escape. One thing Egan knew about Dannemora was that you couldn't escape in the winter. So his first thought was they planned to escape when the weather was at its mildest. Plus, to use the heating system, they would have to wait until the heat was turned off in the spring—too hot, too cold. They had planned for the temperature to be just right. Speaking of pipes, that pipe the escapees crawled in and out of was built of heavy steel. He'd seen photos. Looked like a clean cut. That meant a *powerful* saw.

According to an Associated Press report, an early focal point for inves- tigation was the contractors who had recently worked inside the prison. Could they have supplied tools or even done some of the work attributed to the escapees under the cover of legitimate repairs? It seemed outlandish, but then again Matt and Sweat had pulled off an incredible feat. They *must* have received serious assistance. How else?

This line of investigation went nowhere. The construction workers all said they knew nothing.

Perhaps a loophole in the rules was a contributing factor. Contractors were required to check in and check out tools upon entering or leaving the prison, but rules prohibited guards from searching the person of a worker from the outside, raising the possibility that tools had been smuggled to Matt and Sweat in this manner.

The prison conducted an internal inventory of all the tools on the premises, and none were missing. New York prison commissioner Anthony Annucci said that he had instructed all facilities to make sure they exercise the utmost vigilance and precaution in inventory control and other basic security protocols. This must never be allowed to happen again.

Captain Gabriel DiBernardo, chief of detectives for the North Tonawanda Police Department, had had his fill of Ricky Matt and had hoped never to hear that name again. He considered Matt a man "with no heart, no soul." Only minutes after the escape, DiBernardo received his first call from a reporter. Had he heard the news?

"I'm well aware of it," he said. "So are my detectives, yes. We are well aware and police officers are always armed. It is not a good feeling to know he's out there, but for him to come all the way here . . . but anything is possible with Ricky Matt. Anything is possible. I keep watching the news, and I hope they stop him before he does anything violent again, because he is full of violence. That's his life."[7]

DiBernardo couldn't imagine a peaceful outcome. There would be *blood*.

Did Matt's escape surprise him?

"Heck, no. He is one cunning individual—but how he did it, with power tools; that's mind-boggling to me. I don't understand that."

DiBernardo recalled how he felt the last time Matt was free: "I had a loaded weapon on every floor of my house. He was the most evil, cunning, sadistic person I ever investigated in thirty-eight years."

DiBernardo noted that Matt sometimes worked with accomplices but opined that he was always the one in charge. "Matt was very imposing, a big muscular man and very strong, so others would help him, out of fear."

One of the first people to talk to reporters was Matt's son, who seemed eager to portray his dad as some sort of superman who could escape from any prison, who could take a lickin' and keep on tickin'.

During one prison escape, the son said, Richard Matt made it up to the roof of the prison and got shot in the shoulder. The son knew it to be true, too, because his dad had pulled down his shirt and showed the bullet wound. The guy had bullet holes on his body.

The son concluded, "He's been shot like nine times. It's like they can't kill him."[8]

Turns out, the scars that Matt had proudly shown his son may not have come from gunshots at all but from cigarette burns he'd endured while being tortured in Mexico. Matt also told his son that his scarred forearms came from climbing over the razor wire, not mentioning that at least some of those scars came from a razor-blade suicide attempt.

Randy Szukala was a Middleport and then a North Tonawanda cop, rose up the ranks to become the youngest chief in North Tonawanda history, served twenty-five years, and retired in 2013. When the news of the Dannemora escape hit, Szukala had just been hired as the assistant director of campus safety at Niagara University and was scheduled to begin work on June 10. Now, however, he was in demand, but it had nothing to do with his sterling career. It had to do with the fact that, many years before, he knew Richard Matt. It wasn't a happy memory, but Szukala nonetheless remembered. Again and again, he was asked to feed the ravenous information machine.[9]

Before the day was through New York governor Andrew Cuomo received a guided tour of the prisoners' escape route, with film crew in tow. And investigators winced as they watched the governor stomp around crime scene areas that had yet to be fully processed.

Cuomo learned power tools had been necessary; the escape must have been noisy as hell, so he asked prisoners straight out: if someone was inside the building using power tools, wouldn't they be heard?

The guards heard it; they had to have heard it, the prisoners told Cuomo.

Despite this, Cuomo said that he would be "shocked if a guard was involved, and that's putting it mildly. But we're looking at the civilian employees now and the private contractors to see if possibly a civil employee or contractor was assisting the escape because [the escapees] wouldn't have the equipment on their own, that's for sure."[10]

On June 7, the U.S. Marshals Service issued federal arrest warrants for Matt and Sweat, charging them with "unlawful flight to avoid prosecution," thus allowing federal agents to join the search.

The Adirondack Park rangers, all forty-three of them, would both search and be on call in case the prisoners—or their pursuers, for that matter—happened into an area of particularly cruel terrain and needed to be rescued.

Governor Cuomo went on a conference call with New York State public safety officials and members of the press. He announced a $100,000 reward for information leading to Matt and Sweat's arrest.

A written version of the statement read, "They are convicted murderers and our first order of business is to ensure they don't inflict any more pain on the community. . . . With the public's help, we will return these men to where they belong—behind bars."[11]

While news reporters were busy digesting carefully sculpted statements from "official" sources, feature writers and background researchers combed drawers of clippings to dig up the most recent reminders that correctional facilities were not as expertly guarded as taxpayers would like:[12]

In 2009, a New York tabloid ran a photo of a guard at the city jail on Rikers Island. She was asleep in a chair with her keys hanging from her belt. Next to her stood an inmate flashing a peace sign.

Going out of state, there was even a more recent example. Just weeks earlier, at the Mifflin County Correctional Center in Lewistown, Pennsylvania, a video was released of a sleeping guard, taken by a wife visiting her inmate husband.

The tabloid article said, sure, guards could get sleepy. Did CCF guards snooze their way through the escapees' labors, and how did they manage to stay asleep when the prisoners were using power tools?

The day before the escape, Richard Matt wrote a letter to his daughter. He wrote that he was looking forward to seeing her: "I always promised you that I would see you on the outside. I am a man of my word."[13]

By the time the letter was delivered to his daughter's address on June 9, Matt was in his third day of freedom. Police pounced. Though she and her dad had been corresponding for years, Matt's daughter was adamant that she had no foreknowledge of any escape plans.

She pledged her complete cooperation and requested round-the-clock protection, for fear that Dad would pay her a visit as he'd promised.

"Anything else unusual happen recently?" investigators asked Matt's daughter.

"Yeah, I received phone calls and texts a few days before the escape from a woman who identified herself as a friend of my dad's."

"How many times did she call?"

"Couple of times."

"What did she say?"

"Mostly they were texts. She passed on little tidbits, how my dad was doing. He has a bad back, and it had been operated on following an in-prison injury, and she gave me updates as to how he was feeling. You know, medical updates."

"Anything suspicious?"

"Not at all."

"Did she mention the escape?"

"No, sir."

"Did she give her name?"

"Yeah, she said it was Joyce Mitchell."[14]

Former corrections officer Gary Heyward offered CNN the lowdown on what it was really like inside prison walls.[15] It wasn't just black and white. There were shades of gray.

Heyward recalled an instructor who warned him, like a mother saying beware of bad girls, that there were temptations inside, temptations of the devil, and you had to be plenty strong to stay on the side of virtue.

Heyward started talking to himself, telling himself that maybe the devil would corrupt one guard out of three, but it wasn't going to be him. His rookie year was 1996; the venue, Rikers Island. He was making $28,000 a year—and it turned out the salary was his weak point.

When an inmate offered him $300 for a pack of cigarettes, he was easy pickings. From cigarettes, Heyward's biz grew rapidly, until he was smuggling in half ounces of cocaine. He was caught when an inmate ratted on him, and endured a two-year stretch on the other side of the bars.

It didn't have to be money. That was just his tender spot. A lot of time it was ego or sex. Whatever it was, the inmates would find it. They had a lot of time to think and analyze. A good con man had to be part shrink.

There was another factor, too, Heyward said. The prison itself had an effect on the man. Guys who wouldn't bend a rule on the outside break them without conscience on the inside.

It was the ambiance.

"*Guards become sort of prisoners themselves,* working twelve to eighteen hour shifts alongside the inmates," Heyward concluded. It could happen to anyone.

On June 11, *Fox News* tracked down Wayne Schimpf, half-brother of escapee Richard Matt, who amped up public tension with his up-close-and-personal assessment.

"I believe one-hundred percent that he will not be taken alive," Schimpf said. "There's no way he's going back to a life sentence."

Schimpf was then asked to speak directly to Matt: "I would beg him if he ever hears this or anyone gets it to him, Rick, please turn yourself in."

Matt had to understand how afraid everybody was now that he was on the loose. He had people terrified. "Let everybody be at ease finally," Schimpf said.

Did he have any faith that Matt might do as he'd asked?

No way. But he still had to ask. "I mean, somehow, somewhere, there still has to be some shred of human being in him."

As was true of many eyewitness statements regarding Richard Matt, sex came up.

Schimpf said, "He has a way of doing it. He is a thief, a con man. Any woman that comes across him, he will try to charm them and he can do it."

THREE
DAVID SWEAT
BORN
INTO
TURMOIL

David Sweat was born on June 14, 1980, and grew up in the town of Deposit, New York, thirty miles east of Binghamton. Pamela Sweat, a single mom, raised him and his two sisters. His was an undisciplined home, a world devoid of a child's fun, where fun was for adults only, and even then it was more like pseudo-fun, that is, kicks, and self-medication was the only prescription for ailments from an ulcer to the blues.

Patricia Desmond lived with the Sweats for a while, when David was about six.

"It was me, Dave's Uncle Bernie, his mom Pam, his sister Tillie, and Dave's grandmother (Pam's mom), all living together in an apartment on Second Street in Deposit, New York."[1]

Desmond remembered the ambiance as David was growing up. There was a lot of drinking going on, she said. Mostly drinking but some smoking too, every once in a while. Pot. The landlord lived across the street, but he came over to party with them too.

"David really wasn't raised into the best society. His life was into turmoil," she said.

She thought Dave was a good kid. Pretty normal. A little bit rambunctious, a temper tantrum now and again, but not so often that you'd think there was something wrong with him.

At that time Carl Butts was the boyfriend of Pamela Sweat, David's mother. Butts remembered that, when given a toy, David would burn it, or smash it with a hammer or rocks.

Desmond explained that Dave had reasons to be frustrated when he was little. He was emotionally neglected, in her opinion, with a mom who cared more about her boyfriend Carl than her son.

"When he got older he did become bad," Desmond said. "But I blame that on drugs."

As a nine-year-old boy, David Sweat took a liking to knives. He was an angry kid. He had been bullied at school for a whole year, and one day he decided he'd had enough. Sweat brought a butcher knife to school with him, smuggled it in in his backpack, but he was caught with it and suspended.[2]

According to his mother, it was around that time that he started throwing knives at her. In a fit of anger, he lifted a rocking chair and heaved it at his mother.[3] David's attempts to injure his mom usually came up short. But, she claimed, the psychological damage he was doing to her with his attacks couldn't be measured. Pamela says she had two nervous breakdowns around this time that were David's fault, so she sent him down to Florida to live with his aunt and uncle. Once down there, David was anxious, adding a nervous tenacity to his rebellion. It was as if he couldn't wait to mess up. He promptly stole his aunt's car, wrecked it, and ended up in a foster home. He returned to Deposit while still a teenager and, at that time, he took on a part-time job as a pot dealer.[4]

In 1996, Sweat and another teen put on ski masks, entered a Binghamton, New York, youth group home, locked a woman in a closet, and stole computers and cash. The pair were caught and sentenced to five years of intensive supervision probation.

Broome County, New York, judge Martin E. Smith referred to them as "teenaged idiots." In retrospect, the chilling aspect of this crime was that Sweat was found to have written down, step by step, how the job was to be committed, including a hand-drawn map of near blueprint accuracy showing where the items to steal were and which route they should take to get to them. Sweat liked to plan and plot, diagram and draw.

Judge Smith was not the only official to question Sweat's intelligence. The boy didn't seem to be living in the real world.

At a subsequent hearing, a parole board commissioner questioned Sweat: "You had a big plan to go there and tie up the lady who worked there and steal the stuff. Were you watching too much television or something?"

"Yes," Sweat replied.[5]

The commissioner had seen cases like this before, kids who thought the straight and narrow was sissy, that committing crimes was a way to look good in front of his "troublemaker" friends.

In 1997, Sweat's cousin, Jeffrey Nabinger Jr., already in trouble for breaking the windows on a pickup truck, became Sweat's partner in crime.

Sweat and Nabinger were the same age, first cousins—their moms were sisters—and inseparable. Though they did not facially resemble each other, they were both slight, two peas in a pod.

A lot of neighborhoods have guys like Sweat and Nabinger, guys that have trouble in common, who've lost touch with society, given up on getting ahead, and concentrated only on getting over. They didn't have jobs; they pulled jobs. Sometimes they didn't even have homes. Nabinger tried to make ends meet by selling pot, but it was hard because Sweat liked to smoke the profits. Both went through girlfriends like Kleenex. Sweat fathered a child with one of his girlfriends.

According to court documents unsealed in 2003, the year after the attempted group home robbery, Sweat was convicted of second-degree burglary and appeared before Judge Smith, the same judge who had once called Sweat an idiot. This time Sweat was convicted of second-degree burglary and, now an adult, sentenced to two to four years in prison.[6]

While in prison he was discovered by corrections officers to be making a sort of bucket list of crimes he hoped to commit one day, if a judge was kind enough to give him a furlough. In order to demonstrate his rehabilitation and fitness to return to society, he took a correspondence course and learned how to be an auto mechanic.

When released after serving nineteen months, he went to live with his girlfriend Audrey (pseudonym) in Binghamton, who happened to be the daughter of Patricia Desmond, the woman who lived with David and his mom when he was small.

At age twenty-two, David Sweat was once again enjoying freedom and hanging out with his cousin. He drove a gold 1990 Honda Accord with a moon roof. It was his pride and joy. He'd souped it up, he'd placed red "APC" decals on the windshield and side mirrors,[7] and there was a yellow "R" decal on the rear windshield.

As an adult, Sweat liked guns every bit as much as he enjoyed playing with knives as a child. And he had guns. On June 29, 2002, he told his mom's boyfriend, Roger M. Henry, that a fellow couldn't have enough firepower.

"I use a police scanner to avoid cops, but if I was ever confronted by the police, I would be prepared to blow them away," Sweat said.[8]

Sweat, Nabinger, and Sweat's mom were all there, in the house on Foley

Road near Kirkwood that Henry rented. There was a card table, and on it were two unloaded semiautomatic handguns.

Henry remembered Sweat explaining that he'd purchased the guns himself, but because he was a convicted felon he wasn't allowed to legally buy or carry in New York State. Henry didn't like it one bit and told Sweat in no uncertain terms that he wanted the guns out of his house.

Sweat was a bit showy as he grabbed one gun in each fist and dramatically put one inside the waistband of his pants, the other into a holster. He went outside and put both guns in the trunk of his Honda.

Henry knew for a fact that Sweat and Nabinger were *always* armed and had resumed their criminal careers. During the late spring and early summer, Kirkwood, along with the city of Binghamton and the nearby town of Fenton, underwent a rash of car thefts. Police saw a pattern. All of the vehicles were swiped from a parking lot. On July 2, a difficult-to-hide 1979 Winnebago was stolen from a Binghamton city lot.

It was Sweat and Nabinger appropriating the vehicles, of course—and there was nothing haphazard about the campaign of theft. They had a plan. They would live in the camper, which they had parked deep in the woods behind the Felchar Manufacturing Plant in Kirkwood. When not in the camper they'd four-wheel across the backfields away from prying eyes like Mad Max or the Rat Patrol in stolen trucks.

"They wanted to be modern-day desperadoes," said an unnamed source in an unsealed court record.

It was in those woods, at a place that they had named "One Dirt Road," that the cousins and a third man, twenty-three-year-old Shawn J. Devaul, met late on the evening of July 3. (Devaul had only made the papers once in his life. In 1997, when he was eighteen and living in Binghamton, he suffered head and lung injuries in a car accident in which a fourteen-year-old Chenango Forks girl was killed.)

Sweat briefed Nabinger and Devaul on the plan. He had it all mapped out in his mind. You couldn't have enough firepower, so they would steal guns from Mess's Fireworks store in Great Bend, Pennsylvania. Sweat had acquired a floor plan to the store and knew in advance the location of all of the desired items.

The three modern-day desperadoes climbed into Sweat's Honda and drove to Hallstead, Pennsylvania. There they stole a pickup truck. Sweat stayed in his Honda, while the other two went in the truck, with Nabinger driving. The convoy headed north on Route 11, back in the direction of Kirkwood, and took a right on Grange Hall Road.

In Grange Hall Road Park—where there was a baseball diamond, a playground, a picnic pavilion, and a parking lot—Sweat parked his Honda in the lot and got into the truck. All three men had guns and wore ski masks.

Past midnight now, during the early morning hours of July 4, Nabinger drove to Mess's Fireworks and, with a noisy crash, plowed the back of the pickup truck right through the store's front door. The collision took out the door and part of the wall, and set off the alarm.

Working quickly, the three men ransacked the place, loading handguns, long guns, and knives into Nabinger's Chicago Bulls duffel bag. When done, they threw the bag into the bed of the truck, pulled out of the store, and—convinced that they were home free—headed back to Grange Hall Road Park in Kirkwood.

At the park, they began to transfer the guns from the truck to Sweat's car but were interrupted. At 3:45 a.m., thirty-six-year-old Broome County sheriff's deputy Kevin J. Tarsia—thirteen years on the job, badge #143—was on patrol in Kirkwood, only about a quarter of a mile from his home, when he came upon the three men in a parking lot moving items from one vehicle into another.

Tarsia loved being a highway patrolman, so much so that his nickname was "Taillight." He was a meticulous and tenacious peace officer, a funny guy, fun loving, and engaged to be married. He was "a kind, loving soul," Tarsia's sister Cecilia said.

He parked his car at an angle so that he could point his spotlight at the two suspicious vehicles. The light revealed a blanket of night fog hovering over the park. Through the mist, Tarsia could see that there were at least three men. Two dashed off and hid in a nearby cluster of trees, while the third, Sweat, dove battlefield-style underneath the pickup truck.

As Kevin Tarsia approached, Devaul, completely out of his element, did nothing. Sweat crawled out from under the truck and fired at the cop. Sweat had an unloaded rifle in one hand and a loaded Glock in the other. He would later claim that Tarsia began to draw his own weapon, which was also a .40-caliber Glock.

Timothy Finch, a thirty-eight-year-old town of Kirkwood employee who lived nearby, blinked himself awake to the sounds of loud reports, which at first he thought were firecrackers. It was the Fourth, after all, if only technically.

Still, it was way too late (or too early) for those kinds of shenanigans. He'd heard three "pops" and then, after a pause, three more. Now fully awake, he heard another pause and another series of pops. He heard the screeching of tires, possibly from two vehicles. Finch interpreted the sounds in his mind and didn't like his conclusion. He threw on his New York Yankees jacket, pulled on his Adidas sneakers, and grabbed his cell phone. By this time Finch was fairly certain that this was more than just kids making a racket in the middle of the night. He went outside to investigate, stepping softly through his backyard onto a path that led to the park's baseball field. From a vantage point near third base, he saw a single car in the park with two lights, one a spotlight and the other blinking.

It was too dark and foggy to see that it was a police patrol car.

He called the Kirkwood state police barracks, which were ten miles away, and reported what was logged in as suspicious activity. The police dispatch recorded the call at 4:01 a.m.

According to a reconstruction of the event by police and information from the medical examiner, the thieves shot Tarsia a total of fifteen times. Sweat missed with a couple shots, he struck Tarsia's body armor with others, and one hit Tarsia in the lower torso, putting a groove in his small intestine and damaging one kidney. That shot knocked Tarsia off his feet. As he writhed on the parking lot, Sweat dropped his Glock, jumped into his car, and ran Tarsia over. The officer became caught under the car and was dragged several feet across the abrasive blacktop.

At this point, Nabinger emerged from his hiding place in the trees with a Kahr 9 mm in his hand. He squeezed off only one shot when his gun's magazine fell out. Tarsia's gun had fallen out of his hand when he was struck by the car. Now Nabinger picked it up and fired twice, point blank, into Tarsia's face.

The deputy now lay still on the parking lot pavement, on his back, with his legs twisted under him—the first Broome County sheriff's deputy to die in the line of duty since the department was founded in 1806.

Before leaving the scene, Nabinger walked over to Tarsia's car, pulled the keys from the ignition, and used them to open the trunk. He unzipped Tarsia's equipment bag and stole a pad of arrest forms and a fistful of flares. They also stole Tarsia's Glock. (The arrest forms and flares were later recovered inside a stolen vehicle found at their headquarters in the woods, at the location known as One Dirt Road.)

After calling the police, Timothy Finch remained on the baseball diamond and waited for the troopers to arrive. But no one came. He waited for a half hour, returned home, and went back to bed. His kitchen clock said 4:35 a.m.

No one ever did respond to Finch's call. At 5:40 a.m. a man from Windsor named Michael West was returning home from his job in Conklin when he spotted the patrol car parked at an unusual angle in the park. He called the police, and this time there was a response.

For the three men in attendance at the cop's murder, freedom was brief. On July 6, Saturday, a little more than two days after, someone dropped a dime on them. Nabinger was walking down a street in Port Dickinson when the cop car pulled up. Sweat was in his car, driving in Kirkwood, when he was pulled over. Devaul was caught and arrested in the Village of Greene. Nabinger and Sweat were charged with murder one; Devaul, with possession of a weapon three, a felony.

Police spoke with Sweat's girlfriend Audrey, and she was cooperative, telling the law the location of One Dirt Road. Police went there and recovered the stolen vehicles.

Broome County sheriff David E. Harder was an ex-Marine (Forty-Eighth Rifle Company) and had been with the Broome County Sheriff's Office since 1964. He had been the county's first warrant officer and first narcotics officer, and he was elected sheriff in 1998. He'd been a sheriff's detective for more than twenty-five years.

Now, with three men under arrest following the killing of a cop, Sheriff Harder said, "Devaul was a non-active participant." He watched while in possession of a gun, Harder explained. Nabinger and Sweat killed the cop.

On the day of the arrests, police searched the garbage cans on the back porch of an apartment at 15 Dickinson Street in Binghamton. In the garbage they found soda bottles filled with urine and a hand-drawn map showing the layout of Mess's Fireworks. On the map they found David Sweat's fingerprint.

Early details were scattered. The perpetrators might have stolen Tarsia's gun. It was uncertain if Tarsia's gun had been fired. Local newspapers couldn't find permanent addresses for Nabinger and Devaul. Almost as a sidebar, it was reported the trio were also responsible for the burglary of Mess's Fireworks in Great Bend, Pennsylvania.

Law enforcement strutted a little. All three bad guys were in county jail, no bail. When you lost one of your own, swift justice sent a message. There was nothing more serious than killing a cop. It was a great example of what teamwork could do. They had impressive stats: sixty hours of investigation, some deputies going fifty hours without sleep, one hundred officers on the job, and fifteen agencies playing a role. Sweat's girlfriend was also cooperating. To avoid the death penalty, Sweat pleaded guilty to first-degree murder before Judge Patrick H. Mathews and was sentenced to life without parole (LWP).

He was packed off to Dannemora on October 30, 2003, where he wrote frequent letters in a cramped hand to his mother. In those letters he described how much he was enjoying his new prison job sewing clothes.

Not long after Tarsia's death, a plaque was installed, imbedded in a large rock, located at Grange Hall Road Park in Kirkwood, and each year on the anniversary of his death, they would decorate the site with flowers, flags, and candles. On the tenth anniversary of the murder of Kevin Tarsia on July 4, 2012, WDNG-TV ran a feature story remembering Deputy Tarsia. In it Sheriff Harder said, "It's important to remember any of our dead officers, no matter what agency it is. They do work hard. They put their lives out there every single day. If the residents of the county or city or town, wherever they work, can sleep or rest at night, then they know they're doing their job."[9]

Sheriff Harder updated his Facebook status to pay respect to the Tarsia family and to ask the public to keep the family in their thoughts and prayers.

FOUR
RICHARD
MATT
TWISTED

Richard "Ricky" Matt grew up in the Buffalo, New York, area, in the city of Tonawanda. Tonawanda and North Tonawanda are known in the area as the "Twin Cities," separated only by the Erie Canal. Folks in Tonawanda knew early on that Ricky Matt was a bad egg. He was just like his old man, a chip off the good-for-nothing block, and a twisted twig. But how twisted he was none could imagine, at least not until body parts began washing ashore on Tonawanda Island in the Niagara River.

Richard Matt was born on June 25, 1966. As an infant, he was abandoned in a car. He and his older brother Robert didn't have a real home and were fast-tracked into the foster-care system. It looked for a time like the story might have a happy ending as the brothers were both taken at an "early" age[1] into the home of Mr. and Mrs. Vernon Edin (now deceased), who had previously given a good home to foster kids and were known to offer second chances to kids who'd messed up. The Edins made sure Ricky and Robert went to school and enrolled them in extracurricular activities such as scouts and youth baseball. Matt was considered a bright kid, played the trumpet, and grew into a good-looking teenager who was popular with girls.

The trouble was, when it came to Matt's personality, Nature was beating out Nurture. Ricky turned out to be a lot like his biological father, Robert Sr., who was a career criminal with a long record of assault, burglary, fraud, and theft charges. One police officer referred to Matt's father as a "piece of garbage."[2]

Successes in Ricky's life were infrequent, but they existed. In December 1976, Richard Matt was "Player of the Week" in the Franklin Street Boys' Club indoor soccer league and lauded for his goalkeeping that led his team to victory.[3] He received a certificate and a photo of himself in action.

He was a jock, at age twelve played Little League and Pop Warner football, but by age fourteen Ricky was in juvenile detention for trying to steal a houseboat. The facility couldn't hold him for long, however. In a harbinger of things to come, Matt stole a horse and rode away to freedom on it.[4]

Matt's son, Nicholas Harris, later said that running for freedom was the only kind of life his old man ever knew. "Everybody is born innocent," Nicholas said. "But he was *raised around crime*." It was in his blood. He wasn't born evil—he was just predisposed to it.[5]

Ah, the love of a son for his old man.

North Tonawanda cop Randy Szukala recalled, "Matt would terrorize kids on the school bus. He would just terrorize people. Even in elementary school, junior high. He had issues. Even as a child, his reputation was fearsome."[6] From 1985 to 1991, Matt terrorized the Broadway-Fillmore neighborhood in which he lived.

On May 13, 1986, according to the *Tonawanda News*, "Richard Matt, 19, of 28 Hill Place, was sentenced to one year for third-degree assault."

It got to the point where, if a crime was committed in the area, the first question was, "Is Matt in or out?" If he was out, police picked him up. Chances were good that he was the one who'd done it. He was arrested eight times.

Tonawanda police captain Frederic Foels told the *Rochester Democrat and Chronicle* that Matt started out as a "small-time thug, but one time he beat up a girl pretty bad. He got charged with assault in the second degree—that's a felony. We always knew him as Ricky. Ricky did this. Ricky Matt did that."[7]

Few knew Matt as well as David Bentley,[8] who was a motorcycle cop when he first met Matt in 1979. Bentley was patrolling Niagara Street when he noticed an angry kid scowling at him out the back window of the car in front of him. Matt was thirteen at the time.

Bentley knew, as most cops know, that there are kids who are mad and there are kids who are bad, and it helped to know which you were dealing with at any given time. Bentley thought Matt was mad, not bad—and worth saving.

The officer later learned who the kid was and why he was so angry. Matt had been abandoned. Alcoholism ran in his family. These were things that Bentley understood from his own life. He learned that Matt only first met his biological father when he was eighteen and in jail. A deputy called out the name Matt, and he and an older man both stepped forward. They looked at each other, realized that they were father and son, and the older man barely acknowledged the boy. It was around that time that Bentley, now a detective, tried to mentor Matt. But he didn't get very far.

"When Matt was cleaned up, he was very handsome and, in all frankness, very well endowed," Bentley said, unaware of the meme power of that statement. "He gets girlfriends any place he goes. Trouble was, he was in and out of jail constantly. Burglary. They alleged he committed a horrific rape, but I think he beat the charge on that; stolen cars, everything but drugs."[9]

Richard Matt's older brother Robert was also arrested multiple times during this stretch, but as far as police knew, the brothers were independent and did not do crimes together.

Matt was married and had a couple of kids but never had a legitimate job of any consequence. For a time during the 1980s, Matt promoted a modicum of good will by ratting out other criminals to Bentley.

In 1986, the nineteen-year-old Matt, already described as a repeat offender familiar with incarceration, was serving a year in the Erie County Correction Facility for assault. Instead of graduating from grammar school to middle school and high school, Matt graduated from foster homes to juvenile facilities to big-boy prison.

The prison was in Alden, New York, twenty miles east of Buffalo. A photo of Matt taken there reveals much about his playfully mischievous and thoroughly alpha personality. In the picture, Matt has a cigarette hanging off his lower lip. He's wearing a correction officer's shirt and holding a guard's billy club in his hand. Matt himself gave the photo its handwritten caption: "Who said I can't escape this place?"[10]

On June 15, 1986, Matt made good on that threat, taking advantage of a guard's mistake (he'd left the electronic lock on Matt's cell open). Matt left his cell and scaled a nine-foot brick-and-metal wall topped with razor wire in order to escape. Bleeding from razor cuts, he hopped a freight train.

After a four-day manhunt that covered Tonawanda and Buffalo's West Side, areas chosen because this was where many of Matt's relatives and his then girlfriend lived, police found him with an ax handle in his hand at his brother's apartment at 267 William Street. His brother was attending night classes at a business institute at the time. Detective Sergeant Charles Tirone of the Erie County Sheriff's Office stood ten feet away from Matt and talked to him calmly, eventually convincing him that the smart thing was to drop the ax handle and be arrested.

After four years in Attica, Matt was released, arrested soon thereafter for attempted burglary, imprisoned in Erie for three and a half years, and again loosed on the world in February 1997. Bentley theorized that Matt was bipolar because he had big mood swings. He'd do bad things to people. Then he'd go into a depression and sometimes hurt himself. Matt had a Jekyll/Hyde personality; he was Janus faced—brutal one second, kind the next.

At least twice Matt attempted suicide, but on both occasions Bentley and others arrived in time to save him. The first attempt came when Matt was twenty. Bentley recalled going to a Hill Street address after receiving a call that Matt was going to hurt himself. He went into the place and found blood smeared on the walls, going up three flights of stairs to Matt's apartment. In his apartment Matt was holding a big knife in his hand and had inflicted maybe twenty cuts up and down his arms.

Blood was spewing from the wounds.

Four years later, now twenty-four years old, Matt was again suicidal—and again Bentley was called. This time Matt was in a garage at an address on Tonawanda's Delaware Street. He was almost dead from carbon monoxide fumes in a car. He had plugged up the exhaust pipe and started the engine.

Although Bentley said he knew the Jekyll side of Matt's personality, others all too often encountered Hyde. He was accused of rape in 1989 and of slashing and stabbing a woman who was the mother of his son in 1991.

Matt was also a realist who understood that stints in prison were inevitable, so he took steps even when he was on the outside to make life easier on the inside. For example, he had the Marine Corps motto tattooed on his right shoulder, *Semper Fidelis*, even though he'd never been a Marine. His thinking was that the tattoo would increase the chances that one day, sooner or later, potentially dangerous or amorous inmates would be intimidated by him.

Auto plant worker Gregory Durandetto met Richard Matt when they were both eight years old. Back then, Durandetto said, Matt was a "goofy, fun-loving kid."[11]

Matt's early years as a criminal were linked to his sense of abandonment, Durandetto said. The kid lived in a foster home and had nothing. He stole things so that he could have possessions like the other kids.

One day in high school, Matt pulled up in a car and said to Durandetto, "Get into my new Charger."

Durandetto said, "Hey Rick, that's not a Charger, it's a Challenger."

Matt was taken aback. "You mean I stole the wrong car?" Moping with disappointment, he returned the car.

Another time, Matt stole dozens of pairs of shoes. Most of them didn't fit so he placed them on the lawn in front of the Tonawanda Town Hall.

Like Bentley, Durandetto remembered Matt as a ladies' man, a guy that wasn't nervous around girls the way others were, one who could walk right up to a woman in a bar and efficiently walk out with her. Durandetto liked hanging out with Matt during those years because he would attract more women than he could use and was always introducing his friends to pretty girls.

An interesting interlude in Matt's life occurred when he was in the Erie County Holding Center awaiting trial on the rape charge and became acquainted with another inmate who called himself David Telstar, the adopted son of a middle class Minnesota family. He'd been born as Mark David Matson but hoped one day to marry rich so he changed it to something tonier. The name he chose was David Telstar.

His affluent wife was born Susan Ellen Sperling, but later became known as Desiree Sheinbaum. No matter what she was called, she was the granddaughter of movie mogul Harry Warner and an heiress.

The couple was introduced in 1985 by Telstar's former teacher and ex-girlfriend while Telstar was studying at the Pratt Institute of Architecture in Brooklyn, New York. Telstar moved to Sacramento, married Desiree on Valentine's Day 1986, and started a small graphic arts business.

As it turned out, Telstar's real business was trying to get control of his wife's fortune. By the time Richard Matt met him in jail, Telstar was listed as hailing from Santa Barbara, California, and charged with embezzling $1.3 million from a trust fund controlled by his wife.

Telstar allegedly paid $100,000 to bail Matt out so Matt could murder his wife, her parents, and an attorney involved with the trust. Desiree's father was Stan Sheinbaum, who was at the time a member of the Los Angeles Police Commission.

As it turned out, Telstar's in-laws were not in danger. Once bailed out, Matt reneged on his promise and ratted on his coconspirator. He informed Mrs. Telstar that Mr. Telstar wanted her dead and revealed the plot to the authorities in exchange for lenience regarding his legal woes. Matt, at the time, was under indictment for a 1989 rape and was facing possible charges for a separate assault on a former girlfriend.

Telstar ended up pleading guilty to conspiracy. Matt later claimed he was attacked in a prison in Elmira, stabbed in the leg, as part of Telstar's retaliation. After Matt served as the star witness at Telstar's trial, he appeared on a television newsmagazine called *Hard Copy* discussing his involvement with the case.

Following his 1997 release from Erie Correctional, Matt found a place to live at 114 Minerva Street in the city of Tonawanda.[12] His first job out of prison was working for a food brokerage company in North Tonawanda. The company took food that was near the expiration date and resold it. After only a few weeks, Matt was fired by the company's owner, his boss, seventy-six-year-old William Rickerson.[13]

Out of work with nothing to do, Richard Matt starred in a home movie, an activity far less common then than now, and showed off one of his prized possessions, a South American blow-dart gun.

As the 8 mm film starts, Matt is on-screen and the camera operator says, "This is my friend Ricky Matt right here, he's a freaking crazy lunatic maniac."

Holding the gun, Matt waves to the camera.

"This is the face of a maniac!" announces the friend.

Disturbingly, the cameraman then shoots Matt in the forearm with a dart. Matt smiles as blood drips from the wound and then proves himself to be a man of ideas: "Let's dip these in AIDS blood, and we'll put a patent on them and sell them as deadly weapons," he says.[14]

Matt's old food brokerage boss William Rickerson was not known to be a rich man but did apparently say some things that ended up getting him into trouble. With Matt in earshot, Rickerson made reference to the "$100,000 I have buried in the basement." It might have been a brag or it might have been a joke, but it was definitely not something he should have said with Richard Matt in the room. Matt got it into his head that Rickerson kept great sacks of cash in his home, and from this notion he wouldn't be dissuaded.[15]

By 1997, Matt's new crime partner was twenty-five-year-old Lee Eugene Bates, a part-time strip-club employee who was also a criminal justice major at Erie Community College, studying to be a police officer.[16]

The unthinkable crime that Matt and Bates committed together was surprisingly spontaneous. On December 4, 1997, the pair, all in one night, planned to rob Matt's former boss—the man who had fired Matt five weeks earlier and who said his home contained buried treasure, the guy Matt called the "million dollar Jew"—and commenced executing the plan in a matter of hours.

Matt was visiting his stepbrother Wayne Schimpf when the seed of a bad idea was first planted. Schimpf overheard Matt on the phone having an argument with a former employer, who turned out to be Rickerson, about money Matt claimed he was owed.

Matt got no satisfaction, hung up roughly, and immediately called his friend Bates.

"Come on over," Matt was overheard saying. He then asked for and received a pair of gloves from Schimpf.

Matt and Bates drove to Rickerson's house and pounded on the door. When Rickerson answered, Matt and Bates barged in. Matt did the talking:

"Where's the fucking money?" Matt asked.

Rickerson gave him a bewildered look.

"You heard me, where's the cash?" Matt said. He grabbed Rickerson at the shoulders and roughly spun him around. Matt punched Rickerson in the face and pushed him again until Rickerson fell awkwardly down a set of stairs into the family room.

Bates stood guard over Rickerson while Matt searched the house, turned the place upside down—the bedrooms, even the basement. Matt's mantra was bitten off but steady: "Where's the money? Where's the fucking money?"

The pair beat Rickerson, who wouldn't answer the question. It wasn't that there was money and he wasn't revealing where it was; it was that there was no money. Couldn't they get that through their heads?

They could not.

Then, just as Matt was about to start a fresh round of beating, there was a knock at the door. Matt put his finger to his lips. Everyone was quiet. The knock repeated. Eventually the visitor went away, and the attack continued.

Matt found a letter opener and held it menacingly, at one point prodding the sharp tip roughly inside Rickerson's ear. Rickerson didn't respond to the threat. With frustration Matt hit Rickerson repeatedly over the head with the letter opener, which was kinder than stabbing him with it but still hurt like hell.

The crime was already tons messier than Matt and Bates had planned, so messy that the pair began to revel in it with porcine gusto. Matt opened a bottle of wine and poured it over Rickerson's head. It was kind of funny if you were a sick fuck.

But it was frustrating too. Why wasn't Rickerson spilling the goddamned beans? This wasn't working. None of it was working. At some point it occurred to them that they hadn't bothered wearing masks and Rickerson knew who they were.

How could they silence him? There was only one way, only one that didn't involve trust.

The home invaders decided to up the torture ante. After a solid hour inside Rickerson's home, they wrapped the pajama-clad Rickerson in duct tape at the hands and feet, and carried him outside, taking him out through the sliding door to the patio and then along the side of the house to the trunk of Bates's 1990 Chevy, where they stowed Rickerson.

Bates couldn't tell what was on Matt's mind but was starting to get a real bad feeling. He was in way over his head. The simple fact, which hadn't occurred to them as they hurriedly planned the caper, was that if you robbed someone you knew, the chances were pretty good that you wouldn't get away with it.

As they drove down the road with their captive in the trunk, Matt regularly shouted back to Rickerson, who sometimes answered and sometimes merely grunted. As the ordeal went on, Rickerson stopped responding.

Matt would shout the question and there would be silence. So they drove to Matt's house where Matt and Bates had a conversation.

"We left a real mess back at Rickerson's house," Bates noted.

"Yeah, we should clean it up, cover our tracks," Matt agreed, so they returned to Rickerson's and, with the victim still bound in the trunk, attempted to clean up his house—not quite well enough as it turned out.

Then they were back in the car, back on the road. In the front seat the conversation must have at some point gotten down to brass tacks, as they decided the tool they needed the most. So they drove nonstop to Erie, Pennsylvania, where they stopped and bought a shovel.

By this time, Rickerson's silence act was over. Now, he wouldn't be quiet. He was shouting and trying to draw attention. When they stopped in Erie so Matt could buy a pack of Marlboros, Rickerson was particularly loud. Bates turned up the car radio to mask the cries coming from the trunk: "Let me out! Let me out!"

"I'll let you out when you tell me where the fucking money is," Matt said. He had to teach this guy a lesson. They pulled over in a secluded spot, and Matt grabbed The Club, an antitheft device that attached to a car's steering wheel.

Matt opened the trunk, struck Rickerson a few times with The Club, and slammed the trunk shut again. That would teach him not to try to attract attention the next time they stopped at a store.

They drove all the way to Ohio. When they reached a desolate rural section, they pulled off the road and tried to dig a hole, taking turns with the shovel. But the ground was too hard, and they quickly gave up.

They got back in the car. Next stop: Allegany State Park. Along this stretch it began to snow, hard, big flakes; visibility was a matter of feet, so the already impatient captors were forced to slow down to a crawl.

The storm passed, and their pace resumed at the speed limit. They turned west and pulled over just outside the village of Silver Creek, on the shores of Lake Erie, an area of western New York known as the Concord Grape Belt. They stopped down the road from a place called the Sunset Beach Club, just south of the mouth of the Cattaraugus Creek.

Out of frustration, Matt decided that his captive was still not taking the situation seriously enough, and so he opened the trunk, struck Rickerson once in the chest one more time with The Club. Desperate now, Matt increased the torture. He bent back four of Rickerson's fingers until they broke with a brutally sharp noise, like someone snapping a breadstick in two. Rickerson screamed in agony.

But, for Matt, the location of Rickerson's cash stash was as unknown as ever. As they drove back toward North Tonawanda, Bates was feeling increasingly worse about their predicament. Matt was continuing to make messes that were hard to clean up, messes that, if discovered, would mean an end to life as he knew it.

Disturbingly, Bates noticed that Matt's attention span was shrinking. The more frustrated Matt became, the more difficulty he had focusing. His loop of thinking steadily shortened until his behavior became repetitive.

With ever-increasing frequency, Matt ordered that the car be stopped and stepped to the trunk so he could have the same argument with the moaning Rickerson for the umpteenth time. It was now the wee hours of the morning.

The final argument with Rickerson occurred alongside the road somewhere between Silver Creek and Buffalo. According to Bates, Matt had him pull down a road to a cul-de-sac. Bates stopped the car and opened up the trunk with his key. (Since the only living witness to this scene had plenty to gain by inserting details that made him look good and Matt bad, we have to take some things with a grain of salt.) According to Bates, Matt then yelled at Bates; Rickerson yelled at Matt for yelling at Bates; and Rickerson said, Bates quoting him, "Leave Bates out of it. This is between you and me, Matt."

That, apparently, was the last straw for Matt, who said, "I've had enough of this." Matt violently clutched ahold of Rickerson's head with both hands and viciously twisted Rickerson's neck until there was a loud popping noise.

Matt dropped the limp, quiet, and still Rickerson back into the trunk.

Inside the car and back on the road, morale was very low. They had driven for twenty-seven hours and had made a profit of less than $100, credit cards, and whatever they'd be able to get from the victim's wedding ring.

Quiet now, Bates and Matt drove to Tonawanda Island where they hid Rickerson's body under a woodpile.

The key to getting away with murder was to keep your mouth shut, but murderers often failed to pull it off. Yakety-yak and the next thing you knew, cops were pounding at the door. Matt was no exception. He had too much adrenaline working to stay quiet, and he almost immediately told people close to him that he had been involved in a man's death. He lied about it, decriminalized it, but talked about it nonetheless.

Among the people Matt told was his girlfriend, Johanna Capretto, a stripper living in a motel across the border in Canada. Matt said, "I pushed Rickerson down and he died. I didn't kill him on purpose. I'm not that kind of guy."

The more Matt thought about it, the more he understood that they'd inadequately disposed of the body. So he returned to the dumpsite and pulled the body out from under the woodpile. Laboring, Matt used a hacksaw to dismember the body. The head and all four limbs were sawed off. He threw the remains chunk by chunk into the rolling Niagara River.

Rickerson's friends last heard from him on December 4, 1997, at 8:00 p.m. On December 5 Rickerson missed an appointment, and two employees, William McGee and Eddie Solomon, called police to report him missing.

They knew he would never miss a business meeting without explanation unless something was wrong.

At 12:31 p.m. on December 7, a police officer went to Rickerson's address, accompanied by the two employees, to see what was up. The officer found Rickerson's front door locked and that morning's paper untouched, but the sliding door in the back was open. The officer and the two employees gave the house a quick search and saw no sign of Rickerson or disarray. No written report was made of this search at the time.

At 12:53 p.m. on December 9, a Mrs. Alice Reszel called the North Tonawanda Police Department's Detective Bureau. She said she'd just received a visit from William Rickerson's cleaning lady, a woman named Lois Brant, who said she was unable to get into Rickerson's house with her key and that there was an accumulation of old newspapers and mail at the front door. Officer Ralph LaFreniere was dispatched to speak with Mrs. Reszel.

Police at first tried to find an innocent explanation for the disappearance. Perhaps a sick man had simply wandered off. Maybe a tired man had taken an unexpected vacation. Detectives Glenn D. Gardner and John Snopkowski went to Rickerson's home and gave the place a cursory search. The sliding door in the back was still open, but there were no signs of a struggle and there was no Rickerson. This time, a little investigation was deemed necessary. The detectives spoke with cleaning lady Lois Brant and William Rickerson's daughter-in-law Kathryn, who said that Rickerson would never leave the area without notifying his friends, family, and business.

On the morning of December 10, Gardner drove to Cheektowaga, New York, to the home of William McGee, one of the employees that had first reported Rickerson missing. McGee climbed into Gardner's car, and together they went to Rickerson's warehouse on Military Road in Tonawanda. There they spoke to the manager of the property, Kevin McMahon, who said he hadn't seen Rickerson since late in the morning of December 4, when he gave Rickerson his warehouse electric bill. McMahon gave Gardner and McGee permission to search. No Rickerson.

During the search, however, McGee and Gardner got talking.

"You think somebody did something to Mr. Rickerson?" McGee asked.

"Can't rule it out. Why?"

"Well, because if someone did something bad to him, I might know who it could've been."

"Who's that?"

"Guy named Rick."

"Last name?"

"I don't know."

McGee told Gardner about Rick: The guy had been in prison, a long stretch for something violent. He'd worked for Rickerson for about a month and a half. Rickerson fired Rick around Thanksgiving, accused him of stealing.

"Where does Rick live?" Gardner asked.

"I went there once," McGee said, trying to remember. "We were in the car and he had to go home for a second to change his clothes."

"Do you remember where it was?"

"Sort of," was the best McGee could do. He knew the neighborhood. "Somewhere off of Delaware Avenue," he said.

Gardner suggested they ride around Rick's neighborhood. Maybe they'd see something to jog McGee's memory. For ninety minutes Gardner drove. Eventually they got to Rick's Minerva Street block, and McGee recognized the house at number 114.

"I had another awful idea," McGee said. "We searched the warehouse pretty good but we didn't look in the dumpsters out back." There were two.

So they went back and searched. Nada.

On December 11, Gardner started the day by picking up McGee and bringing him to the detective bureau, so he could give a written statement. That done, Gardner and Detective Edward Schintzius took McGee home and went to Minerva Street to see if they could find Rick. They knew that Rick rented from the homeowners, who were Vernon and Marcela Edin. Gardner didn't yet know that the Edins had also been Matt's foster parents.

As the detectives arrived two men were pulling up in a car. One was Vern Edin and the other Rick Matt. The detectives said they wanted to talk about William Rickerson, and Vern invited the policemen inside to his kitchen. The police then split up the men. Schintzius spoke with Edin, and Gardner took Matt into the other room.

"What do you want to talk to me for?" Matt asked.

"We're investigating a missing person complaint about Mr. Rickerson."

"Why me?"

"We are interviewing all of Rickerson's employees and ex-employees," Gardner explained. Matt was clearly unhappy so Gardner pressed a little harder. "Would you be willing to come down to the police station and give us a statement that might help us find Mr. Rickerson?" Gardner asked.

"I ain't going to answer any questions from any fucking police and I ain't going to no police station."

"Why?"

"Because I hate fucking cops that's why."

"Why hate cops?" Gardner asked.

Because, Matt explained, he had an extensive criminal history, had done time in prison, and was on parole and probation. He felt as if he'd been harassed by City of Tonawanda police since he got out, in particular by a detective named Brady.

Matt told Gardner that it had just been the other day when Brady got his cop henchmen to visit Matt's house first thing in the morning as he was transferring various meat products from his trunk to another car. He'd explained to the cops that he was a meat producer and that the items were not stolen. They called Mr. Rickerson, who told them he didn't want to get involved.

Gardner gave Matt his card, told him to call if he heard anything about Mr. Rickerson, and left. He later learned that the meat products Matt was transferring *had* been stolen and that although Rickerson refused to press charges against Matt for the theft, he did fire him.

On Gardner's list of interesting persons he drew an emphatic line under Richard Matt's name. He checked out Matt's extensive criminal record and spoke to cops who'd dealt with Matt in the past. The key word was violent. Matt once beat and raped a woman during a burglary.

That afternoon Gardner received a phone call from William Rickerson Jr., who was in Toronto, Canada, on the fourth day of a business trip. Considering the circumstances, that his father was missing, he agreed to return to North Tonawanda immediately and be available for a police interview.

That interview with both Rickerson and his wife took place at 9:00 a.m. on December 12 at the detective bureau. Rickerson Jr. gave Gardner the number to access his dad's voice mail. Gardner made a note of some of the messages and deemed others unworthy of consideration.

Gardner and the Rickersons then drove to Rickerson Sr.'s house on Harvard Avenue and again searched the place, this time more carefully. While out on the patio, Gardner saw something, a droplet of something, and it interested him enough that he got down on his hands and knees to take a better look. A tiny brown spec, just one, and so small that a spray might have created it. Yet, it was alone.

Still on hands and knees, Gardner searched inside the house. He went down the stairs to the basement. At the base of the stairs he once again got on all fours to look carefully and found two more brown specs. About a foot away from the specs was a discarded cigarette butt, a Marlboro red. (That butt would turn out to be key evidence, as it was later determined to be Matt's brand and coated at the filtered tip with Matt's DNA.)

He found suspicious stains elsewhere as well: a droplet near the family-room door and a smudge on the kitchen floor at the top of the stairs to the family room. He immediately secured the house and called Captain Gabriel (Gabe) DiBernardo and Sergeant Kevin Locicero of the I.D. bureau. Joined by Detective Snopkowski, Gardner, DiBernardo, and Locicero reentered the house using Rickerson Jr.'s key just before noon. During the search Rickerson Jr. was instructed to stay in the family room, to stay out of the way of the investigation, and to not touch anything.

Locicero realized the crime scene was too big and too important to be handled by one man, so he called in help in the form of Mark Henderson of the Niagara County Forensic Lab and Inspector Joseph Taylor, crime scene specialist.

Reexamining the home now with luminol,[17] investigators found evidence of blood spatter in many places. There had been a bloody mess at one point, and someone had done a pretty decent job of cleaning it up—not good enough to fool investigators though. Possible blood was photographed and samples taken as evidence from nine locations, including the first droplet Gardner has seen out on the patio, which turned out to be barbeque sauce.

Gardner later recalled, "I didn't think finding the droplet of barbeque sauce was worthless to the case at all. It was that droplet that got me down on my hands and knees, and got me to looking down for like evidence, so the barbeque sauce played its part."

The investigators methodically secured the evidence, all the time putting their minds together and mapping out a crime scene. By midafternoon, the home was officially declared a crime scene, at which time Rickerson Jr. was relieved of his house key and asked to leave.

During the thorough search of Rickerson's home, investigators found a shelved book that had been carved out inside to form a hiding place for $5,000 in cash. Rickerson, it seemed, had been telling the truth about having a stash of hidden money. (The money was subsequently given to Rickerson's son.)

On December 13, 1997, Detective Gardner learned more about the incident during which Rick Matt was "hassled" by City of Tonawanda police regarding the transfer of meat products from one car to another. It turned out that a fellow named Lee Bates accompanied Matt during this incident. That afternoon, police took a statement from Christopher Brick, part owner of Brick Brothers' Pizzeria in Tonawanda. He'd been one of the guys whose voice had been on Rickerson's message machine. Brick said he knew Rickerson only professionally, as he purchased food from him for his business.

Detective Schintzius checked out Rickerson's credit card activity. He learned that Rickerson had purchased nothing using his Capital One card since October. The company agreed to call back if any transactions on the card occurred.

They checked his bank accounts and saw no activity since November 25. The bank immediately froze the account and followed the procedure to deny anyone using Rickerson's debit card. Police took another look at Rickerson's warehouse, inside and out, and made a careful check to make sure Rickerson hadn't booked any flights or otherwise made travel plans. At 6:30 p.m., Schintzius and Gardner went to Tonawanda Police Headquarters and spoke to Detective David Bentley, Matt's old mentor. Bentley explained in no uncertain terms that Matt was capable of anything, any crime, without feeling remorse. The thing about Matt, Bentley explained, was that he couldn't keep his mouth shut. If he'd had something to do with Rickerson's disappearance, he was bragging about it to his friends and family.

The next morning, Captain DiBernardo briefed Rickerson Jr. and his wife Kathryn on the status of the investigation. The Rickersons gave lengthy written statements.

On the morning of December 17, investigators once again took over Rickerson's home—this time accompanied by the K-9 search team, featuring Abby the bloodhound. Abby was allowed a whiff of Rickerson's socks in the upstairs bedroom and went to work. The dog took investigators downstairs, out the sliding door onto the patio, and then along the side of the house to the driveway where the trail ended. It seemed that Rickerson had entered a car in the driveway and been taken away.

They knew they had blood in the house, but was it Rickerson's blood? They struggled to find out Rickerson's blood type. The Veteran's Administration had no record of him. In 1987, Rickerson had visited the emergency room at DeGraff Hospital, but folks there didn't know his blood type either.

At Rickerson's warehouse a different sort of emergency developed. The food stored there was decaying. Police called the Department of Agriculture and Markets, who seized the warehoused food for future destruction.

A few weeks after Rickerson's disappearance, Matt arrived unexpectedly at his half-brother Wayne Schimpf's apartment.

"Ricky, what are you doing here?" Schimpf said, not without concern. He knew Ricky well enough to know that he was always trouble—100 percent of the time.

"I'm in a fucking jam," Matt said. "Got a newspaper?"

Schimpf did and Matt pointed out a story about Rickerson's disappearance. He said that he might have killed the missing man by accident. Then he panicked and cut the guy up for more convenient disposal.

Schimpf stared at Matt. Part of him believed it. Part of him thought his half sibling was full of crap. He didn't *want* to believe it, that was for sure.

"How did you do it?" Schimpf asked.

Matt gave his half brother a grin that Schimpf would never forget. "With a hacksaw," Matt said.

"No way." Schimpf felt his heart racing. This was a startling admission, even from the ne'er-do-well Richard Matt.

Matt didn't have time for Schimpf's shock. "Look, I've got to get out of town. Can I borrow your car?"

"No. I need my car. You can't just——"

"You're my brother, you're my blood. I love you—but I'll kill you."

Schimpf had a duplicate set of car keys, so he gave a set to Matt, and seconds later his Explorer was gone—heading south.

At four o'clock on the afternoon of December 22, Lee Eugene Bates came into the police station. The job of talking to Bates went to Detective Edward Schintzius, who had known Bates since he was a kid, as Schintzius's wife attended the same church as Bates's mom. Gardner also took part in the interview.

"Lee, how long have you known this guy Rick Matt?" Schintzius asked.

"About six months," Bates replied.

"Where did you meet him?"

"Ran into him at one of those topless places up in Fort Erie, Ontario."

Bates said Matt had a girlfriend who was a topless dancer. She was Spanish and came from one of those South American countries. He didn't know which one. (The country was later determined to be Costa Rica.)

"Name?"

"Corina." He didn't know her last name. That might not have been her real first name either, come to think of it. Strippers used stage names.

"Can you describe her?"

"Twenty-three years old, five-two, about a hundred pounds, dark complexion. Her English isn't very good," Bates said.

Gardner told Bates gruesome details regarding what a bad guy Matt was and the violence he had used on others: how he'd left a guy (a reportedly gay man) for dead in California, he'd slashed his girlfriend with whom he'd had a child, and so forth. Gardner said that if Bates continued to hang around Matt, it was only a matter of time before he'd get into some real bad trouble.

Bates explained that he'd had no idea what a bad person Matt was.

"As for myself, I consider myself to be a decent person," Bates said.

Regarding this interview, Schintzius later recalled, "He would launch into stories that had nothing to do with Matt, or Rickerson."

One such story that Bates started to tell involved giving a stranger a ride down toward Pennsylvania some time during the winter. The hitchhiker said he was stranded and needed to get home. Bates dropped the guy off somewhere near the Pennsylvania border and then drove back, but it was snowing heavily and he ran out of gas. A truck driver picked him up and drove him to a gas station to fill a can of gas, enough for him to be able to drive to the gas station on his own. But he didn't have any money and had to call his mother and use her charge card to buy gas and a snack. It had been a miserable trip, but he had only taken it in the first place because he was a Good Samaritan and always trying to help out his fellow citizens.

At the time the hitchhiker story seemed completely irrelevant but later was interpreted by investigators as an indication that Bates thought police knew more than they did and had developed a cover story for evidence the police didn't yet have.

On December 27, Detective Gardner spoke with Officer Giannico Marco of the Ontario Provincial Police. Gardner explained that they had suspicions that Matt and Bates might have brought a body into Canada via the Peace Bridge in the trunk of Bates's car; he asked Marco to check their computers to see if they might have recovered the body of an older white male from December 3 to December 18. Marco searched, but results were negative.

On December 28, North Tonawanda police received a tip that Rick Matt and Lee Bates may have cleaned the trunk of Bates's vehicle in the driveway of a friend who lived in Fort Erie, Ontario. When contacted, the friend in question said he had no knowledge of this.

Investigators used border computers to pinpoint the exact time Bates's vehicle had crossed from the United States into Canada. Between November 8 and December 28, Bates entered Canada twenty times, but none of them were between November 29 and December 9.

For weeks there was little progress in the investigation. Then, after the New Year, the weather turned spring-like, ice melted, and everything changed.

January 5, 1998, was an uncharacteristically warm day along the Niagara River. On an average early January day, the temperature might barely break the freezing point. But on this day, the excited TV weathermen were talking about something called El Niño, the temperature had cracked sixty degrees, and whenever possible, folks were doing things outside. Winters in that area being what they were, almost no one was complaining. There were some who muttered that it just wasn't natural for there to be a whole day in January during which the temperature never fell below the freezing mark—bottoming out at thirty-seven degrees, just before dawn. Maybe it was a foreign power messing with the weather.

So, it was without winter coats that, on that day, a fisherman and his son were walking along the Niagara River when they spotted something bobbing like a pale dead fish in the water off Fisherman's Park, between the park and the Waste Water Treatment Plant. Upon closer inspection, they realized that it wasn't a bleached and bloated fish at all but a man's torso, from the bellybutton to the neck—no head, arms, or legs.

The call came in to North Tonawanda police at 2:45 p.m. On Rickerson's missing person report there was a note about a surgical scar he had. Sure enough, the torso had one too. Formal identification of the torso couldn't be done until after autopsy, but in the meantime investigators operated under the assumption that this was Rickerson.

By quarter to four, detectives Gardner and Schintzius were again double-teaming Lee Bates. Schintzius recalled that Bates was a student who dreamed of being a cop one day, so he played to that, tried to talk to Bates cop to cop:

"Look, Lee, I've known you forever, I want to put a young set of eyes on something, help me out with something." Bates went for it and came into the station. When he got there he was Mirandized immediately.

"What's this about?"

"We found Rickerson's body."

Bates's body slumped. The interview was only ten minutes old when Bates began to let the truth slip out. Yes, he and Matt had removed Rickerson from his house. Yes, they took him out through the sliding doors in the back. Matt had stolen a couple of items from the house, a ring and a necklace, and believed that Matt had given the jewelry to his stripper girlfriend in Canada. By 9:30 that night, Bates said he was willing to take a ride out to Tonawanda Island to help search for the remainder of Rickerson's remains.

There was quite a gathering on Tonawanda Island. In addition to the North Tonawanda investigators, Bates's father was on hand. Members of the fire department were there with lighting equipment, and assistant district attorney Ron Winter was on hand as well.

No remains were found, so Bates was returned to the North Tonawanda Detective Bureau where his interrogation continued into the night.

By 2:30 on the afternoon of January 6, police and the assistant district attorney had formulated a plan. They would tape record a phone conversation between Bates and Matt, one in which Bates would be instructed to bring up the subject of Rickerson. Trouble was, they couldn't get Matt to answer the phone, regardless of what number they called.

At 2:40 p.m., January 6, the torso found off of Tonawanda Island was autopsied. Attending the autopsy were Dr. Sungook Baik, autopsy assistant Mark Henderson (who had also been at the Rickerson home crime scene),

Niagara County coroner Joe Mantione, and North Tonawanda detectives Gardner and Snopkowski.

As Snopkowski took photographs, the first incision with a scalpel was at 2:55. The major finding of the procedure was that there were numerous chest and rib bruises. Gardner was on the phone arranging to have tissue specimens transported to the Niagara County Lab and blood and hair samples to a DNA lab as soon as possible. By quarter to four those samples were on their way to their respective laboratories.

Despite being asked the question more than once, Baik refused to estimate how long the torso had been in the water. After further questioning, Baik would say that he didn't think the torso had been lying out in a field for days on end, that it was most likely put in the water with twenty-four hours of the presumed murder. A decomposing torso left out of doors for a stretch of time would have been bitten by animals, and this torso had no animal bites. The contents of the torso's stomach revealed that its owner had not eaten for many hours before his death.

In the meantime, Wayne Schimpf reported that Rick Matt had stolen his Explorer. Police spent hours looking for it locally but couldn't find a trace of the vehicle.

On January 7, investigators—now armed with new info regarding the assault that had occurred at Rickerson's home—returned to the Harvard Avenue address where they successfully dusted for prints on a five-liter wine box that Matt had reportedly pulled out of the refrigerator.

That same morning, local newspaper reporter Tony Farina called Detective Gardner and reported that new body parts had been discovered in Welland Canal, the shipping canal that connects lakes Ontario and Erie.

By January 8, Lee Bates had lawyered up. His attorney was Peter Todoro of Williamsville, New York, and he said that Bates was not to be asked any questions unless he was there. Todoro explained that he was going to need more time to review the case before such an interview could be granted.

Also on the eighth, police set out to find Rick Matt's girlfriend. To do this detectives Gardner and Eddie Garde went to the Niagara Frontier Regional Police in Fort Erie and there talked to investigators Tom Willette and Ronald Cudney. They wanted to find out what the girlfriend knew of course, but they were also interested in discovering if she was in possession of the ring and necklace that had been stolen from Rickerson's house. The men brought along policewoman Jackie Lee when they went to the Pure Platinum gentleman's club to see the woman known as Corina.

Once just outside the strip joint, Lee called the club and asked for Corina. When Corina answered the phone the other officers entered the club and secured her. They explained the situation, and Corina took them to her room, which was right there above the club, on the third floor, room 6. She allowed them to search her tiny room, but no ring or necklace was found. While searching for the jewelry they did find paperwork indicating that Corina, real name Johanna Rodriguez Arguedas of San Juan, Costa Rica, and Richard Matt had applied for a marriage license. She had a valid visa that was good for another twelve months. She said she knew nothing about a ring or a necklace and nothing about Matt or Bates in connection with the disappearance of Mr. Rickerson.

On January 9, police attempted to find Wayne Schimpf's vehicle and locate Rickerson's smashed cell phone. Phone records indicated that the phone had been used close to the time Rickerson disappeared, one call being to the Peppermill Lounge in Grand Island, New York. Police visited the club and found no one there who knew Rickerson, Bates, or Matt. A second trip to the club later in the day yielded results. An eyewitness placed Matt in the Peppermill Lounge "two or three times" always in the company of the same guy. The woman bartender that had been working the night Rickerson disappeared said she didn't remember receiving any calls for Matt's friend, but that didn't mean anything. If the place got busy anyone might've answered the phone.

In the meantime, Matt's stripper girlfriend called Detective Gardner and complained that her boss might fire her or force her to leave the area and go to London, Ontario. Her boss, however, when contacted said that she was "being taken care of" and he was thinking of moving her but only for her own safety with a desperate Rick Matt on the loose and all.

On January 17, an aviation team joined the search for the remainder of William Rickerson. Pilot Phil Newson and Sergeant Kevin Locicero flew low along the east shore of the Niagara River and around Tonawanda Island. They were in the air for an hour and a half but located no body parts.

The Rick Matt trail heated up a bit when the Buffalo Police Department located a forty-three-year-old woman in that city who admitted to smoking crack with Rick Matt around the holidays. She said he'd been driving the Explorer. She knew because he drove her to do Christmas shopping around December 23.

The focus of the search for Matt shifted to the big city. Detective Gardner spent January 18 driving around Buffalo, in the vicinity of Matt's crack-smoking buddy's place, but didn't see him.

Detective Gardner contacted William Rickerson's dentist and learned that, should Rickerson's head be located, it would not be difficult to ID. Rickerson's front two top teeth were fused together, and the tooth next to them was twice the size of a normal tooth, an anomaly that would be easy to spot.

Gardner's next call was to Thomas Vaughan, the assistant superintendent of the Erie County Holding Center. Gardner notified Vaughan that Rick Matt's father Robert was currently incarcerated in that facility, so there was a chance that his much-wanted son might come to visit him there.

Gardner subsequently learned that Robert Matt had been overheard expressing interest in his son's activities and had been discussing body parts that were "spread out all over Western New York."

More importantly, the dad had been heard discussing places where his son might be laying low, in particular a house on Broadway a few houses from the market above a bar, with the tavern being below street level.

On January 21 police executed a search warrant for Matt's home on Minerva Street. Though they found nothing of interest indoors, they did confiscate two shovels that had been in the backyard.

Investigators were still trying to determine Rickerson's blood type. The Department of Motor Vehicles was unhelpful. They found out where and when Rickerson had been married (July 26, 1947, Niagara Falls), but the record of Rickerson's then-mandatory prewedding blood test didn't record his type.

At 3:10 p.m. on January 28, the North Tonawanda Dive Team discovered a leg in twenty feet of water in the Niagara River on the west side of Tonawanda Island. The other leg was found about forty minutes later.

Investigators took Bates for a ride and with his help located the spot where Matt and Bates bought the shovel, and the spot in the woods where they'd started to dig Rickerson's grave.

On the 29th, while divers searched for parts still missing—two arms and a head—the legs were autopsied at the Erie County Medical Examiner's Office. One leg was nineteen inches in diameter, the other only sixteen. Their combined weight was twenty pounds. The divers didn't find parts, but they did pull out of the water a Tartan men's pajama top.

The search for the rest of Rickerson went into overdrive on February 1, 1998, as the dive teams from both Tonawanda and North Tonawanda were hard at work, along with the Western New York Search Dog Teams. No new parts were located, but divers did pull up the PJ bottoms to match the tops they'd found on January 29.

None of this mattered much to Richard Matt. As investigators were building a case against him, Matt was living in the Mexican border town of Matamoros—just across the mouth of the Rio Grande from Brownsville, Texas—pretending to be his brother. He was however, without Wayne Schimpf's car, which hadn't made it out of Texas.

Matt could have minded his p's and q's and been home free, but fat chance. Where Richard Matt went, trouble always followed. In February 1998, he encountered in Matamoros a fifty-three-year-old American named Charles Perrault, a huge guy at six foot six. Matt and Perrault drank and watched brown women work the pole. But Matt wasn't thinking just about the naked breasts. As usual, he had profit on his mind as well.

"I'm a family man, eight kids," Perrault said.

"What you do for a living?" Matt asked.

"I'm a rigger for an oil company in Texas."

Oil. Ka-ching. Matt was now locked in on Perrault, on his story, and on the way he smelled. He smelled of money. As he was prone to do, Matt got it into his head that this guy was holding a wad of cash.

Perrault got up to take a leak. Matt counted five Mississippis and followed him in. Perrault bellied up to the urinal. Matt came up on him from behind and repeatedly stabbed him in the back, killing him.

What seemed to Matt to be such a good idea turned sour immediately. In fact, he was arrested within minutes of the killing, while still running from the bar and—despite his oft-repeated refrain that he'd stabbed the man in self-defense—he was put on Mexican justice's express track.

Authorities said this was a simple robbery/murder. Matt was a "bad guy" with "no feelings for human life," and Matt was almost instantly beginning a twenty-year stretch in a deep-Mexican prison.

On February 4, 1998, Wayne Schimpf's vehicle was located, broken down and abandoned, near the border in Zapata County, Texas. Soon thereafter, North Tonawanda police received a call from the Texas Rangers. This was their first inkling that Matt was long gone, a cool breeze, safe and sound south of the border.

That was the day the Niagara County DA's office began to hand out subpoenas to give testimony at a grand jury hearing regarding Rick Matt, Lee Bates, and the murder of Bill Rickerson. Hearings started immediately.

Lee Bates was interviewed once again for four and a half hours on February 24. This was his "come clean" statement, during which police learned the gruesome details of the attack, torture, and murder of Bill Rickerson. Using an outline created by credit card charges on Bates's mother's credit card on the night Rickerson disappeared, police already had a good idea that the killers had driven back and forth along the Lake Erie shore. Now Bates filled in the details.

Armed with this new info, police searched several stretches of road for Rickerson's smashed cell phone, his wallet, and a pair of gloves that Matt allegedly used during the crime.

On February 28, Detective Gardner drove to Erie, Pennsylvania, to Ferriers' True Value Hardware Store, where the owner, Colby Ferriers, identified the shovel found in Matt's backyard as the one he'd sold on the morning of December 5, 1997. Records showed that the shovel had been Ferriers's first sale of the day, and the store opened at 7:00 a.m.

By the time Wayne Schimpf's vehicle was returned from Texas to western New York, police there learned that Richard Matt had been found and was residing in a Mexican prison.

The story gets a little sketchy here as stories out of Mexican prisons often do, but Matt told his son Nicholas Harris that he was shot while trying to escape and was in a fight and had his teeth knocked out sometime before his capture.

We do know that soon after Matt was locked up, he was allowed a phone call. He called his old pal, Detective David Bentley, and complained about his captors, whining that Mexican prison officials had extorted money from him in exchange for a cell with a bed and a toilet.

While in prison, Matt was interviewed by Channel 4 news out of Buffalo. "How many times did you stab the man in the bar?" they asked.

"I don't know. Until he stopped moving," Matt replied.

During that same interview, Matt denied mutilating and dumping the body of William Rickerson.

"I didn't dump no torso," he said.

Whether or not he ever took a bullet, and how he lost his front teeth, may always be a matter of conjecture, but what is known for sure is that Matt came out of Mexico with a tattoo, a tramp stamp reading, "Mexico Forever," and metallic front teeth, giving his evil smile an extra chill.

Matt had already been behind Mexican bars for years when authorities in Erie County received a communication from the military general who ran the prison. For $10,000, the general said, he would be glad to hand over Matt so he could face justice in New York State.

NYS said thanks but no thanks. You can keep him.

Eventually, the Mexican prison gave him back anyway, and they did it for free. In 2007, Matt was extradited back to the United States along with the kingpin of a drug cartel.

Detective Schintzius recalled that the prison down there was having a problem with Mexican drug cartel prisoners killing gringos. Matt's inclusion in the deal was a surprise to U.S. government officials who not only hadn't negotiated for him but also had refused to negotiate for him.

Suspicion was that Matt was more trouble than he was worth to Mexico, a bad man who always tried to escape, and they were glad to be rid of him. The United States was not displeased, however, as this would give the proper jurisdiction the opportunity to finally try Matt for the Rickerson murder.

Matt moved into the Niagara County Jail. Compared to prison in Mexico, this was like the lap of luxury. There had been a Niagara County Jail since 1810, a stone building on Washington Street in what was then known as the Village of Buffalo, but that one only lasted fifteen years. New jails were built in 1825, 1842, and 1893. The one Matt found himself in had only been around since 1961. It had three stories and 172 cells. During construction, workers unearthed the skeletal remains of nine bodies, most likely occupants of the former county poor farm that had been directly across the street. Best theory was that the remains belonged to victims of an epidemic who had been isolated in an attempt to prevent the disease from spreading.

When it was new the jail was known for its light and modern aura, it's modern pod-system design increasing the inmate-to-guard ratio, all in such sharp contrast to the dark, dank dungeon of a facility that it replaced. But much of that light and modernity had worn away or been covered layer after layer by time's patina when Matt arrived. The pods now seemed less like innovative design and more like overcrowding and understaffing.

During his time in jail awaiting trial, Matt began to draw pictures of people—there was plenty of time for it—and he revealed himself to be a talented artist. When he drew or painted a portrait of a famous person the facial resemblance was nearly photographic.

As Matt waited he wasn't housed with the rest of the jail population but was instead in administrative segregation, or Ad Seg, where prisoners were kept when they couldn't get along with others.

One piece of evidence against Matt lacked a binding chain of evidence. While in Mexico, Matt, it was believed, wrote a letter to Lee Bates, saying that, in exchange for $10,000, he would take the rap for killing Rickerson, and Bates would be off the hook. Bates didn't pay the money, but he did keep the letter. The prosecution hoped that, if it could be proven that Matt really wrote the letter, a jury might interpret it as an admission from Matt that he'd killed Rickerson. In order to prove authorship, Detective Schintzius sat Matt down, with audio and video recording rolling, and asked Matt to write various phrases from the letter nineteen times. The reason for the repetition was that most people can hide their real handwriting for a short period of time, but if asked to write the same passage again and again, the true handwriting would emerge. One of the phrases that Schintzius asked Matt to write nineteen times was "I killed Bill Rickerson."

Matt took great delight in, as he wrote, saying the phrase aloud over and over again, making eye contact with Schintzius. "I killed Bill Rickerson, I killed Bill Rickerson, I killed Bill Rickerson," because he knew that he could say it a thousand times but these were statements that could not be used against him.

Matt's trial was held in a large courtroom in Lockport, New York. He was represented by assistant public defenders Christopher Privateer and Matthew P. Pynn.

Pynn for one was wary of his client's charisma. Matt was a guy who was used to getting by on his charm, an act that could crash and burn in front of jurors with tombstones in their eyes.

Pynn saw Matt as a guy who should have a lot of friends. He was a fun guy but a dangerous guy—too dangerous for most to hang around with. A juror at Matt's trial, Brett Sawyer, felt that charisma as well, saying that the stylish suits Matt wore (donated to his cause by a friend) made him look like a cult leader.

"It seems he has a way of manipulating people to do things," Sawyer concluded.

Even before jury selection began there was fuss. Police received a tip out of the jail that Matt's accomplices were planning an escape, planning to bust him out.[18] Precautions needed to be taken—very, very expensive precautions: the protective layers of glass over the defense and prosecution tables were removed so Matt would not be able to smash them and use a shard as a weapon. (This was deemed necessary after a report that Matt had tried to obtain a "diamond glass cutter" to use in his escape.)

Snipers stood on the roof of the courthouse and neighboring buildings in case the courthouse was *invaded*. At the insistence of the Niagara County Sheriff's Office, Matt wore a stun belt (along with his well-tailored suit) so—in case he acted up—he could be dropped instantly with Taser electrodes that delivered a brutal fifty-thousand-volt electric shock. When Matt was in the courtroom there were never less than six deputies there also.

If he couldn't escape, the report said, Matt was to be considered suicidal. He had been receiving weekly visits from an unnamed woman who had given him money (on one occasion two $50 bills), and the pair had been overheard having conversations that contained the phrases "during the escape" and "help pay off a guard." Matt was quoted as saying that he'd been in touch with Mexican "drug lords" when he was in prison down there and that he was heading straight for the Mexican border when he escaped from the Niagara County Jail. The report noted that Matt had recently purchased a pair of Adidas sneakers with a "hard sole," one that wouldn't tear when he climbed the prison fence.

Random courtroom searches were conducted during the trial to make sure no contraband or weapons had been left in the room. Spectators would walk through a magnetometer before entering the courtroom, but that machine was turned off at night, and there remained the thoroughly unpublicized possibility that something could be placed strategically in the courtroom at that time.

Matt, of course, let on that he found the extra security silly. Escape? Him? And while he seemed to enjoy the fuss, he continued to deny that any of the report's allegations were true and that they were the figment of the imaginations of two homosexual prisoners who were angry because Matt reported them for having a romantic interlude in front of his cell.

FIVE
THROWING
AWAY
THE KEY

Presiding over Richard Matt's trial was the Honorable Sara Sheldon. One of her first decisions was to order a special prosecution to take over for the people in this case, as the local prosecutors, she determined, would have faced a conflict of interest because the new district attorney (DA), Michael J. Violante, played a role in assigning Matt's defense lawyers while he served as the county's public defender in 2007.

Matt was charged with four counts of second-degree murder in connection with the Rickerson murder (one for the murder itself and three for committing the murder during the commission of other felonies: torture, robbery, and kidnapping); two counts of first-degree robbery; and three counts of first-degree kidnapping.

The special prosecution team was made up of two former assistant Erie County district attorneys, Joseph M. Mordino (Joe) and Louis Haremski (Lou).

Mordino was a legend. The sixty-five-year-old prosecutor had successfully prosecuted 250 murderers in the Erie County District Attorney's Office. He'd joined the DA's office after earning his law degree at the University of Buffalo Law School in 1969. He had served as chief of the Narcotics Bureau and the Felony Crimes Bureau, and was deputy district attorney before retiring in 2007. He entered private practice but agreed to come out of prosecutorial retirement for a shot at Richard Matt.

Haremski was chosen because of his twenty-three years of experience working in the DA's office, his excellent working relationship with the courts, and his particularly high conviction rate, especially when it came to domestic violence cases, cases that tended to be difficult to prosecute because of the intense emotions involved, that is, victims remain loyal to their attackers. Before he retired amidst a political shake-up in his office, Haremski had a reputation for working quickly, which was good because he received the call from State Supreme Court justice Richard C. Kloch Sr. asking him to take the case in December, for a trial scheduled to begin in March. Preparation would need to be done efficiently, and it was.

"I am Type A when it comes to preparation," Haremski later explained. "I make a list of ways in which we might lose, and then prevent those things from happening."[1]

Haremski did not come into the case bursting with overconfidence. He certainly thought the case was winnable, but there were issues that would need to be overcome. The case was ten years old, which presented difficulties, and two of the main prosecution witnesses were (1) the defendant's accomplice and (2) a stripper.

He and his wife had plans to go on vacation, and Haremski figured the trial could be completed in plenty of time. (As it turned out, the trial was one of the longest in county history, and the jury came in with their verdict one day before he and his wife were scheduled to leave.)

Jury selection took just a little more than two days. Nine women and three men were chosen, with two male and two female alternates. Haremski delivered the opening statement for the prosecution on Thursday, March 13, 2008. As he spoke he couldn't help but notice the defendant's expensive attire.

"Matt was a snazzy dresser," Haremski recalled. "There were times when I felt like the worst dressed guy in the room."[2]

Years later, Haremski wanted the world to know that Joe Mordino was the mastermind behind the prosecution of Richard Matt.

"I was in awe of him. Joe believed in the Jesuit method of teaching when it came to presenting evidence to a jury: first you explain what you are about to tell them, then you tell them the thing you want to tell them, then you explain what it was that you'd just told them. So Joe would have a witness tell their story, then he would bring out photos and use them to illustrate the story as the witness told it again, and then he'd introduce relevant documents that gave him an excuse to have the witness tell their story yet again."[3]

But it was Lou Haremski who delivered the opening statement for the People, and it too was masterful. There were certain aspects of the crime that Haremski wanted the jury to think about—dwell on, even: William Rickerson was a fighter; he fought for his life, fought every chance he got during his twenty-seven-hour ordeal with his captors, as they took him from North Tonawanda to Ohio and back again. He'd been bound and locked in a car trunk, yet Rickerson never ceased trying to make noise, shouting, banging on the inside of the trunk lid, pulling out the wires to the vehicles stereo, and all the time hearing the same thing. *We know you've got cash; let us know where it is and there's a happy ending.* Somewhere between Alleghany State Park and Tonawanda Island, Richard Matt ran out of patience, lost it, and snapped Rickerson's neck. Then he and Lee Bates went to Tonawanda Island, removed Rickerson's body from the trunk, and covered it with a pile of wood and left. Sometime later the defendant came back with a hacksaw, dismembered Rickerson's body, and threw the pieces into the Niagara River.

Haremski explained that this trial would involve the tragic story of three men: Rickerson, Matt, and Bates. The motive: greed. Rickerson ran a cash business; he carried a lot of cash—at least that was the perception.

Bates developed a penchant for strippers. He hung out at gentlemen's clubs such as Mints and Pure Platinum in Canada. It was something the two defendants had in common. Matt was engaged to a stripper in Canada. Bates and Matt met in a strip club, became friends, and plotted to rob Rickerson, whom they viewed as a walking, talking bank. That was another thing they had in common. They were broke. They talked over an idea at Matt's stepbrother's home, went immediately into green-light mode, drove to Rickerson's home, and pounded on his door.

The prosecutor went over the twenty-seven-hour attack in detail: the home invasion; the beatings; the bondage and the kidnapping; the driving, driving, driving; and finally, the broken fingers—and neck.

It was the pure *evil* of the crime he wanted to impress upon the jury's collective psyche. The cruelty. The sadism. Haremski concluded by stating that, when all the evidence was heard, there couldn't be a shadow of a doubt that Matt was guilty of all charges.

Following a recess, Christopher Privateer addressed the jury for the defense, starting with a lesson in law, specifically the *burden of proof*: the jury had heard *Haremski's version* of events, sure—now they had to prove it. Prove it *beyond a reasonable doubt*. Privateer did not have to prove a thing on behalf of Mr. Matt.

Several sets of juror eyes snuck a peek or two at Matt as Privateer spoke. The defendant was trying to look scholarly, furrowing his brow as he jotted notes in a yellow legal pad.

The defense attorney acknowledged the crime. William Rickerson died in December 1997. He was murdered. That wasn't the question. The question was, Who did it? Only one man had ever confessed, and his name was Lee Bates—the very man whose version of events the prosecution would present as fact. The prosecution's whole case depended on Bates. Take Bates out of the equation, and their case fell apart. And why not take Bates out of the equation?

"Is Bates a reliable witness?" Privateer asked the jury. The defender promised to demonstrate that Bates had changed the details of his story many times. Matt in fact had *nothing to do with the killing*. The defendant wasn't even there. "And that is why we are gathered in this courtroom on this day—because Richard Matt was not at the scene of the murder and had not been involved in the death of William Rickerson."

Opening statements concluded, Judge Sheldon excused the jurors and adjourned for the day.

Privateer had at least one thing right: The prosecution's star witness was indeed Lee Bates, who took the stand on Friday, March 14, in prison khakis and manacles—his attire in sharp contrast to the defendant's dark blue suit, white shirt, and pink tie.

Haremski later explained that the direct examination of Bates was another example of Joe Mordino's prosecutorial brilliance. Bates had a tendency when being interrogated to drift off the subject, and when he did he frequently gave varying versions of the same events, little inconsistencies that defense lawyers lived for because they could pick and pick at them, pointing out to the jury that the witness wasn't reliable. Since cross-examination can only touch upon issues that were first brought up during direct examination, Mordino kept his examination of Bates brief, about a half hour, thus all but eliminating the defense's ability to discredit the witness with his immaterial inconsistencies.

The direct examination of the People's star witness was brief but stunningly effective. Bates gave the jury a vivid and horrifying blow-by-blow of the home invasion, beating, kidnapping, torture, and murder of William Rickerson. Regarding the moment of the murder, Bates said, "Matt had me turn down a road that was a cul-de-sac. I opened the trunk with the key. Rick Matt said, 'You know, I've had enough of this.' He reached in and twisted Rickerson's head. I heard a pop. Rickerson just dropped back into the trunk."[4]

After that, Bates testified, they hid the body on Tonawanda Island.

"Was that the last you heard about Rickerson from Rick Matt?" Mordino asked.

"No, sir," Bates said. "Later on, Matt told me that he returned to the island with a hacksaw and a shovel. He said he dismembered the body and threw the pieces in the Niagara River."

"No further questions."

"Mr. Privateer, will you be cross-examining this witness?" Judge Sheldon asked.

The defense table was caught off guard by the direct examinations' brevity.

"Yes, your honor," Matt's lawyer replied. "I have a somewhat lengthy cross-examination planned."

"In that case . . ." Judge Sheldon tapped her gavel and declared a weekend recess with the cross-examination of the witness to begin on Monday morning, March 17.

That Monday-morning cross-examination started hot: "Isn't it true that *you lied* to North Tonawanda police?" Christopher Privateer asked.

"It is, but I was only doing it to protect myself from Matt. He would've killed me if I ratted him out."

"You blatantly lied, isn't that true?"

"I blatantly lied to police. I was giving them something to get them off my back till they realized I was in danger. I would have told them that I shot JFK and I wasn't even born then."

"Didn't you lie to protect yourself from being arrested?"

"That, too."

"You cut a deal with prosecutors to reduce your sentence, right? Part of your sentence was that you would testify at this trial and that's why you're here, right?" he asked.

Bates admitted that he'd cut a deal, pleaded guilty to second-degree murder, and had received a sentence of fifteen years to life. (Bates was released from prison in 2014.) But there was part of his plea deal that the defense attorney was leaving out. "I agreed to tell the truth," Bates concluded.

"And to correct all the things you told the police and DA that weren't correct?"

"True."

"And what you're telling us now is the true version?"

"Yes."

Privateer took Bates on a meticulous survey of all of the false statements he'd made to police and to a Niagara County grand jury regarding the abduction and murder. The interviews with police were from December 1997 and January 1998; the grand jury testimony, from February 1998. (Inconsistencies in Bates's statements on other subjects were objected to and sustained as improper cross-examination.)

"When you first spoke to police, did you mention anything about the kidnapping and murder?"

"No."

"Why not?"

"Because, one, I was afraid of being arrested. Two, I was afraid of crossing Matt, and three, I was afraid of my family becoming victims of Richard Matt." Bates said that he finally confessed to his role in the crime in January 1998 during a subsequent interview with North Tonawanda police.

"I went in and said, 'Your job is to protect and serve. Matt is coming to kill me.'"

"But you still lied, didn't you?"

"Matt said he would kill me. I saw him kill Bill Rickerson right in front of me," Bates replied.

The other star witness for the prosecution was Matt's half brother Wayne Schimpf, who had under duress donated his car to Matt's escape cause. For his appearance on the witness stand, special prosecutor Joe Mordino took over the examination.

Schimpf testified that the defendant and the murder were not easy subjects for him to talk about, that ten years had gone by and he'd done his best to forget about them. True, the plot to kill Rickerson had begun in his own apartment. True, Matt had called Rickerson on his phone and argued about money. Matt then called Bates and asked to borrow a pair of gloves, which the witness admitted he had ended up supplying. Bates arrived at Schimpf's place, and soon thereafter Bates and Matt left to visit Rickerson in person. The next Schimpf heard about it was many days later, about two weeks maybe, when Matt brought up the subject.

"What did he say?" Mordino asked.

"He told me he was in trouble and didn't know what to do, that he thought he might've killed his boss. He said he accidentally broke Rickerson's neck when he hit him and he fell downstairs."

On a subsequent visit, Schimpf testified, Matt was visiting when he saw a newspaper, the *Tonawanda News*, in which there was a photo of Rickerson and a story about the businessman's disappearance.

"That's the guy," Matt had said.

During a third visit, Matt admitted to his half brother that he had disposed of Rickerson's body by cutting it up with a hacksaw.

Schimpf testified, "He said he would kill me and my fiancée if we ever told anyone. He told me he needed to get out of town."

"What did you do?" Mordino asked.

"I gave him a spare set of keys to my van. He left in the van. I then reported the vehicle stolen so my fiancée would not know what I had done."

Mordino asked, "Why not stop him from taking the van?"

"He just killed a guy. You don't want to confront someone like that."

"Were you always afraid of your brother?"

"No, just on that occasion."

"Other than threatening to kill you and your fiancée, did you have any other problems with your brother?"

"Only once when I was setting him up with a job and I couldn't get ahold of him."

The prosecution's next witness was Schimpf's then fiancée, now wife, Jennifer. She said, "Matt told me that he had confronted his ex-boss and they got into a verbal fight. That escalated into a physical fight and Rickerson was knocked down."

Mordino asked, "Did he tell you Rickerson was hurt?"

"He said he didn't know."

Following a week off, the trial was scheduled to resume first thing Monday morning, April 7, but the day got off to a late start. A meeting in Judge Sheldon's chambers used up much of the morning, with the special prosecutors and Mr. Privateer attending. The problem was a front-page story in that morning's *Niagara Gazette* about the extraordinary security that went into transporting Richard Matt from the jail to the courtroom and back again every day. The article by Rick Pfeiffer compared the defendant to mobster John Gotti, with his sharp suits, and an escort made up of badass law enforcement packing assault rifles.[5] Matt was an extreme escape risk, the paper revealed, and to be considered very dangerous. The article said that security was tighter than in any local trial in recent memory. The source for the info was a good one: Niagara County sheriff Thomas A. Beilen, who explained that the corrections officers who took Matt to and from court were a supplement to the court deputy detail, and all of that personnel was part of the jail's Corrections Emergency Response Team (CERT). This team, the sheriff explained, responded to problems pertaining to the county jail with SWAT-like skills.

Beilen said, "They are trained extensively in how to deal with disruptive, dangerous inmates. The precautions and weapons that they use is just another part of having a high profile, high security defendant."

The story was everywhere as the lawyers came to work that morning, in people's hands and on morning radio. It was hard to miss, and Privateer wanted to make sure the jury hadn't seen it.

The jurors were interviewed one by one that Monday morning and had already been admonished to not read, listen to, or watch the news. Each in turn said they hadn't seen the morning paper.

That same day a forensics document examiner from Rockville Centre, Long Island, Dennis Ryan, testified that Matt had written a note received by Lee Bates's parents from a Mexican prison. Ryan compared the note to known examples of Matt's handwriting (i.e., "I killed Bill Rickerson. I killed Bill Rickerson. I killed . . ."). He listed the characteristics (spacing between letters, letter height, etc.) that formed the basis for his conclusion and led him to believe that Matt wrote it. All of this was a tad dry for the jury—down to twelve members and two alternates after two jurors were excused, each suffering a death in the family—as it had not yet been told the contents of the letter.

On Tuesday, April 8, the prosecution called former detective Glenn Gardner, who said he was, before his retirement, the chief of detectives in North Tonawanda and one of the investigators in charge of William Rickerson's disappearance in December 1997.

He described for the prosecution a visit that he and his partner had made only days into the investigation. They'd learned that Matt had been fired for stealing and, on December 11, a week after Rickerson disappeared, had gone to ask him if he knew where Rickerson was, but Matt didn't answer any questions and instead cursed at them and told them that he hated cops.

Gardner testified that during the early days of the investigation they ran into a number of reluctant sources that were afraid of Matt. But by the middle of January 1998, word was out that Matt had split town, and witnesses became more forthright.

Wednesday was a day off, so Gardner was cross-examined on Thursday by Christopher Privateer. In all, Gardner was on the witness stand for eleven hours split up into two days. Gardner and Matt made eye contact often, but Matt would bore of staring contests and allow his eyes to roam the courtroom absent-mindedly.

Gardner was cross-examined for the most part by Privateer, but there were plenty of times when Matthew Pynn chimed in with a question for him as well, double-teaming the chief of detectives, who found the process grueling but held his own.

Gardner did admit that on January 8, 1998, he had compiled a list of statements made by Lee Bates, which he divided into truths, partial truths, and lies—and that, in retrospect, he didn't have all of the statements in the correct column, that some of the truths turned out to be lies and vice versa.

Privateer's point was that Bates and not Matt had killed William Rickerson, and police had gotten it wrong, assuming that Matt was the guy because they felt, for no adequate reason, that Bates just wasn't the type.

In fact, "Bates just wasn't the type" was a quote from another North Tonawanda detective, Edward Schintzius,[6] who testified about Matt's handwriting tests for the prosecution. While being examined by Joseph Mordino, Schintzius said, "I felt Bates was not the aggressor in this homicide."

Schintzius admitted not locking Bates up because he wasn't a flight risk. Bates seemed like a meek person, and the feeling was that it would be better to have him on the outside, possibly gathering more information, instead of in a jail cell where his capacity as an informant would be diminished.

Gabe DiBernardo, the Rickerson murder detective, said there were reasons to believe certain aspects of Matt's story. Mexican prisons had a reputation for human rights violations, so everything he said was plausible, plus Matt's body really was covered with scars. Somebody tortured him with a cigarette. Matt claimed they held him down and tattooed "Mexico Forever" on his back. The tattoo was really there.

DiBernardo said, "It was our understanding that they don't like Americans down there in the prison where he was held. From everything we heard, we do believe he was abused down there."

That part of the story might've been true, but the rest of it was BS.

DiBernardo said, "From everything we heard from our contacts in Texas, the killing in the strip club was a cold-blooded murder. We were told that Matt saw this man with a wad of cash in his hand, followed him into the men's room, and killed him for his cash." DiBernardo said that he had been in law enforcement for almost forty years, and Matt was the most genuinely evil individual he had ever encountered.

He said, "The things he did to Mr. Rickerson, a seventy-six year old man who had given Rick Matt a job, were cruel and vicious beyond belief. Matt is a cunning and evil criminal, and also the ultimate manipulator and con man."

The prosecution's penultimate witness was retired City of Tonawanda police captain, David Bentley, who testified that late on the night of February 28, 1998, he received a collect phone call from the defendant, who was being held in a Matamoros, Mexico, jail and was apparently not having a very good time. He said he needed money for a better cell.

Bentley testified, "He told me he was in a small cell with four, his word, 'Mexicans,' and there was a drain that they defecated in, a pail that they urinated in and they used the urine to flush the feces. He said he could get a better cell with some money. I told him that he didn't deserve anything better because of what he'd done."

Matt called Bentley twice more over the next two days and said the same thing: "He thought I might give him money so he could get a better cell. He never flat-out said that he wanted to exchange information for money, but he did tell me where he put Mr. Rickerson's head."

The torso had been found floating in the river, and the extremities were found in hacksawed pieces, but the location of the victim's head was still unknown at that point.

"Where did he say the head of William Rickerson was?"

"The defendant told me he put it in a dumpster on Tonawanda Island."

"How long have you known the defendant, Captain Bentley?"

"Since he first got into trouble, when he was sixteen years old," Bentley said. "I've known him for twenty-five years."

"What was your relationship with Matt at that time?"

"I befriended him. He had been in foster homes, as I had. I thought maybe I could bring him out of his negative ways."

"Did you succeed?"

"I did not. I still tried to help though. My wife and I befriended Matt's ex-wife and helped raise Matt's daughter in her father's absence."

North Tonawanda police knew of Bentley's relationship with Matt and reached out to him as soon as Matt became a suspect in the Rickerson case. When Bentley set up the meet with Matt, Matt was suspicious, and asked him three questions: (1) Am I in trouble? (2) Is there a warrant for me? and (3) Are you going to arrest me?

"I told him that I wanted to have a friend-to-friend conversation. In the car, he blurted out, 'Dave, we're talking about a fucking homicide. We're not talking about some little fucking burglary.'"

Matt, as it turned out, never did agree to talk to North Tonawanda police and instead split to Mexico, and the next time he was heard from, Matt was in jail down there.

During cross-examination Privateer attempted to reframe this information so that it could be read as beneficial to Matt's case. It wasn't easy. Privateer's point was that Matt's conversations with Bentley were not indicative of guilt but merely of desperation. Matt was desperate for money while living in a hellish Mexican jail.

The final prosecution witness was criminologist K. Paul Meyers, who told the jury that he'd found DNA on a Marlboro Red cigarette butt found in the victim's basement that matched that of the defendant.

With the defense about to begin its brief case, Matt wrote a letter to the judge. It read, in part, "In the time I spent in prison in Mexico, I was tortured, starved and beaten many times to say the least, just because I was an American. I was hung from a wooden beam by my hands and razor cut over ninety times and beaten until I passed out. I have all of the scars to prove it." The note said that Matt was falsely imprisoned in Mexico, that the incident in the strip-club men's room was self-defense. The guy came at him with a knife; what else could he do? But he was convicted of murder because he was an American. He was never given an opportunity to contest the charges.

"I never seen a courtroom," Matt complained. "I never seen a judge. I was given an attorney who I seen one time and he only spoke Spanish. I did not speak Spanish at the time. I received a twenty-three-year sentence by mail in Spanish from a judge who I never seen or talked to before in my life."

As for that other so-called murder, "I never killed, robbed or kidnapped Mr. Bill Rickerson. The person who did it made a deal with the DA's office and they are going to let that killer out." Matt wrote that, at the time of the Rickerson murder, he was about to come into some money. He'd been planning to marry "a stripper from Costa Rica" who needed to marry an American to stay in the United States, and she was willing to pay for his "I do."

Matt claimed that he was "released" from Mexican prison because authorities down there suddenly realized that he was innocent. The "president" of Mexico initiated a new investigation into what happened in that strip-club men's room. Why did the president care? Because he'd been given a tip by one of Matt's prison guards, a guy who knew him and knew he was innocent. Supporting his claim was the known fact that a caveat of Matt's transfer from Mexican to American authorities was that Matt not face the death penalty for the Rickerson murder.

When the contents of the note were made public, the *Buffalo News* contacted the Mexican embassy in Washington, D.C., regarding Matt's claims. Ariel Moutsatsos-Morales, minister of public affairs at the embassy, declined to comment on the specifics, stating only, "Mexico has clear and effective legal institutional ways for any person to complain and start an investigation if he or she feels that his or her case was mishandled."

Testifying for the defense, Matt's former live-in girlfriend Marta Cruz told the jury that the defendant was a father figure to her three children. She said under oath that she had faith in Richard Matt's innocence.

"Honestly, I don't believe he did it," she said. "I've known him for many years."

After thirty witnesses and a month's time, testimony was over. In his closing statement on April 14, Christopher Privateer told the jury that there was a reasonable doubt as to Matt's guilt, that the evidence supported their theory that Lee Bates had killed William Rickerson, while Matt had merely assisted in cutting up the remains and disposing of the parts in the river.

In Mordino's closing statement, he said,

> Bentley knocked the pins out of the defense case. What does Matt tell Bentley? He cut up the body. He put Rickerson in the trunk. He drove through Pennsylvania and northeastern Ohio, twenty-seven hours on the road. Rickerson ripped out the stereo wires. Not many people knew that. The defendants own actions nailed him. How can you believe Bates killed Rickerson? You can't. Cold-blooded killers don't spill their guts to an investigation. Weaklings do. Bates was a wuss, a big baby—not a cold-blooded killer. Before I let you go and deliberate, I want you to finish the story of the Rickerson case. What you heard in this courtroom in the last month was a horror story. It was a real horror story written and produced by Richard Matt. But you can write the last chapter. You can find Matt guilty. Show him the same mercy he showed Bill Rickerson.

Following closing statements and Judge Sheldon's instructions to the jury, the jury alternates were dismissed, and the twelve arbiters were sent off to the jury room to deliberate. While the jury was out, defense co-counsel Matthew Pynn told members of the press that Matt felt confident that he would be acquitted. Anyone could see that Lee Bates had framed him. It was clear and obvious.

The jury, as it turned out, took only four hours to come up with a unanimous verdict. One ballot and it was over. Matt had fooled no one, not even himself. As the jury forewoman read the jury's guilty verdict on all charges, Matt remained calm, stoic. Perhaps he hadn't been as confident as his attorney had said only hours before. Matt acted like a man who saw his fate coming. After all, he'd gotten his Marine Corps tattoo just for moments like this.

Members of the Rickerson family burst into tears upon hearing the verdict and rushed forward to clutch at the hands and congratulate the members of the prosecution team. Judge Sheldon scheduled a sentencing hearing for May 30 and pounded her gavel.

Only moments later, Pynn was again talking with reporters, saying he had no regrets. They had presented their case just the way they'd wanted to, and of course there would be an appeal.

Privateer said, sure, he was disappointed by the result and he was already running through his options as to how to "see if there is anything that can be done about it."[7]

William Rickerson Jr. told a reporter that he couldn't imagine two more dedicated and qualified people than the special prosecutors, Mordino and Haremski, who'd handled the case.

"I'm grateful to see that Matt will be off the streets," Rickerson added. He added that he had every reason to believe "*that Matt would never see the outside of a prison again.*"[8]

While Mordino said he never had a doubt in his mind that Matt was guilty, Haremski added that "you can never be sure what the jury is going to do regardless of what the proof is."[9]

Asked about the defense's scenario that Bates was the killer while Matt only aided in disposal, Mordino said it didn't make any sense. "Why would you cut up a body if you're not the killer?"

Mordino said Bates was a crybaby, a mama's boy. "He couldn't have cut up the body. He didn't have the stomach for it." The defense, Mordino added, wanted the world to believe that there was a conspiracy to make Matt look guilty, but if you made a list of the things that made Matt look guilty, you realized that they all came from Matt himself.

The bottom line was that Matt couldn't keep his mouth shut. "He was telling people things and every time he spoke he was digging his own grave a little deeper," Mordino concluded.

At the May 30, 2008, sentencing hearing, seven of the twelve jurors returned in person voluntarily to see Richard Matt get his just desserts. They described their duty as jurors as emotionally draining and said they were on hand to "get some closure."

William Rickerson Jr. was allowed to address the court and his father's killer. He thanked the prosecution team and the returning jurors. "Myself, I'm not a terribly vindictive man. But we all have to benefit from this, and the only way to benefit is for this person Matt to never do this again. *He should never see the light of day*. I know that I'll never be done with Matt. It will be my job to visit parole boards each and every time his name comes up and make sure they understand: this guy *shouldn't get out*."[10]

Judge Sara Sheldon said, "Before I sentence you, Mr. Matt, do you have anything you'd like to say to this court?"

"No ma'am, but thank you for the opportunity," Matt said, a last-ditch attempt to flash his superficial charm.

She said, "Quite frankly, this is not a difficult decision," and sentenced Matt to the maximum possible prison term of twenty-five years to life.[11]

Detective David Bentley said that the night after Matt's conviction, he received another written message from Matt, the youth he'd tried to mentor many years before.

"You lied in court to fuck me over for the DA," it read. "You also make it clear that we are not friends. I will remember both . . ."[12]

That ellipse, Bentley assumed, represented a threat.

"Dot-dot-dot. Like there's more to come," Bentley said.

Mordino said that the sentence still seemed too light to him. "The facts speak for themselves, this defendant's record speaks for itself and this case cried out for the maximum sentence. If New York had not abolished the death penalty, I'd have a lot more to say. *Of all the cases I've tried this would top my list for the death penalty.*"[13]

Under most circumstances, when prisoners in jail are convicted of a crime, there is a grace period before they are transferred to the prison where they will serve out their term. But in this case, the Erie County Holding Center could not get rid of Richard Matt fast enough. Matt had threatened police. He had talked to two other prisoners who were getting out about putting a hit on Detective Gardner[14] and another officer. The sooner they got him out of town and on his way to Little Siberia, the better.

Privateer was still convinced that the prosecution's heavy display of security influenced the jury. In addition, he felt, the media influenced the jury to no end.

The jurors in attendance disagreed wholeheartedly. They thought the guards in the courtroom were there for the judge, and when Judge Sheldon told them to avoid newspapers and TV and radio news, they did as they were told. The media, they said, had not been a factor at all.

Matt filed for an appeal, which was turned down in November 2010 by the appellate division of New York State's Supreme Court.

The cost of Matt's murder trial to Niagara County taxpayers was tallied at $216,900. That was the amount paid to Haremski[15] and Mordino,[16] by order of Judge Kloch.

The bill drained the county's contingency fund for the remainder of that year. DA Michael Violante commented, "I know it's a lot of money. I think in my heart, it's money well spent. Richard Matt, if we're lucky, *will die in jail*."

By the time Matt got to Clinton Correctional Facility (CCF) on July 10, 2008, David Sweat had already been there for almost five years. Matt concentrated for his first few years in Dannemora on his legal case. Acting as his own attorney in 2013, Matt filed a federal court habeas corpus action, claiming his civil rights were denied during the Rickerson trial. The violations included the fifty-thousand-volt stun belt he wore.[17]

During their stay in Dannemora, Matt and Sweat were deemed well be-haved and accrued generous privileges. Each had only one blemish on his prison record. Matt was found with tattooing materials and implicated in an extortion scheme, and Sweat reportedly harassed another inmate. But by 2015 they were neighbors, both on the third tier of the Honor Block.

Honor Block. In the civilized, or even semi-civilized, world, the con-cept is easy to understand. In some high schools there was an "honor pass" system. If you were well behaved and went a whole quarter of the school year without being scolded, you received an honor pass, which meant you didn't have to sit in study hall but could go outside and play tennis, work on extracurricular activities, or go to the library. This was more or less how it worked at CCF as well.

But CCF was neither civilized nor semi-civilized. And the criterion for inclusion ignored a prisoner's history. The past didn't count. If you were good lately you got into the Honor Block, so it didn't matter that Matt was a solipsistic sociopath who once chopped up a human being and dumped the pieces in a river, and it didn't matter that Sweat had shot a police officer in cold blood and then run over him in a car for good measure. It didn't matter that Matt had a history of escape attempts, both in the United States and Mexico. He was being a good boy in Dannemora, so into the Honor Block he went.

SIX
THE BLONDE AND THE BURGER

As soon as news and initial details of the escape reached them, investigators realized that the prisoners must have had someone's assistance. They quickly honed their search for conspirators to a select few, one of whom was a woman, Joyce Mitchell, a prison sewing-shop supervisor.[1]

In addition to the corrections officers working at CCF, there were 150 civilian workers who were tailors, cooks, and clerks and fell under the Civil Service Employees Association (CSEA). The tailor shop where Mitchell worked was created in response to the 1929 riot, as an attempt to not just punish prisoners but rehabilitate them as well.

Her name had come up when investigators were interviewing Richard Matt's daughter. A subsequent examination of Mitchell's cell-phone records revealed that, during the days and hours before the escape, her phone was used to call several people connected to Matt.

Mitchell, investigators quickly learned, was a plain and bespectacled middle-aged woman, blonde and a little heavy, who lived with her husband of fourteen years Lyle (also a Clinton Correctional Facility [CCF] civilian employee, a "floater" who moved from tailor shop to tailor shop as his assistance was required) on Palmer Street in Dickinson Center, fifty-five miles from the prison.

Neighbors described them as "good people" but "quiet." Joyce was friendly but kept to herself. While canvassing the Mitchell's neighborhood, detectives learned some potentially illuminating information. Before working at the prison, Mitchell worked at the local school and had been the town tax collector for several years. She had been active at local churches and coached girls' softball. Going back even further on her resume, Joyce demonstrated the sewing skills that got her hired at CCF, while working at the Tru-Stitch Clothing factory in Bombay, New York. She had been working at the prison since March 13, 2008, and was making $57,697 per year.

Mitchell made her first statement at the New York State Police Station

in Malone, New York, on June 7. She was read her Miranda rights and acknowledged that she understood them. She said her name was Joyce "Tillie"
E. Mitchell, and she was fifty-one years old. She was employed at CCF as
an industrial training supervisor. When she first arrived at the prison, she
worked in all of the tailor shops.

"You have to work in all the shops before you get assigned to a specific
shop," she explained.

She said that she met Richard Matt soon after her arrival, in 2008 or early
2009. She'd been assigned to Tailor Shop 1 in October 2013, and when she got
there David Sweat "was already working there as an instructor."

Sweat, she said, was a "good worker" and was always "very nice to me." She
spoke every day with Sweat, and they became close friends, but they never
had a physical relationship.

The investigators were skeptical. They'd looked up Mitchell's CCF disci
plinary records and knew that in September 2014 there were allegations that
Sweat and Mitchell were "involved in an inappropriate relationship." So they
asked about that.

Those allegations, she said, were dropped. There had not been any sexual
contact between her and Sweat, but she later admitted that, at his request,
she'd sent him "X-rated selfies."

Investigators wanted to know, specifically, what was in those photos.

She answered, "I did take some naked photos of my breasts and vagina
and gave them to Matt to give to Sweat. I do not know what they did with
the photos."

Because of the sexual misconduct allegations, Sweat was not allowed to
return to her shop. He was reassigned to Tailor Shop 8, where he worked
right up until the escape.

Mitchell talked about the escapees. They were different from other inmates.
For one thing, Matt and Sweat were a *team*. She thought them extraordinarily
bonded for inmates. They were always together and shared everything, she
said.

The allegations of misconduct involved Sweat, she explained, but it was
Matt that she liked. She and he got along well. They talked every day, and
he treated her with respect and was nice to her. He made her feel *special*.

As the relationship between Mitchell and Matt grew, which happened in
a matter of weeks, the first favor Matt asked involved sending messages to

his daughter Jamie. He gave Mitchell his daughter's phone number. Mitchell contacted the daughter on several occasions on his behalf, and they had "casual conversations."

Matt was known for his artistic abilities in Dannemora, and one thing he wanted Mitchell to find out for him was if his daughter had received a painting he'd sent her.

Mitchell said, "I know it was wrong but I called his daughter Jamie and told her who I was and that I was not supposed to be doing this, but I was doing it as a favor for her father. The daughter asked Mitchell to let her dad know that she got the painting and was doing fine.

After that, whenever Matt wanted Mitchell to contact his daughter, Mitchell would text Jamie. They exchanged texts regarding everything from Matt's artwork to complaints about his sore back.

In November 2014, Mitchell asked Matt to paint a portrait of her children, which she planned to give to Lyle. After the first time she spoke with Jamie, she went on the Internet and looked at some of Matt's pictures.

"They were very good," Mitchell said. Matt, she discovered, could draw faces with photographic accuracy.

To pay for the painting, Mitchell gave Matt—in advance—a pair of speed-bag boxing gloves with the padding to protect the knuckles. To make sure she bought the correct gloves, Matt provided her with a prison-approved catalog.

He next requested two pairs of glasses with lights on them, so he and Sweat would be able to paint at night. She ordered the glasses off eBay. The eBay account was under her husband's name, but Lyle did not know about it.

Mitchell noticed that the gifts kept flowing in one direction. In addition to the boxing gloves and the eyeglasses, she also brought him brownies, cookies, and other food—but her wedding anniversary came and went, and she had still not received the painting of her children. She asked Matt what was up, and he told her he had accidentally spilled something on the painting and had had to start over.

It was near the end of April 2015 when her relationship with Matt changed. They were together in Tailor Shop 9. They were there "to get a part off a machine," but Matt apparently had something else in mind.

"Matt grabbed me and kissed me," Mitchell told investigators. "It startled me. He kissed me with an open mouth kiss. I was scared shitless."

"Scared but excited?"

"Yeah. I didn't say anything because I was scared for my husband who also works in the facility."

Shortly after that incident, also in April, Matt asked Mitchell to bring him a star-type screwdriver bit. He did not explain why he needed the bit, nor did she ask him. She purchased the bit—at either Kmart or Walmart, she couldn't remember—and brought it to him.

There came a time when they were again alone in Tailor Shop 9. Using the bluntest possible language, redacted in copies of the written statement released to the public, Matt commanded Mitchell to give him oral sex.

She said she was "frightened," and so complied.

"He pulled his [redacted] out and I put my mouth on it for maybe a minute," she said. "He did not ejaculate."

Once the sex started, it became part of a routine. Matt would put on his "large coat" in which he had cut a hole in the pocket. He inserted his penis through it and would tell Mitchell that she should pretend she was going to give him a piece of hard candy.

"While doing so," she said, "I should reach into his pocket and squeeze his [redacted] really hard."

That happened three or four times, she said, adding, "The only other physical contact I had with Matt was when he kissed me at the bottom of the first set of stairs. He never touched any of my private areas."

At some point Mitchell learned that Matt and Sweat had a project, and it involved getting out of their cell and into the cellblock's infrastructure. Despite this knowledge, and here was a key legal point against her, she continued to provide them with tools.

"Around the beginning of May 2015, Matt asked me to get him two hacksaw blades," she said. This was after she bought the bit, so she was used to going to the tool department for Matt. She bought the blades at Walmart, brought them to work in her bag, and gave them to Matt.

At first Matt told her that the project was perfectly innocent, that he and Sweat were making frames for Matt's paintings.

"Sometime around this time," she said, "I also bought them batteries for the glasses I had given them. I found out about the hole because Matt was coming into work tired. I asked him about sleeping and he said he was up all night. After a couple of days, he told me that he and Sweat had cut the holes and were going down in the pipes."

She guessed without being told that they were visiting the pipes as part of a plan to escape. She wrote, "Matt told me they had found a toolbox with power tools under the facility. They were using them to get out through the pipe system. Matt told me they were getting out and we were all going to be together. By this he meant Sweat, him and I."

Eventually she got around to being an active participant in the escape plan: "I was already bringing stuff in to him, and didn't really feel I could stop."

Matt asked Mitchell to call a phone number and ask for Diane or Diana. When she had them on the phone, she was to act as if she was confirming an appointment.

"I was to say I would like to confirm a doctor's appointment on Saturday or Sunday at 4:00 p.m. at Alice Hyde Medical Center."

She was to give the other party a description of her vehicle and set up a meeting place and time. In response to her message, these outside parties would deliver to Mitchell a package—Matt explained that it was not going to attract attention because it would be the same size and shape as the lunch bag she usually brought to work with her—which she was supposed to pass along to Matt.

"I do not know what was supposed to be in the packages and I never picked any of them up. I started to call the number that night at 6:06 p.m. but got scared and hung up before it rang. I received a call back from the number at 6:25 p.m., but I blocked the call."

The next day Matt asked her if she had called the number, and she told him she had not.

"He told me to call that night. On May 13, I called at 6:20 p.m., but hung up before it rang. I dialed again at 6:21 p.m. and hung up after seven seconds. At 6:36 p.m., I called and asked for Diane or Diana.

The guy who answered the phone, she said, sounded Spanish and told her there was no one there by either of the names she'd mentioned. Mitchell reported this conversation to Matt the next day, that she had mentioned both names and gotten no satisfaction. Matt said he would "check into it."

They were up to May 14 now. Matt gave her a new name to ask for at the same phone number. She called at 5:30 p.m. and got an answering machine that didn't mention the user's name but asked the caller to leave a message at the beep.

She hung up and called the number again two minutes later. This time a live female answered. Mitchell asked for Bree, and the woman on the other end said, "I am she."

Mitchell gave her the message, using the guise of pretending to confirm an appointment. She said Sunday at 4:00 p.m., which Mitchell now knew meant the time she was to meet for a pickup.

But, Mitchell admitted, she messed up. She forgot to give the woman a description of her vehicle as she had been instructed to do. On May 15 she told Matt what happened, and he told her to call back that night. She said she wasn't comfortable doing that so he said, okay, just let it go. State police later interviewed a woman who admitted that she had received "crazy phone calls" from a woman seeking to confirm a mysterious appointment, but she denied being part of the prison conspiracy.

Mitchell's statement now skipped ahead to Wednesday, June 3, when again Matt insisted that she call the number that night, and this time she did, first at 7:58 getting the answering machine, and then on June 4 at 5:48 and 6:34, no answer either time. It went to voice mail, but she left no message. She called twice more that night, at 6:44 and 7:27, again no answer, and again she left no message. She gave up.

On Friday, June 5, Mitchell said, she got up and went to work with her husband. They took the Jeep, as they almost always did, and got to work a few minutes after 7:00 a.m. She reported for duty that morning in her tailor shop. The inmates arrived between 7:45 and 8:00, and Matt was among them.

Matt said, "We're getting out tonight." All of them, he added, Mitchell, Matt, and Sweat. Matt told Mitchell to pick them up in Dannemora near the powerhouse at midnight. He asked her to bring him a cell phone, a GPS, a hatchet, and a shotgun that he could saw off.

The plan was that she was going to leave her husband and meet him there and they would all quit Dannemora together. Matt did not say where they were going to go.

That day she got into an argument with a correctional officer in the shop. He wanted to write up the inmates in her shop for standing around and griped that Mitchell was not giving them enough work to do.

She ended up calling her boss and asking for the sergeant. Her supervisor called, and she ended up arguing with him also. So it had been a stressful day when she left the prison with her husband at 3:30 p.m.

They stopped for an early supper at King's Wok Buffet, located across the street from the Malone Police Station. They arrived around 4:15 p.m. Joyce paid for the meal at 4:58 p.m. using her credit card. The bill came to $22.14. She left a $5 tip.

So it wasn't a rushed meal. Joyce might've thought at first, as they went to the buffet, that this might be the last meal she would ever have with Lyle. Sad. It was the end of an era. She had reason to be nostalgic: it was her torrid affair with Lyle that broke up her first marriage.

She realized she couldn't do it. She had what she referred to as "a moment of clarity," and she knew: running off with Matt and Sweat was a bad idea. The escape might not even work.

Her mind was clear now, and she saw all. If the inmates did succeed in getting under the wall, and she joined them on the outside, it could be for her a fatal mistake. If the escapees themselves didn't turn on her, she might end up getting killed by the police who would pursue Matt and Sweat as if they were John Dillinger and Bonnie and Clyde combined—and when spotted, they would be gunned down mercilessly, thoroughly ventilated, in the name of justice. If she were standing next to them, well, she would be ventilated too.

No, she had to back out.

Then her brain raced in the other direction: Maybe *not* showing up for the rendezvous was just as dangerous as following through. Hell, she might end up getting killed anyway. She might end up getting killed no matter what she did. What if Matt and Sweat became so pissed off that they made a stop at the Mitchell home before desperately fleeing? By standing them up she jeopardized the escape. Matt and Sweat would be super-pissed.

That was when her heart began to race.

She told Lyle that she wasn't feeling well. Her heart was jackhammering out of her chest. She was on the verge of hyperventilating. Fearing cardiac arrest, she stretched out in bed and tried to control her breathing. The wave of anxiety proved unmanageable, and she had a full-fledged panic attack.

After a while, she managed to relax a little bit and maybe even dozed for a few minutes, but then she woke fully up and it started up again. She'd painted herself into a corner.

Lyle was terribly concerned. He asked if she wanted to go to the hospital, and she said yes. Sometime between 9:00 and 10:00 p.m. Lyle drove her to the emergency room at Alice Hyde Medical Center.

She was in the ER until 2:00 a.m., at which time the hospital decided to admit her overnight. Lyle left at that point, returning home to let the dog out. She was given a room around 2:30 and called Lyle. He said he would stay home as long as he was there and see if he could get some sleep.

She shut off her phone until around 6:00 or 7:00 a.m. when she called her husband and asked that he bring her medication to the hospital. He got there around 8:00. The next time she looked at her phone it was 11:30 a.m., and there was "a bunch" of messages from her family saying that the police were looking for her.

"I ended up checking out and coming to the New York State Police Station in Malone at 1:00 p.m. I was questioned but did not tell the whole truth," Mitchell admitted.

That afternoon she and Lyle had run into an investigator at Walmart, and she told the officer that she needed to speak with him. This statement was the result, and she was now telling the truth.

She reiterated that she'd first heard Matt and Sweat talking about "getting out" two months previous but had only known the plan to go through their cell wall for the past three or four weeks.

She didn't know where they were headed. She didn't give them any items other than those she'd already specified. To her knowledge the escapees had neither a gun nor a cell phone.

She concluded with head hung, "I am really sorry for what I have done."

Conversations with Mitchell continued the next day, and the next and the next. Her interrogators thought she still knew things she wasn't saying.

At one point she said, "The day they were supposed to escape I was supposed to give my husband two pills. These pills were intended to knock out Lyle so I could leave the house."

Matt, she went on, gave her the pills on May 25, and she hid them in a bathroom drawer next to the medicine cabinet at home. Matt told her that she'd have to trick Lyle into taking the pills somehow and that they would "incapacitate him." (She flushed them down the toilet instead, thank you very much.)

Once Lyle was asleep, she was supposed to drive to Dannemora and meet

Matt and Sweat. She would pick them up and drive to her home where Matt would kill 'the glitch.'" Matt, she explained, referred to Lyle as "the glitch"—as in the glitch in the system that would need to be removed so that their lives could go on smoothly. Matt, she maintained, wanted to kill Lyle because he wanted to have Joyce all to himself. With Lyle dead, they were going to drive six or seven hours to a densely wooded area where they would lay low for a week. Then they would separate. Sweat would go off on his own so that Matt and Joyce could be together forever. But instead, she panicked.

"I really do love my husband and he's the reason I didn't meet," she said. She merely enjoyed the attention that the inmates gave her, dreams "of a different life. I was caught up in the fantasy," she said.

Matt had given her a list of things she should bring with her when she picked them up: a cell phone, a GPS, clothes, a shotgun, a rifle, tents, a hatchet, sleeping bags, and fishing poles. She hadn't accumulated the items because she had no intention of showing up.

On June 10, state police superintendent Joseph A. D'Amico announced that Mitchell was cooperating with the investigation, "may have had a role" in assisting them, and has not been charged with committing a crime.

At some point, Mitchell reportedly backed off her statement that she had no idea where the escapees were going, telling authorities they might be "headed toward Vermont," a piece of information that was disseminated to law enforcement and then promptly leaked to the press by Vermont governor Peter Shumlin.

Mitchell's interrogators had her cooperating, so again they held off on arresting her.

Predators have a sixth sense regarding the nature of their prey. Matt and Sweat must've started tingling the instant they encountered Joyce Mitchell. An unnamed coworker told *People* magazine that Mitchell was known for her one-track mind.

"She would talk about men," the coworker said. "That's all she would talk about."

This wasn't the first time Joyce had been involved in scandalous behavior involving men. According to the ex-wife of Mitchell's ex-husband, Mitchell was part of a love triangle involving her ex- and current husbands.

Helen Premo told *People*, "She cheated on Tobey with the man she is married to. They all worked together. [Tobey] was a basket case when I met him. He was devastated."

Premo theorized that monotony rather than libido was at the root of Mitchell's sexual restlessness: "It's kind of boring where they live. You're not going to find a lot of excitement. It's near the Adirondacks. Even so, she was married, had a wonderful son, a house, a good job, a decent life—and she *blew* it."

The sexual relationship between a staff member and a prisoner, and its pertinence to the Dannemora escape, caused officials to take a look at the staff-inmate phenomenon. According to the Bureau of Justice Statistics, there were hundreds of consensual sexual relationships between guards and inmates each year. More than half of those incidents involved female staff members.

Governor Andrew Cuomo weighed in: "I understand prisons run on a delicate balance, and having a good relationship between guards and the inmates, guards and the employees, employees and inmates is important, but there's a line, and when the line is stepped over, then action has to be taken."

Writing for *Syracuse Daily Mail*, reporter Geoff Herbert went in search of Joyce Mitchell's past. What was it about her that placed her in the epicenter of the summer's biggest story?

Herbert found Tobey Premo—Mitchell's high school sweetheart and first husband in St. Regis Falls, a town about fifty miles from Dannemora. Premo worked as a farmer in Massena, New York, and no he wasn't surprised at her alleged involvement in the escape.

Premo and Mitchell knew each other as kids, enjoyed their first kiss on the school bus, were married for five years, and during that time she had at least two affairs. It was her cheating that destroyed their relationship. The last affair was with Lyle Mitchell, the man who became her second husband, but there was at least one more before that, with a guy she worked with.

"I know because the guy's girlfriend came and told me about it," Premo said. There was a pattern. Fidelity wasn't a concept Joyce was comfortable with. "She cheated on me, so I could see her falling for someone in prison."

Tobey and Joyce had a son, also named Tobey, who went with mom following the split and was subsequently adopted by Lyle Mitchell, so his name is Tobey Mitchell. (Tobey Sr.'s characterization of Joyce as a home wrecker and cheater irked Paige Mitchell, Joyce's daughter-in-law. She told the *Press-Republican* that it was Tobey Sr. who was to blame, having abandoned her husband when he was one year old. "As far as I'm concerned, anything he's got to say is bullshit," Paige said.) Premo said that he hadn't seen Joyce or Tobey since the split but that didn't change the fact that he'd loved her, she'd been his wife, and then she cheated and screwed everything up. He said he was a little surprised at Joyce's recent behavior. At fifty-one, he would have thought her sex drive would be kaput.

Soon after the escape, *NBC News* located the son Tobey, now a member of the Vermont Air National Guard. Tobey offered a more positive—if not informed—image of his mother. He didn't think his mom would knowingly help inmates to escape.

"She's not going to risk her life or other people's lives to help these guys escape. She's always been a good person, and anyone will tell you, my parents are the nicest people," Tobey said.

Investigators were impressed with the extent of Joyce Mitchell's promiscuity. Mitchell had admitted to manual and oral sexual activity with Matt. She'd been investigated previously for photo fun time with Sweat. Multiple affairs broke up her first marriage. And that, for all they knew, might be just the tip of the hanky-panky iceberg.

Joyce's action-packed statements were more than entertaining. Investigators found them illuminating as well. She gave investigators insight into the prisoners' situation and made it easier for them to predict what Matt and Sweat might do. When the prisoners popped up out of the manhole and found that their getaway car was not there, they had to either ad lib or revert to a plan B. And if there was a plan B, Mitchell knew nothing of it.

When New York State governor Cuomo discussed this portion of the plan with reporters weeks later, his characterization of Mitchell and her involvement smacked of romantic hyperbole. He said that Mitchell claimed to be "in love" with one or both of the prisoners, that she planned to go to Mexico with them, and that this was "a fairy tale that I wasn't read as a child."

When no more blood could be squeezed from the stone—on June 12, while both prisoners were still free—Mitchell was charged with a felony for promoting prison contraband. She appeared in Plattsburgh City Court dressed in blue jeans and an electric green tee shirt. She was represented by Plattsburgh general practice attorney Keith M. Bruno, and the hearing was presided over by Judge Mark Rogers.

The charges specifically alleged that she provided for the escapees hacksaw blades, chisels, and a drill bit. Mitchell allegedly hid the tool inside hamburger meat that she placed in a freezer. She then allegedly asked a corrections officer to deliver the meat to Matt and Sweat, which the officer allegedly did. (This will be discussed more thoroughly in the next chapter.)

This was the last time Bruno would be seen at Mitchell's side. When she next appeared in court on June 15, Bruno would announce that he was withdrawing from the case because of a conflict of interest. Mitchell, from then on, would have a more media-savvy lawyer. Mitchell might not always have been the brightest bulb, but she did eventually see the writing on the wall. She was in deep trouble and was looking at a long stretch of being front-page news. Her new lawyer was Steven A. Johnston, who told reporters, "All I'd say is she's very upset. She's distraught." At the June 15 hearing, Mitchell informed the court that she was aware of and approved her change of counsel with a series of monosyllabic answers. Johnston said he was troubled by all of the cameras in the courtroom. Could city court judge Mark Rogers put a stop to it? A meeting in chambers followed, and when the parties returned to the courtroom Judge Rogers admonished the media to refrain from shooting video.

On June 22, on the anniversary of the 1929 Dannemora riot, Jessica Layton of WNYT-TV spoke with Erik Jensen, a former CCF inmate who knew Matt and Sweat. Jensen explained his own presence behind bars with a simple, "I got greedy."

Jensen knew Sweat from the tailor shop and had been impressed with Sweat's skills: "He could sew any piece of clothing. He was very talented," Jensen recalled.

Jensen and Sweat bonded over their shared passion for art. "He wasn't loud. He was quiet, reserved. He was an artist just like me. We compared our artwork."

He was also one of the smartest people Jensen had ever met, and he believed that Sweat was the mastermind behind the escape. Jensen knew Sweat to be a "master manipulator," who was so familiar with some prison workers that he had a lot of special privileges and seemed more like a coworker with those people than a convict.

"I didn't know that he killed a police officer. I would not even think he was in there for murder by the way he conducted himself. He was well-spoken when he did speak, and he was the head of the tailor shop."

Jensen described Sweat as a guy "with a lot of pull" and wondered out loud, "How do two guys like Matt and Sweat land on the honor block?"

In another interview weeks later with North Country Public Radio, Jensen said that he blamed the escape on the prison's "complex culture" that left "openings and weaknesses" that the escapees were able to exploit.

Jensen said that before he got to Dannemora, he had served hard time at other New York State facilities. But when he arrived at CCF he was told that things were going to be different there. Tougher. He was told that if he put his hands on any officers, if he disrespected any officers, they would kill him, and no one would care. If Jensen and another prisoner wanted to kill each other, they were cool with that too. Like a saloon owner telling brawlers to take it outside, Jensen was told that if he wanted to commit violent acts against another inmate he should "take it to the North Yard."

That area, Jensen recalled, was controlled by gang activity, which he (like prison employees) largely steered clear of. He avoided the gangs but did get caught up in an "enforcement action," in which officers swept the yard. During that action he was kicked in the back and had teeth knocked out. (Jensen showed the interviewer his dentures, which still had his prison ID number on them.)

He recalled the first time he reported to Joyce Mitchell's tailor shop. She gave him paperwork to fill out. David Sweat was her right-hand man, in charge of all the other inmates in that shop. Jensen loved it there. It was a kinder and gentler place than anywhere else he'd been in CCF. Because the atmosphere was so relaxed, "a lot of things were going on that shouldn't have." He recalled officers returning from hunting trips with photos to show the inmates, with pieces of venison for the prisoners to eat. The level of "relationships and fraternization" was "extremely high." Jensen said he noticed that Mitchell and Sweat were particularly close and knew that Mitchell routinely brought Sweat presents from the outside, things such as food and tattoo supplies.

Jensen was aware that Mitchell admitted to having sex with Matt but denied having sex with Sweat. He waxed skeptical. He'd seen Mitchell and Sweat sneaking off into storage rooms with the door closed for as long as forty minutes, to be alone to do something, and everyone assumed it was to have sex. When they reemerged the other inmates would crack jokes. Mitchell and Sweat would laugh but neither confirmed nor denied that they'd been intimate.

Mitchell told police that it was depression that led her into inappropriate behavior with the future escapees, but Jensen said it didn't look that way to him. It looked to him as if Mitchell was simply a flirt, the kind of woman who couldn't walk past you without bumping into you and giving you a little rub. It looked to Jensen as if Mitchell was having fun.

Jensen told the public radio reporter that there was a system: simple exchange. You gave a guard something—a can of tobacco, a box of assorted candies, and so forth—and he would let you out of your cell for a while.

In design, and for the most part in execution, the system was friendly rather than sinister, and Matt and Sweat knew the system inside out. The staff was simply "outplayed" by Matt and Sweat. It was normal for prisoners to spend hours on end plotting to "get over or get out." Sweat was smarter than most. He figured out a way to do both.

On Tuesday, July 28, Mitchell appeared in court wearing for the first time in public a black-and-white prison jumpsuit. Her hands were shackled. At the bench was the Honorable Kevin K. Ryan, a no-nonsense judge with a rim of silver hair and a long, kind face.[2]

Judge Ryan asked for her plea. Mitchell practically whispered the word, "Guilty."

The plea was Johnston's idea. He'd advised her that there was overwhelming evidence that she did what she had admitted to. Also, he was fearful that additional charges might be lumped upon those she'd already been charged with, and Johnston wanted to nip that in the bud. A deal was the way to go.

Wylie liked the idea too. He said, "I determined that although there were possible charges in which to charge Ms. Mitchell with, that the people were confident that the charges within the court information were charges that would be proven beyond a reasonable doubt. And in the interest of justice, I negotiated a plea and recommended a sentence."

By cutting a deal, Mitchell waived her right to appeal and avoided the rape charges that Johnston was afraid of—in connection with her sexual activity with Matt[3]—and a murder conspiracy charge in the plan to murder her husband.

The deal with the district attorney's office also meant that Mitchell agreed to cooperate with the ongoing inspector general's investigation, which had staffers in the courtroom.

The inspector general promptly released a statement: "Nothing short of her full cooperation will be tolerated. And I am confident that when she fulfills that obligation, I will provide a thorough and complete accounting of all of the factors contributing to this elaborate breakout, with an eye toward ensuring this never happens again."

After the hearing, DA Andrew Wylie said, "Because the evidence was so overwhelming, she wanted to expedite her case proceedings and move on with the matter."

Sure, that was why she wanted to cut a deal. But why was the prosecution willing to bend?

Wylie said that he wasn't 100 percent positive that he could convict her solely on her statements to investigators, so it was in the "interests of justice" to cut a deal.

After the hearing, Johnston said he didn't believe his client conspired to murder her husband. He agreed to the deal on behalf of his client because he wanted to avoid a scenario in which the DA would charge Mitchell separately for each occasion in which she smuggled contraband into the prison.

The day after Mitchell's court hearing, a British reporter did his genealogical homework and learned that Joyce Mitchell's maternal grandfather, Kenneth Snyder, had been an inmate in Dannemora. At age twenty-one, Snyder was earning $8 a week plus board and lodging as a farmhand in Moira, New York, when he stole eight chickens from a hen house and was arrested, along with two of his brothers (Cleon, thirty-three years old, and Frederick, nineteen) and another man (Roscoe Cox, twenty-five).

The police report at the time said the crime was "due to drinking." That official report noted that Snyder was Catholic but hadn't been to church in more than a year. His habits were described as "intemperate." District attorney Ellsworth N. Lawrence said the four men had done more than just once steal some chickens. They were, he believed, responsible for a series of burglaries and had been passing bad checks as well. The brothers were convicted and sentenced on February 27, 1939, to two to four years in what was then known as Clinton Prison. Roscoe Cox received a sentence of ten to twenty as a second-time felon. After a few months in Dannemora, Snyder was moved 250 miles south to a lower-security facility, Wallkill State Prison. Snyder only served fifteen and a half months of his sentence when he was released on parole in June 1940 and weeks later impregnated a fifteen-year-old girl, Ruth Jesmer, whom he married. The child, born in April 1941, was Joyce Mitchell's now seventy-four-year-old mother, also named Joyce.

Snyder by all accounts went straight and raised a family. The couple had seven children, four girls and three boys, and remained married for almost half a century until Snyder died in 1989. Ruth Snyder died in 2012 at the age of eighty-seven. Kenneth and Ruth were buried beside one another in St. Mary's Cemetery in Brushton. Their gravestone read, "If you listen with your heart, you will hear the music of the woods." Mitchell's mom Joyce Snyder lived in Brushton.

Not everyone was happy about Mitchell's plea deal. Janet Duprey of the New York State Assembly said the deal frustrated her, that it seemed a small penalty for the expensive and dangerous consequences of Mitchell's actions. There'd been no justice. Public commentary, Duprey opined, tended to express outrage at the process, in favor of the criminal instead of public good. Mitchell's dalliance and infatuation endangered hundreds of law enforcement personnel, created physical and emotional stress for the residents of Clinton and Franklin counties, and cost taxpayers millions of dollars. Duprey hoped that this quick plea deal would encourage the inspector general's office to finalize its investigation and issue results, that it was time to punish the accountable and vindicate the innocent and allow them to get back to work. Several correction officers were still on administrative leave, she noted, locked out of the prison. The majority of them were not involved in any way with the crime. Their professional and personal lives were turned upside down because of Joyce Mitchell's actions.

Those actions, Duprey said, affected the inside of Clinton just as much as the outside, maybe more so. Additional stress had been dumped upon the shoulders of correction officers who already worked in a tense and anxious environment.

During her last tour of CCF, Duprey had been pleased to see signs of improving morale. Still, uncertainty regarding the fates of their innocent coworkers made a tough job even harder. Short staffing was as bad as ever. Overtime—long, long hours—was the norm. It was a schedule detrimental to an officer's family life, tough on spouses and children. Everybody suffered. She was talking about pros that took pride in serving with dignity and ensuring community safety. It wasn't fair because, for the most part, they couldn't defend themselves. Rules bound them: public comments about prison issues were forbidden. Duprey concluded, "As I've done throughout my career, I will be the voice of those who are not given the opportunity to speak for themselves. Let's give them the courtesy of justice and closure, too." As a postscript, Duprey said she was also bothered by the fact that, according to present law, Mitchell was still set to collect on her pension. That was a subject that brought out the politicians, all bobbing their downward thumbs.

Assemblyman Dan Stec of Queensbury said the law needed to be changed, sooner the better, "to prevent these kinds of situations in the future."

Assembly minority leader Brian Kolb of Canandaigua blamed assembly Democrats for their ineptitude as Mitchell cashed her pension checks. Kolb opined that it was the dang blasted Democrats who walked away from a bill, already passed by the senate, which would have called for pension forfeiture for state employees who'd been found guilty of exploiting their positions.

Duprey had a plan. The only option, she said, was to draw up a constitutional amendment, take it to the voters. To do that, she warned, they would have to pass the legislation in two consecutive legislative terms, and the first chance voters would have at the issue was November 2017. The state senate, she added, was planning public hearings regarding the escape, but those wouldn't start until after the conclusion of the inspector general's investigation. And who the heck knew when that was going to be?

Another point of contention was that Mitchell had been given a public defender. That subject made legislator Mark Dame see red. As soon as the legislature received the bill, he was going to start a protest. Mitchell, he noted, was pulling in $58,000 in annual salary, also taxpayer's money. That the state was picking up her legal tab was adding insult to injury.

Duprey's kvetching sat uneasy with the district attorney. Wylie said that he had rarely, if ever, heard the type of "political demagoguery" as in Duprey's statement. Mitchell, the prosecutor pointed out, had waived her right to a grand jury proceeding and pleaded guilty as charged to each count. She was scheduled to be sentenced, and he couldn't emphasize this enough, to the *maximum sentence allowable in New York State.*

What more did Duprey want? She had apparently already determined that Mitchell should be prosecuted for unnamed crimes that she failed to cite. Wylie noted the irony: a member of one of the "most criticized legislative bodies in America" lecturing to those who worked tirelessly to bring justice to those involved. It was astonishing and insulting to all involved law enforcement.

"I saved taxpayers thousands of dollars," Wylie said. He had no agenda, just the desire to represent the people. One day he would like to have a sit-down with Duprey and explain to her a few points she was missing, like how prosecutors rarely used words such as "closure" because of the large number of victims they served.

"There is almost never closure," the DA said, "only a sense of justice delivered by prosecutors that fight for you, not politicians who try to exploit you."

The sordid side of the story was what was keeping it on the front page. Talk about "well-endowed inmates" and prison sex was titillating and left the public hungry for details. Questions arose, such as where does one go to have a romantic interlude with a prison staffer when incarcerated in a maximum-security prison? Such facilities weren't known for their hiding places—were they?

To get an answer to this question, Ian Mohr of the *New York Post's* gossipy "Page Six" column posed the question to "Club Killer" Michael Alig, who had served seventeen years in Dannemora for murdering his drug-dealing friend in 1996.

Alig said that it was easier to have sex with a woman at the prison than with a man. Women who worked on staff had access to private rooms, such as the storage rooms or the meat freezer.

Many things happened in the meat freezer because there was only one entrance, it could be locked, and there were no windows. There were other locations as well, blind spots. Officers were positioned every approximately one hundred feet, so there were in-between spots where the guards couldn't see you.

"Inmates know where all those spots are," Alig said.

Regarding the escape itself, Alig noted that CCF was an old prison but one that was *really hard* to escape from. Just because Matt and Sweat had pulled it off did not mean that any inmate could do it again. The odds were remote of once again finding two inmates with the intelligence and complementary skills of Sweat and Matt.

How did the prisoners break out without being heard? Alig said it wasn't that amazing. CCF was never quiet; in fact, the prison was "louder than a nightclub" with "music blaring at all hours."

That accounted for the logistics of the tryst, but what about the psychology? Why would a female staffer at a maximum-security prison risk her career to have sex with a prisoner who, in the final analysis, is probably a sociopathic dirtbag?

ABC News asked that question to Robin Kay Miller, a fifty-three-year-old former prison employee, who was writing a book about her prison experiences. Miller said, "Inmates are con artists. They know how to play the game and they know how to manipulate."

During the summer of 2015, a North Carolina jailbreak also had a sex angle featuring a female staffer. Thirty-three-year-old Kendra Lynette Miller was charged with having sex with and aiding and abetting a fugitive in connection with the escape of Kristopher McNeil, who'd been convicted of second-degree murder, from Brown Creek Minimum Unit in Polkton, North Carolina.

Just how common was this phenomenon? Not that all staff-prisoner relationships resulted in escape of course, but how much sex was going on? The U.S. Department of Justice, Bureau of Justice Statistics, released a report in 2014 that revealed that almost half of the substantiated incidents of sexual victimization involved guards and inmates, 48 percent, as opposed to the 52 percent that involved prisoners only.

The majority of the staff-involved cases involved female staffers, and these were far more consensual than male-on-male encounters. The study found that 84 percent of the female staffers who had sex with inmates "appeared to be willing." That number was only 37 percent when male staffers were involved.

Trying to put things in perspective, Glenard S. Middleton Sr., vice president of the American Federation of State, County, and Municipal Employees, pointed out that the great majority of prison staffers did not have illicit relationships at work and that those staffers were having their reputations stained by "an irresponsible few."

Mitchell may have seemed to some like supporting cast in this drama, but for the reactionary media, including tabloid and supermarket newspapers, it was Mitchell's involvement that made the story perfect. She could have been more photogenic, it was true, but she gave the story its sleaze. One typical headline from the *National Enquirer* read, "Crooked Prison Worker's Sex behind Bars." The *New York Post* kept the story on their front page for weeks, routinely referring to Mitchell as "Shawskank."

During the first week in July, Lyle Mitchell's lawyer Peter Dumas spoke to WPTZ-TV with an update on his client's side of the story. Lyle last visited his wife only a few days earlier, on Independence Day, at the Rensselaer County Jail in Troy, New York. Lyle, Dumas said, was "blown away" when he first heard about the jam his wife had gotten herself into. Still Lyle tended to give a rosy spin to recent events. He credited Joyce with saving his life. By not going through with her part of the escape plan, she had prevented his murder. Dumas said, "Toward the end, Joyce had told Lyle—and we have no reason to doubt it—that she told Sweat and Matt that she wasn't going to go through with it. At that point, they threatened her by threatening Lyle, saying that they were going to have someone on the outside do something to him or someone on the inside when he was back at work, so I think it was a point of control. He's still in love with her, but I don't know that he is going to be very supportive." When Lyle confronted his wife, she warned him that the escaped men had been plotting to kill him. Dumas said, "The inmates had a plan to do harm to Lyle. She doesn't agree with that. She doesn't want Lyle hurt, and I think some of the threats were made to her from the inmates at that point." (Of course, this was a markedly different spin on events that the version Joyce told investigators during the first days after the escape, when Lyle was referred to as a "glitch" that needed to be removed so that she and Richard Matt could live happily ever after.) Lyle, Dumas said, wondered early on whether the tools his wife had smuggled to the prisoners were his. He went out into his garage, inventoried his tools, and found nothing missing. Joyce had apparently been telling the truth when she said she's gotten the tools from the store.

Police had asked Lyle if his wife had displayed any unusual behavior in the days and weeks before the escape. According to his attorney, Lyle had noticed nothing helpful along those lines. Dumas said, "I hate to use a cliché, but love is blind." The Mitchells had known each other a long time, twenty-one years. They'd been married for fourteen of those. In addition to living together, they worked at the same place. Lyle loved his job and knew Sweat and Matt." The revelations following the escape were not Lyle's first inkling that something might have been going on between Joyce and the inmates. When Joyce was investigated two years earlier for alleged improprieties with David Sweat, Lyle confronted the prisoner. Sweat told him there was nothing going on. The investigation into those earlier allegations did not result in Joyce losing her job, but Sweat was moved out of her tailor shop so that he and Joyce would be separated.

Dumas said that, although Lyle was "not standing by his wife" and was not "supporting any allegations of her innocence," he was interested in making sure she wasn't hurt. "There is a big part of his life that he is wondering if it was a lie all the time. There is a big part of his life that is gone now, pulled out from under him."

Dumas also offered details of the first time Lyle and Joyce met face-to-face following her arrest. They spoke at that time, Tuesday, June 16, for over an hour.

Joyce's son, Tobey, whom Lyle had adopted, asked him if he was still going to be his father. "Of course," Lyle reportedly sad. "I have been your father for twenty years and I am going to keep on being here for you."

Joyce Mitchell was convinced that once the public heard her story they would insist that she be treated with mercy. So, on August 14, Mitchell granted her first interview as a celebrity, interviewed by her TV favorite, Matt Lauer of NBC, over several hours. The interview took place at the Clinton County Jail in Plattsburgh where Mitchell was being held.

Members of the media had been hounding Mitchell for cooperation from the moment they'd first heard of her. Her lawyer Stephen Johnston said there had been an onslaught of requests: "Generally, my response has been it's essentially her decision and not mine, but my recommendation is she not give interviews until after sentencing," Johnston said, perhaps realizing that his client was a gal who, as the song said, just couldn't say no. (As it turned out, the interview was broadcast before her sentencing hearing.) Johnston said that, to the best of his knowledge, Mitchell had not been paid by NBC.

All interviews with jail inmates had to be approved by both the prisoner and Clinton County sheriff David Favro. Favro said Mitchell had become a "popular topic" with reporters, but despite the intense demand she insisted on speaking with Lauer exclusively. The sheriff also let slip that, on multiple occasions, Lauer and NBC people had been in touch with Lyle Mitchell's lawyer and eventually sat down for a chat with the ex-husband as well.

The Lauer interview was *supposed* to be strictly hush-hush, because the attorneys agreed it shouldn't become known until after Mitchell's sentencing. But it didn't stay hush-hush for long. News slipped out on August 20. DA Wylie was holding a press conference and said, "Are there any people here from NBC. I guess they got an interview with Joyce last week at the jail."

Lauer did interview Lyle. Joyce's husband, it turned out, had his own version of his wife's confession that he wanted to share. Lyle told Lauer that he had been at the police station when an investigator approached him and said that his wife was involved. She was in it, maybe deep. He had asked Joyce what was going on, and she'd told him that she had "done some things," that she had gotten in over her head, and that she was terribly frightened. She told him that she didn't know what to do, that she was in shock, disbelief, that the escapees had threatened her, that someone—from either inside or outside the facility—was going to do something to him, harm him, or kill him.

Lyle said that his wife swore on her son's life that she never "had sex with Matt or Sweat." She told him that Matt had "tried to kiss her" and she might have "just showed a little affection" to him in return. Clearly Lyle was uninformed regarding the hole Matt cut in his coat pocket.

Asked about the future of his relationship with his wife, Lyle rattled off a string of questions: "Do I still love her? Yes. Am I mad? Yes. How could she do it? How could she do this to our kids?"

Sure, he was aware that his wife could be sent to prison for more than seven years, but he hoped it wouldn't be that long. "I'm just hoping that she'll be home in less than two," he said dejectedly.

Lyle divulged that the plan included slipping him sleeping pills so Joyce would be able to drive the getaway car and run away with Matt and Sweat. Joyce, he said, told him that it was her love for him that made her back out of that part of the plan.

"I love my husband, I am not hurting him," Lyle quoted his wife as saying.

During the NBC interview, Lyle registered no shame, humiliation, or embarrassment. He couldn't wait for Joyce to get out of jail. He didn't see any reason he and Joyce shouldn't continue living in the same community where they'd always been.

Lyle's attorney, Peter Dumas, was quick to point out his client's unadulterated innocence, that he had no advance knowledge of the escape and was not planning to cover up for his wife. Dumas said, "He is not going to testify for her, he's not denying anything that she's done. Everything that Joyce has told Lyle, he's gone to the police and he's let the police know about it."

The first portion of Matt Lauer's interview with Mitchell didn't air until September 14, 2015, on NBC's *Today* show. This was before Mitchell's sentencing. Her lawyers had originally agreed to air the interview only after the sentencing, but it had been apparently Mitchell herself who decided that it should air before. By her way of thinking, she was going to speak directly to the public and they would see that she wasn't such a bad person and they would see to it that the justice system went light on her.

As it turned out, she greatly overestimated her charisma and the effect her blubbering rue would have on her TV audience. During the interview, Mitchell admitted lying to the police when she first spoke to them the day after the escape, but she corrected the lie quickly. The very next day she went back to talk to the police, this time with Lyle at her side, and "told the truth."

Mitchell blamed mental illness for her crimes: "I was going through a point in my life—a lot of people go through depression and I guess they saw my weakness and that's how it all started. The attention made me feel good. I just got in over my head. And I couldn't get out. I did wrong, I deserve to be punished, but people need to know I was only trying to save my family."

Lauer asked how she got the contraband to the prisoners. She replied that she was supposed to have her bags searched when she came in and out of CCF, but that never occurred.

Mitchell was contrite, so sorry about "everything that everyone" went through because of her. She never wanted any of this to happen. "I would take it all back if I could, but I can't," she said.

She said she was stuck in a position where she *couldn't tell anyone*. She was breaking the law, prison rules, and her marriage vows simultaneously. Where could she turn? There was no one for her to talk to, no one to tell.

Lauer asked her why she didn't call the police. Mitchell replied that now, in twenty-twenty retrospect, she could see that that would have been the right move but not at the time. She was too scared.

There was still an element of denial, she admitted. Part of her thought all of this was unreal, that it never happened. It was a bad dream. How, she asked, could it have happened when she always loved her husband?

Lauer asked, "Did Richard Matt have complete control over you?"

Mitchell replied, "Yes, he was good at that."

She understood that, because of the way certain things were reported by the media, many folks out there thought she was a nymphomaniac who'd had sex with both Matt and Sweat. Not true. She'd been brought up on charges regarding an improper relationship with Sweat, but those allegations were false. With Matt it was more complicated. She never had *consensual* sex with Richard Matt. She understood that having sexual contact with a prisoner was a crime. In fact it was considered a form of rape, with her being the rapist, but it wasn't that way at all. On the contrary . . .

Her eyes filled with tears. "Mr. Matt grabbed me a couple of times and kissed me. There was one point where he wanted me to perform oral sex on him." A tear rolled down her cheek. She paused to wipe it away. "And I said no—and when I said no he grabbed my head and pushed me down."

She did as she was told because she was being terrorized. Matt once asked her where her mother lived, where her son lived, and then she knew he would hurt her family if she didn't do as he said. Matt used terror expertly, she explained. He wanted people to know what a bad man he was, why he was in prison, that he'd cut up a guy like bait and threw the gory pieces in a river. Should anyone question his credibility, he even went so far as to keep a newspaper clipping of the Rickerson murder on him, so he could verify his evil boasts.

Lauer asked Mitchell how it started in the first place, her relationship with Matt and eventual assistance with the escape?

Well, she might've been flirting—no, she was flirting, and for her that was all it ever was. It started out so innocently. She brought in cookies and brownies for Matt and Sweat. She remembered feeling as if she were smuggling the baked goods in. Guards were supposed to check her bag when she entered the facility, but no one ever did.

And it was fun and a little naughty, and she never wanted it to be anything more. They made each other feel a little special, she and her two favorite prisoners. They were making each other feel good, sure. But she was never *in love* with Matt.

She recalled a conversation:

"You know, Joyce, I do love you," Richard Matt reportedly said.

"I love my husband," was her reply. It was "a little while" after that exchange that Matt decided to "get rid of Lyle."

Why was she flirting? To fill an emptiness she was feeling inside. There had been a time, she admitted, when she was starting to think her husband didn't love her any more, so she perhaps became a tad restless.

"I guess they saw my weakness and that's how it started. I'm not the monster that everyone thinks I am. It's just the opposite. I'm just somebody that got caught up in something that she couldn't get out of. Everybody tells me that I am way too nice. I guess I got a little too comfortable."

She wanted America to know that she only gave in to the prisoner's demands—sex, chisels, drill bits, hacksaws, and hats with lights attached to them—because she feared for her family's safety.

Of course, there came a moment when it stopped being fun and games, just sex, consensual or otherwise, when she knew that there was more here than two guys painting and creating art, and when Matt first let her in on the fact that he and Sweat were *planning to escape* and they needed her to help by supplying tools.

She had said no way: "I can't get you that."

When she did comply with Matt's requests, it no longer had anything to do with making him feel special, or him making her feel special. It was pure extortion. He had threatened her husband. She had no choice but to do everything that he demanded.

Why did she stand the prisoners up at the manhole?

She said it was because she'd finally figured it out, how it would go. "They would have killed me," she said. "They would have had the vehicle and they wouldn't have needed me."

A preliminary analysis of events led investigators to a somewhat surprising conclusion. *The weak point in maximum-security prisons in New York State was not in the infrastructure of those buildings but rather in the character of their employees.*

To outsiders, the reality was startling. There were employees in the corrections system that had forgotten their adversarial role with the prisoners. A sense of community, that they were all inside these walls together, had grown over the years, perhaps over the generations.

It was a trait that was naturally almost always exploited to the fullest by the prisoners. A prison employee told *NBC News* on June 12 that the act of recruiting prison employees for favors by convicts was called "grooming." Any employee that showed compassion toward a prisoner became a target. You had to be patient, take things slow, but sometimes it worked. Favors given the prisoners were usually minor, extra recreation time, newspapers, and food—all absolutely innocent, until it wasn't. Employees became too comfortable with the prisoners, turned the filter off when they said things, gave up too much personal information about themselves—and that was the first and most important ingredient in a recipe for disaster.

Such had been the case with Joyce Mitchell, who apparently—using a combination of verbal and nonverbal communication—had conveyed to the escapees a notion of her unhappy marriage and sexual neediness.

The source added that once a prison employee broke the rules on behalf of a prisoner, they were "owned." If the employee failed to give in to escalating demands, the prisoner threatened to "rat them out," a move that could cause the staffer his or her job, or even jail time.

The problem was so real that corrections officers were trained in how to protect themselves from prisoner manipulation, not an easy task as prisoners were smart and would always find a con game suited perfectly for the targeted staffer, their *mark*. In Mitchell's case, she was made to feel sexy by the prisoners and responded with sexual favors, tools, and a promise of driving the getaway car.

In convict-speak, the successful manipulation of a guard was called "downing the duck." The duck was the guard or staffer. Downing meant doing things in a manner that didn't raise suspicion.

Inmates, because they are serving time, many of them great chunks of their lifespan, have an innate patience that serves them well when it comes to executing con games.

"You have to take it slow," was how they put it. They would first get an inkling of what the duck was willing to do before asking him or her to do it. Guards and civilian employees are not all alike. Some are bad; some are good but gullible. Either one would do. It starts out with something simple, supplies above and beyond the ration, such as extra writing paper or toilet paper. It might seem an easy task for a guard to avoid manipulation, but guards and prisoners are together all day. Guards may see certain prisoners more frequently than they do members of their own family.

The first step toward owning a guard was for the prisoner to get him or her to stop seeing him as a criminal but rather seeing him as a person with problems, a basically good person who just needed help. That was the biggest psychological leap. The method sometimes worked to shockingly excessive degrees. In 2003 a gang member incarcerated in Baltimore pretty much took over the facility and impregnated *several* corrections officers.

Mitchell's story was not a new one, and romance was common. Twenty years ago a convicted killer escaped from an Oklahoma prison with the aid of a female warden who fell in love with him while they worked together in a prison pottery program. But the amount of TV time and newsprint inches dedicated to that story was a minute fraction of that given to Joyce Mitchell, who would remain the icon—at least in the foreseeable future—for illicit prison sex and betrayal of justice. Folks in the Buffalo and Binghamton areas who had worked so hard to get scum like Matt and Sweat behind bars could only shake their heads at the ease with which this self-deluded woman had handed those prisoners the key to get out.

Although the investigation into the escape cast a large net, there would be only one other interviewee to admit culpability in the escape. On June 19, prison officials, without mentioning names, announced that a corrections officer had been placed on administrative leave as a result of the probe into the escape. The next day, in the interview room of the New York State (NYS) Police Barracks at Plattsburgh, FBI special agent Timothy Coll and investigator Scott T. Fiordaliso of the NYS police interviewed fifty-seven-year-old Gene E. Palmer, who was accompanied by his lawyer Andrew Brockway. Palmer said that he had provided Matt and Sweat with forbidden items for months and that he had a base salary of $72,644.

Palmer told investigators that he had been assigned to A Block for eight years and had known Richard Matt since he arrived there in 2009. During his polygraph examination, which he passed, Palmer admitted to giving a screwdriver and a pair of pliers to Matt in exchange for artwork. Matt was a very talented painter, and Palmer had functioned as a sort of agent for him, helping him sell a portrait of Tony Soprano to a Florida woman for a nice piece of change, two grand. Palmer admitted to his interrogators that he had purchased and then provided paint and paintbrushes for Matt on two occasions. The items were purchased approximately two years earlier at Michael's in Consumer's Square in Plattsburgh. He provided items at that same time for Sweat as well: white zinc paint, white titanium paint, and acrylic paint. Eight months earlier, he'd provided tools for Sweat on four separate occasions. Among those tools were a ninety-degree angled pair of needle-nose pliers with a red handle and black metal tip and a flat-head screwdriver described as being four to five inches in length with a red and white handle.

Palmer admitted that back on May 29, 2015, about a week before the escape, Joyce Mitchell had left a package for him to give to inmate Matt. It was left in the freezer located in Tailor Shop 1. It was a green-colored, woven cloth bag, containing two tubes of paint and more than one pound of frozen ground beef.

How big was the package?

Palmer said about a foot long, five inches wide, and two inches high. The beef was packaged with a white piece of Styrofoam and plastic wrap. The plastic wrap did not have a price sticker on it.

"Did Mitchell say why she was giving Matt meat?" an investigator asked.

"No."

"Did you ask her?"

"No."

"Did this seem unusual?"

"I knew we were in a gray area with the meat," Palmer said.

Palmer said he approached Matt, who was locked in his cell at the time, and passed to him the hamburger meat and the remaining items in the bag.

That was the extent of the items he'd provided for the escapees, although he admitted that he did allow Sweat to change the electrical wiring in the cell electrical boxes, because "he asked me to and I was doing him a favor."

He also allowed Sweat access to those boxes, which were located in "the catwalk located in company 3 and 6 to A block." Palmer denied foreknowledge of the escape and intentionally assisting with the escape. In exchange for the favors, Palmer said, Matt provided him with paintings and information on the illegal acts that inmates were committing within the facility.

"Did they tell you why they wanted to change the wiring?"

"Yes, they said it was to enhance their ability to cook in their cells."

Not all of Palmer's indiscretions involved sneaking stuff to Matt and Sweat. After the escape, when he realized he might be in serious trouble, he destroyed evidence as well. Some of the paintings he'd received were allegedly burned sometime during the first two weeks of the manhunt both in his own backyard and at a second location in Cadyville.

He'd also, before the escape, taken measures to help Matt and Sweat from being caught with the contraband. During cell inspections, Palmer hid the painting supplies. "I had inmate Matt bring the two oil-based paint tubes that I had previously purchased for him out of his cell. He followed me onto catwalk 3 and 6. I took the paint tubes from him and hid them on top of the air vent," Palmer admitted.

On June 24, Palmer appeared in Plattsburgh Town Court, with Justice Kevin Patnode presiding. There he was charged with promoting prison contraband, first degree, a class D felony; two counts of tampering with physical evidence, class E felonies; and official misconduct, a class A misdemeanor. His misconduct charge related to his receiving paintings from Matt in exchange for pliers and a screwdriver. The tampering charge stemmed from Palmer's alleged destruction of evidence.

Palmer was scheduled to appear in court two days later but didn't because he was changing lawyers. Andrew Brockway told Justice Patnode that he had been dismissed and from that point on Palmer would be represented by the Albany firm of Dreyer Boyajian. With his new counsel, Palmer waived his right to a preliminary hearing on June 29, and evidence in his case was initially scheduled to be heard by a grand jury.

Palmer opted to waive the grand jury process as well. He was briefly jailed and then released when he posted $25,000 bail on his credit card. He was scheduled to have an arraignment hearing in Clinton County Court in November.

Palmer's entire defense rested on the notion that he didn't know about the escape plans, didn't know there were hacksaw blades in the meat, and so forth. He knew he was breaking rules, of course, but was ignorant of anything egregious.

There were solid indications that Palmer was not feigning naïveté. Men who knew him vouched for his character. Former coworker and CCF historian Walter "Pete" Light told me that he believed Palmer to be an honest guy, a straight shooter. There was such a culture of bribery—gift giving or gift exchanging some might call it—between prisoners and guards that Palmer's story was completely feasible. Light explained: "His big mistake was, once he realized what had happened, he tried to destroy evidence." In other words, it wasn't the crime; it was the cover-up.

Plus, lack of suspicion had been part of Palmer's prison mindset for years. In 2000, Palmer was interviewed by North Country Public Radio and referred to the prisoners as "children" and "damaged puppies." He said CCF often reminded him of a strange "kindergarten." So, he was perhaps just the sort of person who would do favors for the prisoners without considering the possibly dire circumstances.

During that same public radio interview, however, he proved to also be in touch, at least in hyperbolic terms, with the dark side of his workplace. "With the money that they pay you, you'll go bald, have high blood pressure, become an alcoholic, divorce, and then kill yourself," Palmer said.

Through the social media, the world learned that Palmer had a life outside the prison. He played guitar in a band and had since at least 1978. His axe was a customized black Les Paul, and he also sang and played keyboards.

Despite Mitchell's teary TV admissions and Palmer's straight-shooter reputation, the stories they told simply did not add up and did little to explain how the escapees had gotten under the Dannemora wall.

Mitchell told NBC that she provided hacksaw blades to Matt and Sweat only once, that she purchased four blades and broke each in half so she gave the prisoners eight half blades, placed them in the hamburger meat, froze the meat, smuggled the frozen meat into the prison, and placed it in a prison refrigerator. Palmer took the meat from the refrigerator and gave it to the prisoners.

The prisoners received those blades six days before the escape, yet experts have estimated that it took two months of steady work to cut through a steel wall using half-blade hacksaws and drill bits. The remainder of the work would have required another two weeks to one month to accomplish. Even if the stories being told by the arrested CCF employees were the absolute and complete truth, the story was woefully incomplete.

In the days after the escape, New York State Governor Cuomo took several tours of CCF. Many experts blamed the escape on the governor's own budget cuts, but his Inspector General's report, which came out a year later, put the emphasis on pervasive slacking among CCF employees. Courtesy Governor Andrew M. Cuomo

The hole at the back of David Sweat's cell through which he crawled out eighty-five times. He only crawled back for eighty-four of them.
Courtesy Governor Andrew M. Cuomo

With only primitive tools with which to work, Sweat drilled, sawed, and chipped out an escape route to freedom. Courtesy Governor Andrew M. Cuomo

With Sweat and Matt still on the loose, Governor Cuomo listens in as State Trooper Major Charles Guess addresses the press. Courtesy Governor Andrew M. Cuomo

Between the rear of the cells in Honor Block, and the outer wall of the building were surprisingly roomy grate catwalks. The grates enabled one to see the catwalks above and below. Sweat said he once had to hide from a corrections officer who walked on a cat walk above him, and had to dodge when the guard dropped a lit cigarette butt.
Courtesy Governor Andrew M. Cuomo

The prison's infrastructure came with convenient ladders. They were put there to simplify maintenance, but for Matt and Sweat those ladders simplified escape as well.
Courtesy Governor Andrew M. Cuomo

The entrance hole cut by David Sweat in the prison steam pipe. On their way out, the prisoner left a post-it next to the hole. It had on it a racially offensive drawing and the words, "Have a nice day!" Courtesy Governor Andrew M. Cuomo

The femme fatale of our story, Joyce Mitchell, makes a fashion statement with her prison stripes and bulletproof vest. Here she confers with her lawyer Steven Johnston in a Plattsburgh, N.Y. courtroom where she is about to be charged with promoting prison contraband and criminal facilitation. Reuters/G.N. Miller, N.Y. Post/Pool

Clinton County District Attorney Andrew Wylie became one of the faces of the story, first during the manhunt and later as justice prevailed. Here he is addressing a press conference following Joyce Mitchell's arraignment. Reuters/Christinne Muschi

Twenty-three days into the manhunt, stalwart members of law enforcement, exhausted from long hours and waterlogged from relentless rain, continue to beat the bushes in search of the missing desperadoes. Reuters/Chris Wattie

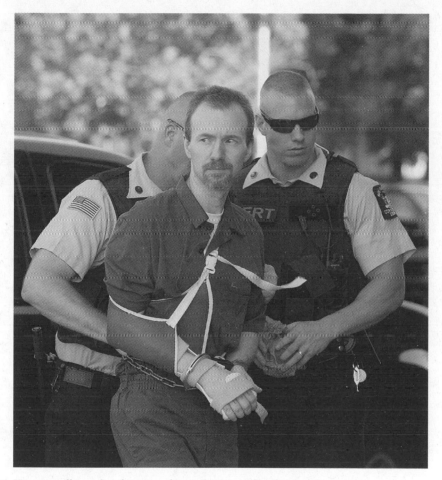

His arm still in a sling because of a gunshot wound suffered at the time
of his capture, a demonic-looking David Sweat is led into Clinton County Court.
Reuters/Christinne Muschi

The Border Patrol personnel assisting in the hunt for Matt and Sweat were from the Swanton Section, an area that included all of Vermont, six counties in New York, and three counties in New Hampshire—all in all 295 miles of border. Here a Border Patrol search team choppers to the front line of the hunt in a Black Hawk helicopter. Photo courtesy U.S. Customs and Border Protection

SEVEN
THE
HUNT

The first thing New York State Police did when learning of the escape was visit Maggy's Marketplace, a store that included a drug store and a Dunkin' Donuts, located just across the street from Clinton Correctional Facility (CCF).[1] On the first visit they were there to check the security tapes, which were unhelpful. On the next thousand visits, they were there for provisions, becoming such a constant presence that owner Mickey Maggy set up an office in the store for them. The store was also noteworthy for the ample size of its parking lot, which became a home away from home for media vans and other news crew vehicles.

During the first days of the hunt, authorities were fairly certain that the escapees were on foot. No cars were known to have been hijacked or stolen. Since the prisoners would be forced to move under cover, it was suspected that they had not gotten far, and the Essex County Sheriff's Office methodically searched farms and fields around the town of Willsboro, New York.

By June 7, there were already multiple law enforcement agencies involved in the manhunt: New York State (NYS) Police, NYS Department of Corrections and Community Supervision (DOCCS), the NYS Department of Environmental Conservation, the NYS Forest Rangers, U.S. Marshals, and the FBI were jointly conducting grid searches. About one hundred state troopers were assigned to the case—including uniform, investigative, and specialty units (such as K-9 and aviation units). Two hundred fifty corrections and law enforcement officers were on the job. "All available assets" were involved.

Governor Andrew Cuomo promised that law enforcement was going all out to recapture the bad, bad men. True, 250 able bodies were in on the search, but that was a number not as impressive as the governor had hoped, considering the size of the forest that needed to be searched. There were miles and miles of harsh country, thick foliage, steep inclines, and low valleys of thick mud that could pull a man's boot right off his foot. With only 250 personnel searching, the escapees felt like a pair of mobile needles in a lush, green haystack. Luckily, that number was growing, and each day the escapees remained free, the number of manhunters grew larger.

Cuomo called for the public's help. Anyone who saw the escapees or evidence of the escapees—anyone who knew anything that might assist their investigation—should report that info ASAP.

On Monday, June 8, the hunt got its first taste of frustration when an abandoned car and the sighting of two men near the woods in the Dannemora area both turned out to be unrelated to the escape. That same day activity inadvertently picked up by a TV crew caused a bit of a furor. In a segment shown on the *Fox News* channel, anchor Greta Van Susteren was interviewing a reporter who was standing outside the prison with the big white wall in the background. As the reporter filed her report, in the background a person could be seen crossing the road toward the prison while carrying something, a bundle, climbing a set of stairs next to the wall, attaching the bundle to a rope, and then, apparently using a pulley system, pulling the package up the wall, presumably to someone at the top who was waiting. A viewer who was videotaping his TV set captured the moment and put it online, claiming that they had witnessed contraband being smuggled into the facility right under everyone's noses. The video went viral, scoring five million hits, despite the fact that Dannemorians said that the system was routinely used for wives and other friends and loved ones, to get supplies, food, and so forth, to staff who were working long shifts on the other side of the wall.

In the face of imminent danger, law enforcement approached its massive task with ultimate vigilance. The search for the escapees unfolded with an urgency just shy of frantic. The law was in a rush to finish this, convinced that it was only a matter of time before the escapees hurt or killed someone during their flight .

Even though the early days of the search came with few encouraging events, Sheriff David Favro saw no signs of discouragement from his personnel, or from other agencies. It was a methodical, massive task, one that called for teamwork. His men were setting up checkpoints, sealing off areas, and holding down positions at the edges of woods in case the escapees were chased out by lines of searchers.

Sheriff Favro said that, if there were any interjurisdictional glitches in the manhunt, they came from on high. On the ground, the officers and agents worked shoulder to shoulder, and morale never flagged. Because of the man-versus-nature element of law enforcement up north, there was already complete cooperation between agencies. If you walked into a diner Up North, you were apt to see a Clinton County sheriff's deputy having coffee with an officer from the border patrol. It was an everyday occurrence. Chances were good that they had worked together many times, not necessarily busting crime but just *helping people*. In that part of the world, where the elements could be so terribly harsh, there was a strong sense of community in which people came together in times of crises. The big ice storm of 1999 came to mind, where the line between agencies and jurisdictions melted away. Everyone just did the best they could to save people. So it all came as second nature with Richard Matt and David Sweat on the run. They worked together.

"Every day those prisoners were on the loose, we had hope," Favro later explained. "Energy was always at a very high level because every day we thought this was the day we were going to catch those guys."

The border patrol personnel assisting in the hunt were from the Swanton Sector, an area that included all of Vermont, six counties in New York, and three counties in New Hampshire—all in all 295 miles of border. That was too much border to be manned, and much of it was monitored electronically via sensors and cameras. Within hours of the escape, the border patrol stepped up vehicle inspections on cars that were "outbound," that is, crossing into Canada.

By June 9, the number of officers in on the hunt had risen to 440, and the search was most intense along the Clinton and Essex county border. While U.S. Customs and Border Protection joined the effort, rain fell in sheets, when it fell. Mostly it flew sideways, lit up like a strobe by impossibly close lightning strikes. Drivers on Middle Road saw two men cross the roadside ditch, and a hundred officers responded with urgency as the site was close to train tracks.

The next day, searchers conducted a door-to-door search of the homes in the village of Dannemora. In case no one was home, officers left a note asking the occupants to get in touch. They wanted to be doubly certain that no one was being held hostage.

Fifty digital billboards, donated to the cause by Lamar Advertising, featured photos of and information regarding the escapees. The billboards were located in New York City, Albany, central and western New York State, Boston, Massachusetts, and Erie, Pennsylvania.

There was a brief moment of optimism on June 11, when forest rangers stopped at a convenience store alongside Route 374, a major highway about three miles from the prison, during a steady soaking rain. The rangers spotted a trail into the woods that led to a patch of matted-down grass. K-9 units picked up the scent of both prisoners at that spot, so police closed the road between General Leroy Manor Road and Rand Hill Road, and conducted an intensified search. School was closed. Search planes flew low over trees. Search teams were dropped into position from helicopters. But . . . nothing.

On June 12, in the town of Cadyville, a man named Brent Cringle was surprised to see five police cars behind his house. The reason: around 7:30 a.m. two men were seen jumping a stone wall in his backyard. Cringle offered the police a tall ladder that they could lean against the wall for a better vantage point. Helicopters swooped in, and everyone in the area prayed that this was the hunt's grand finale. Door-to-door searches were conducted up and down Trudeau Road. Nearby Saranac Central School was closed for the second day in a row. But if it had been the prisoners jumping the wall, they had once again disappeared.

Back in Dannemora, someone had the theory that maybe the prisoners had never come up out of the sewer system. Perhaps they'd not liked what they saw when they popped their heads above ground and had decided to stay subterranean, so a K-9 team, starting at the exit manhole, went down into the system without positive results.

Because leads knew no geography, reports of possible sightings sometimes took the search far afield. On June 13, witnesses spotted two men in Steuben County, near the New York–Pennsylvania border. The pair was seen walking near the Gang Mills rail yard on Rita's Way in the town of Erwin. On the fourteenth, two men with a similar description were spotted walking along County Route 115 in Lindley, New York. The men were headed toward Pennsylvania.

Back up north, joining the search by this time were the Department of Environmental Conservation, the Clinton and Essex County Sheriff Departments, and the Plattsburgh Police Department. The number of personnel involved in the search grew to eight hundred.

In Plattsburgh, citizens were showing their support for the hunters by tying blue ribbons around just about anything that stuck up out of the ground: mailboxes, trees, light posts, and telephone poles. A restaurant on Route 3 called Michigans Plus was serving breakfast all day long for manhunters with befuddled body clocks. A sign out front read "Come help us support with blue ribbons! We have enough for everyone!"

Back at CCF, the buses bringing visitors into the prison were searched meticulously, and before those buses were allowed to leave, a mirror on wheels was run underneath.

In every police station, phones never stopped ringing. *Every stranger* was being reported as suspicious. By the thirteenth, the Saturday after the escape, law enforcement had investigated seven hundred leads, without a single encouraging result. In the next forty-eight hours, three hundred more leads were checked out.

On Sunday, a door-by-door canvassing restarted, this time to both search for escapees and remind the locals to remain vigilant.

There was discussion about whether the school of the Saranac Central School District should open the next morning. (The schools did open but with an enhanced law enforcement presence and no outdoor activities.) It was estimated by the state police that the search thus far had covered approximately 8,300 acres, or thirteen square miles.

On June 14, David Sweat turned thirty-five years old. The escapees had been on the loose for about a week when Brian Mann filed a report for North Country Public Radio in which he described the internal culture of CCF and how it may have contributed to the escape.

Mann had first gone inside the walls ten years earlier, to write a story about the history of the prison. Looking back at his notes from that visit, he was struck by one comment: "Everywhere we go, prisoners are handling knives and power tools." (Lane Filler of *Newsday* commented, "If you can operate power tools there, it's not really a prison. It's a Home Depot you got locked in by mistake.")

Mann noted that there was an element of outrage from people wondering how two prisoners—worst of the worst—could gain access to power tools. But Mann knew the truth. He'd seen it.

CCF was like that. Prisoners were allowed to use tools, power and manual, on an everyday basis. He'd since learned that many correctional facilities were like that. Prisoners were routinely put in charge of maintenance and repairs, a "cost-effective way to keep old prisons running." The trouble was, the use of prisoners in this capacity had another unintended effect. A bright prisoner (like Matt or Sweat) could use those experiences to learn a lot about the inner workings and design of the prison.

And, Mann noted, if one prisoner learned something potentially useful about the prison, it wasn't long before everyone knew. The prisoners had ample opportunity to share secrets, such as which heating pipe passed through the outer wall to the outside (it was the one that headed toward the power plant on the other side of the wall), information that could be used to hatch an escape plan.

During one tour of the prison, Mann was guided by Gene Palmer (the same Gene Palmer who furnished Matt and Sweat with hamburger meat that contained hacksaw blades), who showed the reporter the "North Yard," which is a 7.5-acre section of the grounds that—and the italics are his—"*inmates mostly control.*"

On the North Yard were accommodations for recreation. There were ball fields. For years there was a ski jump. But also there was that same culture of tools. Inmates who stay out of trouble were given their own plot of land in the North Yard, and that was their turf to do with as they wish.

They built gardens, birdhouses, and other structures. They set up barbeque grills. Some built little white picket fences, like those in the American dream, to separate their turf from that of their neighbors. The idea appealed to prison management because it gave them a way to reward prisoners who behaved.

Without that, there was no incentive to cooperate with prison rules. In light of the escape, however, everything looked differently.

On the fourteenth, district attorney Andrew Wylie said that he expected there would be more arrests—plural. Since only one additional arrest was made, there was speculation about who got off the hook. Best guess is that Lyle Mitchell was considered a possible accomplice at one point.

Richard Matt's son, twenty-three-year-old Nicholas Harris, continued to tell reporters of his dad's powers. Not only could he take a bullet and crawl over razor wire, but also, he told the *Buffalo News*, his dad had a genius IQ, which was why he was so good at escaping from prisons: he could outthink any effort to contain him.

Harris said he first learned that his dad had escaped from Dannemora when his family's home in Angola was swarmed with a combination of state troopers and homeland security agents.

"I thought I had done something wrong and they were coming for me," Harris admitted.

He had vague memories of his father from when he was a child. His clearest memories stemmed from a time a few years earlier when he visited his dad at the Niagara County Jail in Lockport.

"He makes an impression that lingers with you," Harris said. "My father always wanted to have a relationship with me."

Harris said that, during that visit, his father seemed "weighed down" from years behind bars. Harris had carefully considered having a continuing relationship with his biological father, but in the long run decided against it.

"I was raised by a stepfather. I was mature enough at that age to know I already had a father figure," Harris said. "I decided a relationship with Richard Matt would not be healthy."

Harris told the reporter how he came to be. His mother (Vee Marie Harris) grew up in Tonawanda and knew Ricky Matt from when he was a kid.

Matt, five years her junior, had a crush on Vee and would say to her, "If I were older, would you be my girl?"

He'd act as if he was shy—lower his head and kick his toe against the ground. She said he was a baby. Come back when you grow up. And he did, when he was in his twenties and a good-looking guy. They started dating, and when she was thirty, she got pregnant with Nicholas.

On Tuesday, June 16, the section of State Route 374 between Leroy Manor Road and Rand Hill Road was finally reopened, the grid search of the woods there complete. The search, according to the state police, was "expanding and shifting" to "other areas around Dannemora." It was said that the new search locations were determined by "information gathered during the investigation," although it is difficult to imagine what that info might have been. As for the old search area, there would still be periodic patrols of the woods off Route 374.

Revised versions of the escapees' mug shots were released, with their beards enhanced to show how they might look after ten days on the run.

On June 18, the manhunt moved to seasonal camps and abandoned buildings in the region. Some law enforcement teams swept hiking trails and railroad beds. One hundred sixty unoccupied buildings would be cleared along with 585 miles of trails and beds. As the search moved outward, patrols near the prison continued unabated, with 160 troopers providing the security 24-7. More than 1,500 leads had been followed. The Franklin County Sheriff's Department joined the search.

By June 19, Sweat and Matt made the big time, as U.S. Marshals added them to the "Fifteen Most Wanted" fugitives list. At a press conference announcing the addition, U.S. Marshals Service director Stacia Hylton said the list was reserved for the worst of the worst, and there could be no doubt that Matt and Sweat fit into that category.

New York State Police superintendent Joseph A. D'Amico said the most-wanted list was another way to notify the public and generate new leads. City dwellers might find it inconceivable that there were people in the area that still didn't know about the prison escape, but the North Country attracted those who enjoyed absolute isolation.

U.S. Marshal David L. McNulty of the Northern District of New York promised to leave no stone unturned. The marshals also announced that they were offering a reward, $25,000 per escapee, for information leading directly to his arrest. That was in addition to the $100,000 already offered by New York State.

Also on June 19, repairs of the holes the escapees had used to get out were completed, and CCF ceased being on lockdown.

The manhunt forged on, vigilant but drastically overmatched by the vastness of the North Country—and in the meantime the escapees were thinking less of putting miles between them and the prison and more about the comforts of home.

They broke into a series of desolate hunting camps and cabins. They stayed for two or three nights in a remote camp known as Twisted Horn, which was near Black Cat Mountain in the hamlet of Mountain View—about twenty-five miles due west of Dannemora.

The pair squabbled and bickered. Should we stay or should we go? Matt felt that living in an unused cabin was the way to go. There was protection from the elements, staying still was a lot easier on the legs than walking through woods for many hours at a time, and well, it was comfortable.

Sweat strongly disagreed. He thought that moving from place to place was the way to best avoid capture, and comfort would mean nothing if they were caught and thrown back in prison.

"What will we do if someone comes to the cabin and we are here?" Sweat asked.

"We have two choices. We kill them or take them hostage," Matt said.

Sweat claimed that he argued against violence whenever Matt brought it up, and Matt was bringing it up with increasing frequency—especially when drinking. He was into violence and enjoyed thinking about hurting people and killing cops.

Sweat became sick of it. Matt sounded as if he was at war. Sweat just wanted to be free and must've eventually gotten his way. When trouble did come to the cabin, the escapees didn't hurt and kill. They didn't fight. They fled.

Each time they came upon a cabin in the woods, they would make sure the place was empty and then break in and ransack the place. They took items to facilitate their flight: food, clothing, weapons, and a transistor radio, which they used to follow the news of the manhunt and avoid capture.

Sweat would later say that he came very close to the men who were hunting him on a number of occasions. Once he climbed a tree and hid in the tree stand, constructed for deer hunters, while law enforcement officers walked past the tree directly below.

Tree stands are designed to be good hiding places, so that deer would approach without realizing how close the hunter was. Unless the searchers had been looking specifically for a tree stand in that tree, Sweat would have been all but impossible to see.

The search was not without its problems, especially during the first week. Interagency communications were poor, and sometimes police got their information from the news media, which was seemingly competing with the police for investigative leads.

Sheriff Favro said, "There was a lot of confusion at first. I would have expected more daily briefings with local executives. At one point the team of U.S. Marshals threatened to pull out of the operation when they were relegated to checkpoints rather than front-line search areas."

I later asked Sheriff Favro what the biggest difference was between the days of the Dannemora manhunt and an average day as Clinton County's top cop. He said it was the influx of media into his life.

"Dealing with reporters and becoming one of the voices and faces of the manhunt awakened in me a new sense of responsibility. It has always been, on a one-to-one basis, my job to make citizens feel safe and secure, that they are protected by able people who couldn't be working harder. Now I had to do that same thing, comforting the public, only on a larger scale, going on the air and letting people know that everything that could be done was being done to catch these guys and to make sure they didn't have a chance to hurt anyone. So, I never said no to the media—and it made for a few long days. But the voice and face of comfort had to be there, even if it meant doing *The Today Show* at five o'clock in the morning and the Channel 5 news at eleven at night."

On the afternoon of June 20, a witness spotted two men walking along a railroad line that ran alongside Route 20 in the Alleghany County town of Friendship, New York, 355 miles from CCF. An interagency search unit was dispatched to the area immediately. A portion of Interstate 86 and Route 20 were closed. Folks in the area were told to be alert.

The media had to shift locations, also, to follow the new lead and were told by the state police to congregate for periodic briefings at the news briefing room known as "SP Amity" in Bellmont, New York.

Perhaps the one innocent civilian most inconvenienced by the escape was thirty-one-year-old Joshua Lamitie, born and raised in Malone, who during the spring and summer of 2015 was working two jobs to support his kids.[2] Lamitie's first inkling that his life was about to become complicated came a few days after the escape when a friend of his commented on his resemblance to David Sweat.

"Dude, you should probably shave," the friend said, but Lamitie just thought it was funny.

The joke became less funny a few days later when he was walking to his job at the Little Caesar's in Malone when he saw a border patrol car go by very slowly, the officers looking at him suspiciously.

After work, he went to a garage sale in town, not meaning to buy anything, just looking around, and the owner of the house became so concerned about his presence that she called the authorities.

Not long after he got home, his girlfriend was looking out the window and said pleasantly, "Oh look, they've got the dogs outside."

As it turned out, there were more than just dogs. Two U.S. Marshals were there in addition to the K-9 team. One marshal talked through the window to the girlfriend first.

"You see anyone wearing a maroon hoodie?" the officer asked.

The girlfriend answered innocently, "No, but my boyfriend has a red one."

The marshals immediately knocked on the front door with their guns drawn. Now Lamitie was sympathetic to law enforcement, up to a point. They were in a heightened state because of the crisis. On the other hand, he still didn't think he looked that much like Sweat.

"There was a big height difference," he later said to this investigation. "I'm five-three. Sweat was considerably taller."

Nonetheless, the marshals made Lamitie come out of the house, slowly—no sudden movements.

"Keep your hands in front of you where we can see them," they said, using their command voices.

Lamitie was starting to get nervous, first that one of them might get jumpy and pull the trigger on the M-16s they held at the ready and, perhaps more reasonably, that he would be detained or arrested for criminal resemblance.

"Those guys scared the shit out of me," he later said.

Instead, they asked to see identification, which Lamitie had on him. That diffused the situation. The officers apologized for his inconvenience and went on their way.

A few days later Lamitie was walking down Main Street in Malone when a cruising police car stopped. He pulled out ID right away, and the officers were satisfied. He figured that had to be it, but it wasn't.

The next day he was on his way to work, wearing his full work uniform, and taking a shortcut, he walked through the parking lot of the local Burger King at the same moment that a border patrol car was pulling up to the drive-thru for lunch.

Lamitie could feel the officers' stare burning the back of his neck, but he kept walking, trying to look as casual and innocent as he could. Then he heard a barking voice: "Stop!"

He removed his hat and turned around. The officers were out of the car and heading toward him aggressively.

"Really?" he said. "This is the *third time*. Do I look that much like him?"

They said he did. The combination of the beard, light skin complexion, and haircut was striking. So, no one wanted the manhunt to end more than Joshua Lamitie. He yearned for a time when he could once again walk the streets of his hometown without feeling frightened and accused.

An expert on all things Matt was the now sixty-seven-year-old David Bentley, retired Tonawanda detective, and former Matt mentor. Bentley was very concerned that people were going to get hurt, that the chance of violence only increased the longer Matt was out. If he couldn't find someone to hurt he might hurt himself. Bentley had *seen him* inflict wounds on himself, cut himself, break his collarbone, and not seek any treatment. He was fearless—or numb. He sure as hell didn't respond to pain. Bentley urged the public to be wary, not that he himself was afraid: "If he were to come to my house I am prepared to defend myself, and I think it would be a bad day for him."

Major Charles Guess said at a press conference that he had a message for Sweat and Matt: "We're coming for you and we will not stop until you are caught." There was no conclusive evidence that either of the inmates had left the immediate area. But even if they had, searchers had nationwide resources, a coast-to-coast network dedicated to apprehending the escapees. The team, in fact, extended past national borders. They had international resources, looking at the path of this escape.

Spinmaster Guess said, "We're getting closer with every step we take."

An objective look at the situation didn't yield as rosy of a picture. During the early days of the hunt, the search bopped from place to place, responding to a seemingly never-ending series of false leads. Eyewitnesses were trying so hard to be helpful.

The hunters couldn't afford to ignore any of the phoned-in leads. It was frustrating, but not as frustrating as what followed. As the search headed into its second week, the phone calls came further apart. The torrent of possibilities dwindled to a drizzle. The trail, never particularly warm to begin with, now completely cooled, becoming every bit as chilly as the June rain that fell day after day.

The weather report said more of the same: rain, rain, and more rain. Major Guess wasn't worried about inclement weather. It leveled the playing field. When searchers mucked it out, the escapees slogged also. Unless Matt and Sweat had found shelter, searchers figured they were cold, wet, tired, and hungry. That meant even more danger, more desperation.

Survival expert Shane Hobel, founder of the Mountain Scout Survival School in the Hudson Valley said, "It's cold out there. There's the factor of running out of food, running out of water, and certainly running out of places to go."

Hobel said a typical backpacker could hike between ten and fifteen miles per day in that terrain. The escapees would need to account for the seven cardinal rules of survival: "shelter, water, fire, food, tracking, awareness, and movement."

Were they up to it? Hobel doubted it. These guys were used to living indoors.

As it turned out, shelter was on Matt and Sweat's priority list. They stopped and stayed at a series of cabins during their walk through the woods, some better than others, and all luxurious compared to their Dannemora digs. One cabin in particular, near the hamlet of Mountain View, must have seemed like a second heaven. They came upon it on June 18 and stayed three days.

Everything was remote in those parts, but this cabin seemed particularly isolated, enveloped by trees and miles from anything else. It was well furnished and stocked with just the stuff necessary to soothe a couple of guys who'd been roughing it. In the rustic, wood-paneled room was an American flag, several buck heads mounted on the wall (one of them wearing sunglasses), a couch, indoor stove/outdoor gas grill, a reclining chair, and bunk beds. They might've stayed longer, but it lacked one essential: there wasn't much food.

The cabin was off a dirt trail known as Wolf Pond Road and leased by a group of corrections officers. One of them was forty-seven-year-old John

Stockwell, an officer at Upstate Correctional Facility and previously an employee of Lyon Mountain Correctional in 2008 and 2009.

On Saturday, June 20, Stockwell kissed his wife Nancy goodbye—they were celebrating their twenty-eighth anniversary. She told him to be careful; he grabbed his gun and rode his all-terrain vehicle into the woods, his five-year-old black Labrador retriever Dolly running alongside, to check on his hunting cabin. As he approached the cabin, Dolly stopped, her ears perked up, and the hair on her back bristled. (Later, Stockwell would credit Dolly for saving his life.) Seeing the dog's manner, he approached the cabin cautiously and saw movement in the window.

"Who's in here? Whoever you are, you better come out right now," Stockwell said.

He couldn't tell if there was one man or two, and he couldn't be sure that they were the escapees, but whoever it was ran for it, heading out via the back deck. From his vantage point Stockwell couldn't see anyone flee, but he could hear the sounds of something crashing through the brush.

With the intruder apparently gone, Stockwell tentatively entered his cabin and once inside saw further evidence of invasion: A jar of peanut butter and a water jug were out. The coffee pot had been moved. The area map that Stockwell had tacked on the wall was gone.

The intruder had also left some DNA-rich items behind: toothbrush, razor, and a soiled pair of Conecraft-brand, prison-issue underwear, an indication that one of the escapees might be suffering from dysentery, perhaps from drinking standing water. There was also a bloody sock, proof that the escapees' flight was taking a toll on them physically. And there was toothpasty foam in the sink, no doubt saliva rich.

Most disturbingly, the .20-gauge shotgun that he'd hidden between the mattress and the bed frame of one of the bunks was gone.

Stockwell tried to call police from the cabin, but his cell phone couldn't get service—so he left his cabin and rode his ATV for twenty minutes before calling. Investigators arrived swiftly, and the items left behind were carefully processed and sent immediately to a lab.

The evidence was given A1 top priority. Results were back lightning quick, in less than a day. The DNA was a match to Richard Matt. News of the match was a much-needed morale boost for the hunters. Many felt renewed energy and a sharpened focus.

The trail was now hot, and along it the hunters found discarded peppershakers. Matt and Sweat knew at least one survival technique. The escapees were still attempting to pepper their trail and mask their scent from the K-9 teams.

Along with renewed hope came fresh misery. A storm blew in, and the search took place in blinding rain, bowling-alley thunder, and brilliant flashes of lightning. The helicopter units were grounded.

The number of law enforcement personnel participating in the hunt continued to grow, to about 1,200. These now included conservation officers from the Department of Environmental Conservation, officers from the Vermont State Police, and the Franklin and Washington County sheriff's departments. The number of pursued leads had grown to 2,400. While it was true that state troopers were investigating sightings in other parts of New York State, the great bulk of the search as of June 21 remained close to Dannemora. That all changed the next day. With DNA results just in, the whole kit 'n' caboodle moved.

On the twenty-second, a media staging area was set up in the Owls Head area of Franklin County, now thirty miles west of the prison. Reporters were directed to park their cars in the Owls Head United Methodist Church parking lot on Ragged Lake Road. Police urged those who had cabins in the woods to check on them, carefully of course, to see if there were any signs that they'd been broken into.

By this time, the escapees were approaching a record-setting length of freedom. Only once in the previous twenty-five years had an escapee from a New York maximum-security prison gone longer without capture: George Gatto, who broke out of Eastern Correctional Facility in Napanoch, New York, and ran for twenty days before being caught.

Of course the people Up North were frightened that the desperadoes would one night knock on their door or crawl in their window. But the fear was just as rife in the hometowns of the escapees, where the pair had left behind friends and enemies. Now, everyone who'd known Sweat and Matt thought they might get an unwanted visit. Some fears were unwarranted, some not.

Among those who had plenty of reason to worry were Patricia Desmond and her daughter Audrey.[3] The daughter was Sweat's live-in girlfriend at the time of the Tarsia murder. She had subsequently cooperated with police, telling them the location of Sweat and Nabinger's "One Dirt Road" woodsy headquarters.

Patricia Desmond explained, "She told them where the guns were and stuff. We were worried that coming after my daughter was on his to-do list. He didn't have a lot of friends when I knew him. He was kind of a loner. He didn't have that many places where he could go, so it seemed likely he'd visit Audrey. It was terrifying."

Patricia had another reason to be worried. Her son was in Dannemora, and investigators were aware that he'd known Sweat on the outside. Sweat had lived with *his sister*, and the assumption was that he knew something about the escape.

"Don't get me wrong," Patricia Desmond later said. "I think Sweat and Matt had a lot of help, *a lot of help*, but my son didn't know anything. He was in the annex. He had seen Sweat a few times in there, but not regularly. Still, [investigators] made his life hell."

Patricia knew through her son that bad things happened inside the prison after the escape.

"They almost beat one kid to death," she said.

On Tuesday, June 23, David Sweat's mom, Pamela Sweat, sat cross-legged on the couch in her Conklin, New York, home, talking about her son with reporter Megan J. Brockett of the *Binghamton Press and Sun-Bulletin*. The escape, she said, was surreal to her. She couldn't believe he did it.[4]

David had written her regularly, and she'd handed all of the letters to the police. Sorry, she had no photos of her son. She'd thrown them all away.

"I don't want nothing to do with him. He has tormented me since he was nine years old, and now he's thirty-four[5] and I feel like he's still doing it. I've always had trouble with David even when he was growing up. I've always told my kids: You do the crime, you do the time."

David's escape didn't just hurt her; it hurt her whole family, as well as her son's friends who were close to him. It really hurt Kevin Tarsia's family because he took their son away from them.

Sweat's sister, Tillie Tuttle, was asked how she felt when she heard of the escape. She said that she was shocked, that David had been in that prison for fifteen years. He had a certain status there. Why would he want to leave? She had no idea. She didn't know what went through his mind.

Ever since the escape, an unmarked police car had been parked across the street.

Only hours after the escapees were chased from their home away from home—on Monday night, June 22—a resident on Fayette Road on Titus Mountain saw two men sneaking through the woods behind his house. Alicia Monette of Mountain View told WCAX-TV that the eyewitness was her uncle, who had been sitting on his back porch and was certain he saw the men.

Reacting to the influx of law enforcement, Monette said, "It's very quiet up here normally, and this is crazy. It's very scary. Our kids can't go outside and play. We've got to keep everybody in. It's horrible."

On Tuesday, which featured more torrential rain and gusty wind, the search focused even more sharply, now upon the seasonal camps in the forested land surrounding Studley Hill. When the manhunters arrived in the area, they realized their daunting task. The area was full of hiding places, not just hunting camps but abandoned buildings along Johnson Road as well.

The Titus Mountain Family Ski Center was transformed into a police command center. The new search area was even more rugged and mountainous than earlier search areas. The thickness of the undergrowth made mobility a challenge. What was needed was a search team of men and women who were part goat and armed with machetes.

Dene Savage at the ski center said that when he heard the manhunt was coming to northern Franklin County, it was a "no-brainer" that their Upper Lodge should be used as manhunt control. The law agreed.

Folks at the ski center said they would do whatever they could to be helpful. Community members and businesses likewise pledged support. It was everyone versus Matt and Sweat.

All of that law enforcement needed to be fed, so the ski center's food-and-beverage manager called local vendors—Mo's Pub and Grill, Glazier's, Freihoffer's, and KFC—and they all kicked in with food. Titus Mountain staffers worked double and triple shifts making sure every hungry cop returning from the field was fed. No one complained; no one questioned whether or not they were "on the clock."

Within a day, word was out that Titus Mountain was the place, and donations rolled in: 1,200 sandwiches, two hundred pounds of fruit, hundreds of gallons of soup and coffee, and baked goods. In addition to meals being served on location, mess kits were put together for men to take with them into the field, along with "grab and go" stations.

Savage said, "I witnessed everyday people helping however they could, from a smile and a thank you to our officers to random acts of kindness where people put Dunkin' Donuts gift cards on the windshields of police cruisers."

The ski lodge had turned into a wondrous mess hall, but it was perfect as a command center for other reasons as well, first and foremost communications. The location came with radio towers and repeaters that helped, according to Savage, keep a "myriad of agencies on the same page."

The only problem with the location was that, as was true of much of the North Country, cell-phone service was spotty. When the phone companies were informed of the difficulties, they stepped up and installed a new phone tree to help. The marshals built a 150-foot radio antenna.

Radio communications were supervised and coordinated by the U.S. Customs and Border Protection force, a sixty-thousand-person agency that fell under the auspices of the Department of Homeland Security and wasn't to be confused with border patrol. The Plattsburgh edition of the agency flew a Cessna and Citation jet and had prevented approximately 1,400 people from illegally crossing the U.S./Canadian border during the previous five years. Agents had been trained to spot fresh tire tracks and footprints from the air.

The manhunters agreed that being thorough and methodical was the only way to go. They had to take it one woods at a time, one clearing at a time. To think about the search as one humongous thing—all of those miles and miles of bug-infested forest and swamp, the rugged mountains, and the gaping ravines—was to become overwhelmed by the enormity of the task at hand.

As for the bugs, there were mosquitos, of course, but even more bothersome and painful were the brazen and ubiquitous blackflies that swarmed and bit at anything that moved. Subtler were the Lyme-disease-carrying ticks that were in season throughout the Champlain Valley.

And although none of the hunters had encountered it, there was talk of quicksand. You had to be careful where you stepped or you could be up your waist in the stuff, it was said. Bears were a concern as well, but locals knew that bears seldom attacked men, unless it was a mama bear protecting her cubs.

In the meantime, as the hunt carried on with renewed vigor, the escapees weren't getting along. By invading seasonal hunting camps and cabins in the area, Matt and Sweat had managed to procure food, a gun, and other supplies. However, while Sweat remained focused on the escape, Matt became increasingly distracted by the comforts of freedom—alcohol, heat, and hot water.

Among the items the men found as they ransacked cabins and camps was alcohol and marijuana, which left Matt unable or unwilling to move as fast as Sweat wanted him to.

As the adventure grew increasingly grueling, the age difference between the escapees appeared to grow. The younger Sweat felt the older Matt was holding him back. The escape was wearing Matt down. His feet hurt, his sciatica was flaring up, and he needed frequent rest stops.

Sweat wanted to keep his wits about him, stay sober. Matt did not. In fact, Matt seemed reluctant to sober up. In great physical discomfort due to his ordeal, Matt sought to perpetually self-medicate. Every time they broke into a new cabin, finding the booze was Matt's priority. Sweat was sick of it.

Sweat finally came to a decision on June 23 and abandoned Matt.

Of course, searchers knew none of this. What they did know was that a surreptitious police surveillance camera mounted on a spruce tree five miles southeast of Malone captured images of two men moving through the woods. One of the men, who was carrying a gun and seen in profile, resembled Matt. The other (the image showed only his back and one leg) was assumed to be Sweat.

Twenty minutes after the camera picked up the two men, helicopters hovered over the site. (Five armed helicopters were being used in the overall search, with the Dannemora school ball field as the helipad.) SWAT teams rushed to the scene. The men in the photo were spotted—without difficulty, as they were not hiding.

Three machine guns on one chopper were trained on the men. A combined force of state troopers and FBI special agents cordoned off the area. The men in the photograph were surrounded and identified themselves as a couple of locals who were visiting nearby houses and cabins to make sure none had been broken into.

Minutes later an officer gave the order to stand down. False alarm.

This would have been the end of the story except this last part, the false-alarm part, didn't make it to, or register with, the reporter from the *New York*

Daily News. That tabloid obtained the surveillance photo that had caused the excitement and, eager to scoop their primary competition, the *New York Post*, tweeted it, captioned as being an image of the escapees on the run.

That tweet read, "Exclusive: Photo of the escapees from a trail camera." The image appeared on the front page of the June 29 Metro Final edition.

The men in the photo were actually forty-seven-year-old Eric Couture and fifty-four-year-old Charlie Coutu, both residents of Franklin County. Oddly, the surnames were unusual yet similar. Couture was carrying his twenty-gauge Browning BPS pump shotgun and a pair of binoculars in the photo. Coutu was carrying his .30-30 deer rifle at the time, but the weapon was not visible in the photo.

Other newspapers were, of course, eager to exploit the error and quoted Couture as saying, "They need to know what they're doing before they print stuff." The *Albany Times Union* ran a photo of Couture and Coutu having a good laugh as they read the *Daily News* with their miscaptioned photo.

It had been common during the manhunt—among police, politicians, and press—to associate the Canadian border with freedom. If the prisoners crossed that line, they would be home free.

Not so fast, said Ted Rath, a reporter for the *Toronto Sun*.

Rath noted that even if the prisoners were armed and made it into Canada, they would need luck to survive, and a lot of luck to remain free. Getting across the St. Lawrence River alone was tricky. There was the strong current, plus the river was a shipping lane so there was potentially decapitating boat traffic. Royal Canadian Mounted Police (RCMP) boats and helicopters patrolled the waterway on a fluctuating schedule to prevent predictability. (Law enforcement watched closely because of the area's history of cigarette smuggling.)

On Thursday, June 25, at 2:00 a.m., a Roslyn, Long Island, woman named Carla Gerber was alone, in bed, in her remote summer home in Malone, New York, near the Canadian border, when she heard three knocks at the front door.

A chill went up and down her spine. She was near paralyzed by fear. By this time everyone within fifty miles of Malone was on the lookout for the desperadoes who were somewhere out there, desperate for freedom and dangerous as any wild animal.

She later came to believe that her fear saved her life. If she had answered the door, she was convinced, she would have been taken hostage or simply killed.

The other thing that saved her was the light from a passing police car, which apparently scared her visitor away. She called the police, and in minutes her property was teeming with official vehicles.

Fingerprints and a bloodstain were found on her door.

The quality of this information was not released to the public. It was acknowledged however that communities north of the village of Malone, toward the Canadian border, were to be the primary focus of the investigation. People in those areas were told to expect a strong and visible law enforcement presence.

EIGHT
ONE
DOWN

Richard Matt couldn't resist hitting the bottle. After all, it was his birthday, his first birthday on the outside in how long? Who the fuck knew. He'd found a deserted and generously stocked cabin in Owls Head where the squatting was perfect. His shelter could have been further from the road, but beggars couldn't be choosers. Too bad he couldn't stay. The setup was sweet, but Sweat had been right about one thing: the hunters were out there, and to stay in one place for too long was tantamount to surrender. This on-foot stuff, however, was bullshit. He needed a car.

So he took one last glug off the bottle, grabbed his now-loaded .20-gauge shotgun, and, on shaky legs, weaved his way out the door. After escaping through a pipe and three weeks on the run, he had aches and pains all over. He'd had back surgery and suffered sciatica that felt like a red hot knife sticking into his buttock and running down his leg, but for the moment the alcohol was doing a fine job of masking his discomfort.

He felt good. David Sweat had split, saying Matt was too slow. Sweat said he needed to get to Canada pronto, and he didn't have time to wait around for the painfully weary and frequently inebriated Matt.

Now, pretty drunk, Matt assessed his situation. Behind him were a swamp and a ravine. In front of him was a road, Route 30, where the cops were. He didn't feel he could walk much more. Staying just far enough off the road to remain hidden, he decided to make sure the shotgun worked.[1]

Brett and Dottie Gokey and their family, a total of seven people, from the North Country, were a convoy on Route 30: two campers en route to a Meacham Lake campground in Brushton, New York.

They heard a crack.

Brett, behind the wheel of the head vehicle, thought maybe he'd blown a tire. Both vehicles pulled over into an expansive field. All tires were kicked and determined to be fine, so they continued on their way and might have forgotten the incident entirely if, upon stopping at the Meacham Lake campground, they hadn't discovered in the side of one of their campers a hole caused by a .20-gauge shotgun slug. The hole was at eye level.

"Holy crap, that's the noise we heard," Brett Gokey exclaimed. He grabbed a friend who was along on the trip, and the pair drove back down Route 30 to report the incident to a gathering of law enforcement they'd seen lining the road south of their campground. Police immediately closed the road. As Gokey was doing this he heard another report in the distance—as it turned out, the last of Richard Matt's ammunition.

Hours later, it all came down.

Later, Brett Gokey told a local TV station, "Seven people could have died. It was just a camper that got shot? It's not that. It was my family and friends. We could have died."

Dottie Gokey said she couldn't think about it without wanting to cry. "We were all perfect targets," she told the *Press-Republican*.

Neil Gokey said, "I could've been dead. My girlfriend, who was riding with me, could've been dead."[2]

Robert J. Willett and Leland "Paul" Marlow Jr. owned a camp called Humbug Hunting Club off Route 30 near Humbug Mountain in Malone. Both worked for the state Department of Corrections and Community Supervision. Willett was a corrections officer at medium-security Bare Hill Correctional Facility in Malone but had worked at Clinton Correctional Facility (CCF) in 2012 and at Green Haven in 2010 and 2011. Marlow had worked as a nurse at the maximum-security Upstate Correctional Facility in Malone since 2008.

Willett was checking his camp on Friday, June 26—something he had done regularly since the prison escape. During this check, Willett found a bottle of grape gin that had been opened on the counter. Some of the gin had spilled onto the counter surface, and the cap had somehow gotten under a frying pan on the table. Nothing else seemed disturbed.

He called the police at 1:30 p.m.

While investigators were searching Willett's cabin, they heard what sounded like a shotgun blast not far away. The sound of the shot spawned a full alert, and the law headed in that direction.

Photographer Jon Chodat, whose house was very near this scene, grabbed his camera and went out to see. What he saw, he later recalled, was "a myriad of trucks and vehicles and helicopters flying over. A whole bunch of trucks came up with dogs and teams of soldiers in camouflage."

Now that Matt had fired the shotgun, the same shotgun that he'd found hidden in a bunk at John Stockwell's cabin, perhaps in an effort to stop a vehicle so he could hijack it, he wanted to do it again. It was experience to have one shot under his belt, gauge the kick. He couldn't be hesitant and uncertain during a gunfight. Maybe that's what he wanted most: to turn the hunters into the hunted. The thought might have appealed to his inebriated mind.

The report of the shotgun shot into the side of the trailer brought the helicopter units into the area, but Charles Guess ordered them away, which turned out to be a vey smart thing to do, as the hunters' ears turned out to be even more important than their eyes.

Matt was only a short distance from the cabin with the spilled grape gin and close enough to the road that he could see men with guns. He lay down on the ground near Elephant Head Trail and aimed the gun. Then Matt made his final mistake: he coughed.

Christopher Voss was a clean-cut former Army Ranger, a current agent of the Texas border patrol based in El Paso. It was not unusual for Voss's squad to travel and join in large manhunts. His squad went, but they weren't always happy about it. Voss was strictly a draftee when it came to participating in the search for the escaped prisoners. He'd been there for weeks, searching through foliage much thicker than anything found in El Paso.

Voss heard the call. Gunshot in the woods. At first he thought it was just another false alarm. There had been so many. It was always teenagers, or hunters. The thing this report had over many others was immediacy. When did you hear the shots? Just now.

Voss and others responded to the Lake Titus area and searched the woods near Highway 30. But it was a dead-end.

"All the teams pulled out of the woods," Voss recalled. "We all regrouped up on the highway there to figure out the next course of action. At that point, it did not look like we had anything to work on, until one of the state troopers came up to me."

"I think I just heard someone cough," the trooper said.

"Where?" Voss asked.

"Up there along the wood line."

The team fanned out in response and executed a southerly sweep of the woods. In short order there was a physical sighting: man in the woods, lying on his stomach. The spotter shouted out a code word, a precaution to keep friendlies from shooting one another. The man on the ground did not respond to the code word.

Voss called out, "Put your hands up!" He moved to his right to get a better angle on the guy, and for the first time saw the subject. The guy was only about ten to fifteen yards away, lying on his chest, still partially obscured by vegetation.

"He was motioning something but I couldn't quite tell what it was yet. I was still obscured by some of the terrain," Voss remembered. Voss stepped out of the woods and into a clearing where he could get a better view.

"He must have had his head down because all I saw was his head come up, and I noticed immediately that there was a shotgun pointed right at me," Voss said.

Voss's training kicked in. He raised his M-4 to his eye and shot the man three times, a nice grouping, all in the head, killing him.

Voss and others charged to the man, who was clearly dead, with brains sticking out of a hole in his head.

The call went out on the police radio: "Down hard."

Despite the fact that Matt was clearly dead, the first thing they did was pull the shotgun out from under him. Then they pulled up the back of his shirt. Sure enough, there was the tattoo they had been looking for. They had their man. It was Richard Matt.

The codified call went out on the radio, announcing Matt's demise: "Mexico forever," it said.

Matt's body reeked of alcohol and was in a fetal position on the ground. It was in front of a dirt bank wearing combat fatigues and a waterproof jacket. In addition to the gross appearance of his head, the ground in front of the body was covered with gore.

"The goal is always to arrest a target without any loss of life. But he gave me no other option. There was nothing else that really could be done. Later we learned that Matt had been shooting at campers. I'm pretty confident that somebody could've been hurt or killed if we didn't encounter him that day. Any loss of life is regrettable," Voss said.

Voss's mind would not change even when he learned that Matt had not brought extra shells with him. His gun was not loaded. He'd used up all of his ammunition.

The men at the scene did not allow themselves a moment to relax. They didn't know that the escapees had split up. For all they knew an armed Sweat was still nearby, perhaps putting a crosshairs on someone's temple.

Strictly routine, Matt's shooting death came under legal review by Franklin County acting DA Glenn MacNeill. "Any kind of shooting incident like that requires appropriate investigation," MacNeill told the *Watertown Daily Times*.

His office was looking at the shooting itself. There wasn't a defendant. They were in the process of gathering information, waiting for forensic evidence.

In addition to the killing, MacNeill was investigating the pair of break-ins committed by the escapees during the manhunt, both cabins in the woods owned or leased by correctional officers. If Sweat were to be taken alive, preferable but not a given, he might have to face breaking and entering charges in Franklin County in addition to his legal problems in Clinton County. These were matters that were legally important but practically insignificant when discussing a man already serving life without parole (LWP).

Working under the assumption that Matt and Sweat had still been moving as a team, or had only recently separated, the hunters tightened their search, concentrating on looking into every nook and cranny within a perimeter around the site of Matt's death.

Although Matt was shot around 3:45 p.m., he was not legally pronounced dead until many hours later. When Franklin County coroner Brian Langdon heard about the shooting, he knew he had a few hours before he would be called in.

Sure enough, the scene of Matt's death was subjected to careful processing and thorough photography before the coroner was allowed in. Searchers found Matt's bloody socks nearby. Beside him was a canvas knapsack. Among the supplies in the bag was a can of sardines.

Langdon was escorted through the darkness by law enforcement to an area of extremely thick woods where Matt's body lay. It was 10:55 p.m. His job was to verify that the man was dead, not to determine the cause or time of death. That would be done at the autopsy. Langdon filled out a death certificate and signed it and a series of other documents. A seven-hour delay between a man's death and the signing of his death certificate might seem like a long time but not when a crime scene was involved. Evidence needed to be systematically recorded, and that took time.

Langdon found Matt's face intact, but the condition of the head left no doubt that the man was deceased. Matt was wearing heavy work boots, dark-colored camouflage pants, and a dark-green summer jacket.

The coroner later said that he was taken by the appearance of the body. Matt had been showering and had picked up sturdy protective clothes.

"He looked clean and well-kept," Langdon said. "He wasn't sleeping in any cave or anything like that for three weeks, that's for sure."

From the moment Langdon declared the body dead to the commencement of the autopsy, it was his job to protect the remains, a duty he took very seriously. It was more important to protect the remains than to pass judgment on the person. He oversaw the lifting of the body into a body bag, sealing it up, carrying it to the highway, and placing it in a hearse. Following a stop at the Spaulding Funeral Home in Malone, the body was transported with a police escort to the Adirondack Medical Center in Saranac Lake, taken to that facility's morgue and placed in a double-locked compartment. It was a formal process, everything recorded and photographed, and Langdon maintained a solid chain of evidence by witnessing every step.

Langdon was then allowed to return home for the night, but first thing on Saturday morning he was back at the morgue to witness the transfer by funeral parlor hearse of the body from Adirondack Medical to the Albany Medical Center for autopsy, which he also witnessed.[3]

The autopsy was performed by Dr. Michael Sikirica, the Rensselaer County medical examiner. Sikirica's only public comment on the procedure was that he was doing the autopsy on behalf of the Franklin County coroner.

At autopsy, blisters were found on Matt's feet and multiple bug bites throughout the body. It was confirmed that Matt had been eating and drinking while on the run. His blood-alcohol level was 0.18 percent, more than twice the drink-driving limit. He had been fittingly dressed for the outdoors; indeed if he had not worn as much protective clothing as he had, the swarms of insects in the woods might have bitten him so badly that it would have affected his health. No surprise, the cause of death was gunshot wounds to the head.

The postmortem procedure lasted four hours, during which evidence was carefully gathered and logged in. When it was complete, Langdon again took charge of the body as it was transported back to the proper jurisdiction, that is, to the Alice Hyde Medical Center where it would remain until burial decisions were made.

Barring some unknown circumstances, police now knew Sweat was alone. From a hunting perspective, this could work both ways: make him easier to find because he no longer had someone to watch his back and harder to find because he alone could blend in easier than two escapees together. He could look like just another guy.

Bonnie J. Sherman (pseudonym) was a woman who lived about a mile from the scene of Matt's shooting, a proximity that made her life exciting for a while. She didn't know what was going on at first—gunfire in the distance; she didn't think much of it. You heard gunfire all the time in that neck of the woods. She first learned about Matt's death at five in the morning on Saturday when she had to get past five roadblocks in order to help set up a garage sale in Malone.

She was alone in the house, her husband was away, but that didn't frighten her. Police had searched her property thoroughly. She had three dogs, and they would give her a heads-up in case someone was creepy crawling in her window. Sherman also had a loaded gun at her bedside, so no, she wasn't nervous.

Louis Haremski, the special prosecutor who helped put Matt away, told Lohr McKinstry of the *Press-Republican* that he felt better after hearing the news. Matt had sworn back then, during his Niagara County trial, that if he ever got free he would "gut a cop" and never again be taken alive.

"I wasn't surprised he'd been killed," Haremski said. "I felt relieved. It's unfortunate that it ended that way."

The fact that Matt had repeatedly drawn attention to himself—fatal mistakes, it turned out—gave Sweat an advantage. As the police perimeter closed on Matt, Sweat managed to get outside of it—and he was already six miles north of Malone, heading for the town of Constable.

Without Matt weighing him down like a ball and chain, Sweat moved easily and with great stealth until he was fifteen miles north of Owls Head. There would be no more breaking into cabins. He avoided all signs of civilization, shaved so that he wouldn't look like his own wanted poster, hid during the daytime, and traveled at night. He wasn't precisely sure where he was, but he knew he had to be getting very close to Canada.

On Saturday, June 27, law enforcement came up empty with their circumference around the scene of Matt's death. With a new round of bad weather approaching, they established new lines, casting a larger net. The search area, once condensed to three square miles, grew to twenty-two square miles. The area—located between Malone and Duane, about fifteen miles from the Canadian border—encompassed a vast forest, swampy and hard to navigate because of the thick brush. K-9, aviation, and tactical units were all on duty. There was urgency that Saturday because the weather forecast was for severe storms that night, with rain hard enough to wash away the scent of a man and render the bloodhounds useless.

There had been a sense of excitement that the end was near after Matt's death, but that had subsided. Clinton County sheriff David Favro was blunt about it to a New York City reporter.

Any developments?

"Not a heck of a lot," Favro said. "They're still kind of holding out in that area and hoping for the best."

Roadblocks were set up throughout Franklin County, large and small arteries alike. At one of those roadblocks, state troopers built fires to stay warm in the frigid air near Lake Titus. In the darker corners of the towns, floodlights were installed, illuminating sidewalks and doorways with artificial day.

Franklin County sheriff Kevin Mulverhill had a more positive take. He said the end was near: "Anyone in the woods and on the run from the law is not getting a full eight hours sleep. He's not eating well and he has to keep moving. He is fatigued, and he is going to make a mistake."

The hunters assumed that Sweat was heading toward the Canadian border. They started there and moved south. During this time Sweat found a tree stand, such as those used by deer hunters, and stayed in it for a couple of days. He would later recall that hunters passed directly under him. The spot was so good, he said, that he spent two nights there.

NINE
THE CAPTURE OF SWEAT

It was 2:00 a.m. on Sunday, June 28, and Evan King, Alicia Howard, and brothers Patrick and Conor Gordon were in a car making a fast-food run to the McDonald's in Malone.[1] As they drove, their headlights picked up an incongruous sight. Pushing himself along the edge of the road was a visibly fatigued man on a child's kick scooter.

Their first thought had nothing to do with escaped prisoners. They thought that this was a man who'd perhaps had a roadside emergency and was trying to get help.

So they stopped.

"Are you all right?"

The man replied, "I need a ride."

For a moment, they considered letting the man and his scooter in the car, but there was something about him, something off. A "bad feeling" made them change their mind. They pulled away, and King watched the man recede in the rear-view mirror. Soon thereafter, they figured it out. That man might have been that escaped guy, David Sweat. So at 2:33 a.m. they called a police tip line.

Only twelve hours later, at approximately 3:20 p.m. on Sunday, Sergeant Jay Cook was supervising a search team on Coveytown Road near the town of Constable. The location was thirty miles from Dannemora and sixteen from where Richard Matt had been killed the previous week.

Cook was only a mile and a half from the Canadian border, driving his vehicle on patrol, when he spotted a man in a camouflage outfit. At first Cook thought it might be a park ranger who was lost (a ridiculous notion in hindsight as park rangers don't get lost).

Dressed in camouflage, Sweat was overwhelmed by desperation and deviated from his game plan. He'd been spooked by the men searching for him directly below his tree stand. He let it get to him, and he abandoned what was clearly a superior position.

Then he'd tried and failed to secure himself a vehicle during the night. That hadn't gone well. Those kids had seen his face and driven off. He had to move *now* and thus abandoned his rule of moving only under the cover of darkness.

Cook stopped the car and watched as the man in fatigues walked into a newly cut alfalfa field belonging to Tom MacDonald and Denise Yando, who shared a farmstead there with their dog Shasta. Neither MacDonald nor Yando heard Sergeant Cook stop his vehicle on the road outside. Yando was watching TV, and MacDonald was taking a nap in a reclining chair.

From about twenty-five yards away, Cook called out to the man in the alfalfa field: "Hey, you, stop!"

The man replied, "No, I'm good."

He made a gesture with his hand that Cook interpreted to mean, "You've got the wrong guy."

But Cook had a strong visual on the subject and recognized the man as Sweat. He later recalled thinking, "I've got the right guy. This is Sweat. It's on."

When Sweat realized he had been recognized he made a run for it, heading for a line of trees. The officer knew that if the prisoner made it to the trees, he would likely evade capture and quickly cross the border into Canada.

"Stop or I'll shoot," Cook called out.

Sweat did not stop. But Cook did. A marksman, Cook stopped to take aim. He took a deep breath and squeezed off the first shot. The bullet struck Sweat but did not bring him down. Cook fired again, again striking his mark, and this time Sweat fell to the ground.

The officer found Sweat to be unarmed and seriously injured. He'd been shot twice in the upper torso and had suffered a collapsed lung. By this time, Tom MacDonald was awake and looking out the window.

"We saw police cars going by like crazy," he recalled.

Just then one of his neighbors pulled in and shouted, "Hey Tom, you know your hayfield is full of police?"

There were state troopers at the scene that had spent the past three weeks hunting Matt and Sweat, who were now working just as diligently to make sure David Sweat survived. He was the last survivor able to tell the world what happened, so his survival was essential to the historical record.

Sweat was administered first aid at the scene and found to be carrying a bag that contained maps, tools, bug repellant, Pop Tarts, water, and a can of Vienna sausages. He was taken by ambulance to the Alice Hyde Medical Center in Malone, where he remained for several hours before being flown to Albany International Airport and then driven by ambulance to the Albany Medical Center where he was listed in critical condition.

Law enforcement would have preferred that Sweat's destination stay secret, at least for a little while, but that was not to be. The same press corps that had gone into alpha story mode hours after the escape had, displaying an unusual attention span, remained tenacious for the duration. With Sweat still in transit, a CNN reporter called the Albany Medical Center and spoke to Tania Allard, the hospital's vice president of communications. She said yes, it was true that Sweat was on his way to that facility, but she refused to say when he was expected to arrive.

At the Albany hospital, Sweat was placed in a locked ward. He couldn't talk because of heavy sedation and, because of his chest wound, was only able to make what investigators termed "mumbling and gurgling noises."

Soon enough, however, he regained his ability to speak and over the next few hours laid out many of the missing pieces as to how Matt and Sweat managed to escape and stay on the run for three weeks.

Among other things, Sweat told his questioners that he had had a troubled childhood, and as part of efforts to keep him on the straight and narrow, he was trained in how to survive in the wilderness, knowledge that came in handy during his flight.

During his stay at the hospital, a joint team of security from the Department of Corrections and the Albany Medical Center guarded Sweat.

Governor Andrew Cuomo traveled to the Titus Mountain Ski Center, where police had set up a command center in the center's Upper Lodge, and from there he held a press conference during which he noted Sergeant Cook's courageous actions and proclaimed him a hero.

As the law enforcement officers left Titus Mountain, their home away from home during the manhunt, and returned to their actual homes and headquarters, they witnessed a heartwarming thing: citizens standing on their front lawns holding handmade signs that read simply "THANK YOU."

In the meantime, the hospitalized Sweat told investigators that, when Joyce Mitchell failed to show for the pickup at the manhole, he and Matt scrapped their plan to flee to Mexico and decided to head north and hopefully cross into Canada.

He said that twice he had almost been discovered. The first time came when he and Richard Matt were hiding near a cabin in the woods when three people showed up. The other came when he was in the tree stand.

He told investigators that he'd known all along that Matt was the weak point in the plan. He was older, heavier, and less disciplined. He'd had to lose weight in order to squeeze himself out of the prison in the first place. Not only were there touch-and-go moments during the escape itself, but also, once on the run, Matt proved to be out of shape, unable to keep up.

Sweat was angered when they found a cabin to hide in and Matt began getting drunk. They argued over the issue. Sweat had reached his breaking point, and the convicts split up. Every man for himself.

Sweat gave investigators—from the state police to the Department of Corrections and the inspector general's office—details of the escape plan. The idea was his, he bragged, stating that he'd been considering ways to get out of Clinton Correctional Facility (CCF) long before he became next-cell neighbors with Richard Matt in January 2015. The notion that they could not have started their escape plan before the prison's heating system was turned off was wrong, he said.

They began before that, and when the heat next to the steam pipe became too intense he'd made like MacGyver and rigged his own air conditioning system using a fan he had in his cell and electricity from the lights in the catwalk. Investigators suspected he was telling the truth as all of his statements matched the physical evidence.

Each night, Sweat said, work began at 11:30 p.m., right after the evening head count. He would crawl through the hole in his wall, through a catwalk and down a ladder, and then roam the tunnels. He became intimately familiar with the tunnel system. He said he used a hacksaw blade to cut through the wall of his own cell. The second step was to cut a hole in Matt's cell.

What about the noise? A neighboring inmate inquired about that, Sweat recalled. Sounds like sawing, the guy had said. It was Matt who came up with the plausible excuse. He was an artist, you see, everyone knew that. That noise was just him stretching canvas and cutting wood to make a frame.

Each morning Sweat would return to his cell and close up the hole in his cell wall before the 5:30 a.m. head count—and this went on night after night until it was routine.

As is true of beating any maze, the first route taken is rarely the correct one. There had been much trial and error. An earlier attempt to get past the Dannemora walls via the sewer system had turned into a dead-end.

Sweat was well into his nightly explorations when he finally discovered the correct pipe. Looking down its side, he could see that it traveled through the wall and emerged on the outside about twenty feet away.

From that point, it was just a matter of gaining access to the inside of that pipe, making sure it was big enough to crawl through, and then cutting a hole to get back out of the pipe. And then there was finding a way to get back up to the surface once on the other side, preferably at a private spot.

Back then, Sweat recalled, Matt had discipline. He changed his body for the escape. That took some heart. When Matt joined Sweat in the Dannemora catacombs, there was a problem at first. He was too thick to fit inside the key pipe. So Matt stopped eating and dropped between forty and fifty pounds so he could slink and slither his way through the narrow passages along with his more svelte partner.

Sweat was asked what tools he used to chip away at the concrete of the wall. He said he used a sledgehammer and other pilfered tools. The tools were in a gang box, the lock of which he'd picked with a tweezers and a paperclip.

"Where did you get the sledgehammer?" his interrogators asked.

"Must've been left behind by a construction worker," Sweat replied.

Because it was so dirty down there, Sweat got into the habit of wearing a second set of clothes down the hole with him as coveralls—green pants, long-sleeved brown shirt, and a do-rag fashioned from a ripped tee shirt—so that he would look relatively clean when he returned to his cell each morning.

While it was not true that he waited until the spring to start digging his escape route, Sweat did admit that the job became much easier on May 4 when the prison shut down the heating system.

The second to last step was to cut an entrance and exit hole in the pipe that passed through the prison wall, only possible when the metal wasn't blistering hot from steam and full of water. Hacksaw blades were again called into use. He tied rags around the end to be used as a handle, so the work could proceed without damage to his hands.

It took four weeks to cut the holes in the pipe. The exit hole in the pipe was the hardest work of all. Because of the cramped circumstances, Sweat had to cut with his left hand despite being right handed. After that, the final step was to cut the lock on a manhole on the outside and to climb up to freedom. They conducted one dry run, coming up out of a different manhole from the one they eventually escaped through.

Sweat admitted that far more thought went into how to get out of the prison than toward what to do after they were out. They had assumed that Joyce Mitchell was under Matt's thumb. They believed she would be there to give them a ride, and when she didn't show up they found themselves without a well-considered plan B.

Matt panicked, and it was all Sweat could do to calm him down. They decided to get away from the prison as fast as they could so they headed into the village, crossing through backyards. Almost immediately they ran into a homeowner who shouted out a challenge: "Hey, get off my property."

Sweat apologized and said, "We're just lost. We don't know where we are. We're on the wrong street."

At that point, fresh out of the hatch, they were wearing a combination of civilian clothes and prison clothes. Sweat was carrying a guitar case that he'd packed with items he had squirreled away: clothes, twenty packs of peanuts, forty granola bars, twelve sticks of pepperoni, and pepper to throw off the bloodhounds. Sweat thought the guitar case was a brilliant touch on his part, far less apt to attract scrutiny than a prison duffle bag.

Chased out of the backyard, they ran to the village's main drag and took Route 374 up the side of Dannemora Mountain, which was tough on Matt's legs, and they turned onto Hugh Herron Road. At first they were both willing to rough it: go into the woods, deeper and deeper, and further from civilization, walking through swamps and streams to confuse the dogs. Sweat remembered coming across a road and a sign that read "Saranac." They could see lights in the distance so they switched directions. After that, he couldn't be specific about where they were at any given time.

Sweat said that he and Matt had seen the movie *The Shawshank Redemption*, and their joke was that it took them far less time to figure out an escape route than it took the character of Andy Dufresne played by Tim Robbins in the movie. Sweat had two nicknames for Matt. He called him "Hacksaw" to his face, a reference to William Rickerson's dismemberment, and "Fatso" behind his back.

Interrogators wanted to know how he camouflaged the noise from the power tools.

"Weren't no power tools," Sweat said.

"How did you cut your way out of your cells, and through the steam pipes?"

"Just hacksaws, man." Well, not just hacksaws. He finally admitted that Mitchell had supplied other items as well: two chisels, a steel punch, and two concrete drill bits. Other tools came from a contractor's storage box.

"How did you get it open?"

"Picked the lock."

Some of his tools he made himself, using scraps of metal he found down there.

"Mitchell was supposed to meet you at the manhole?"

"Yeah."

"What then?"

"We were going to get in her car and drive to Mexico."

"You were going to kill her husband?"

"That was her idea."

"You have sex with her?"

"No way."[2]

Authorities didn't necessarily believe him, noting that Mitchell had been investigated previously for an inappropriate relationship with Sweat, an investigation that led corrections officials to move Sweat out of Mitchell's tailor shop. The allegations involved Mitchell and Sweat going together into the "spare-parts room," disappearing for a while, and coming back without any spare parts.

Sweat conceded that Mitchell liked him. He couldn't walk past her desk without her starting up a meaningless conversation about some nonsense. It was annoying.

"She wouldn't let me leave," he complained.

Sweat admitted that, during the days and weeks leading up to the escape, he wrote Mitchell notes on Post-its professing his love for her and how much he was dreaming of taking her into his arms when they got on the outside together. Sweat called them "love lust" letters, written to "placate" Mitchell.

"How about Matt? He have sex with her?"

"Yeah."

"She brought you food?"

"Yeah, the only reason I'm working is to buy food so I don't have to go to the mess hall. So when a civilian offers you food, you take it."

Getting food from the outside enabled the escapees to work on the holes they were cutting in their cells while the other inmates were in the mess hall.

"What would you have done with Joyce Mitchell if she'd shown up?"

"I don't know, tie her up, drop her off somewhere, get far enough away and report her whereabouts."

"You weren't going to kill her?"

"I wasn't. Matt might've."

Asked how he camouflaged the hole in his cell wall, Sweat said he taped the metal piece back in place and painted the tape to match the wall. His job was a lot neater than Matt's, Sweat bragged.

Sweat said that, during the planning of the escape, Matt told him that Mitchell was crazy and would do whatever they wanted her to do. He should just make a list of things they wanted her to do and she would do them. And that was what happened. Except she didn't do the last thing on the list. She didn't show up with the car.

While working his way out, Sweat wasn't always alone on the catwalks. One time a guard walked on the catwalk directly above him, and he had to hide and then dodge when the guard dropped a lit cigarette.

Sweat explained that finding the escape route was easier—*much* easier—than he had anticipated. He had expected a series of locked doors and gates that turned out not to be there. In fact he didn't encounter a major obstacle until he reached a wall between B and C Block. There was a period of discouragement before he discovered a large pipe that went through the wall. It was marked LPS (low pressure steam) and big enough to crawl inside. It was a happy moment. Steam pipes, he knew, went *out*. They left the facility. Sweat always split his time between cutting and exploring. He wanted to be sure that once he chose a route, it was the easiest route.

Sweat told investigators that he tried popping a hole in the steam pipe by hitting it with a sledgehammer, but the sound was loud enough to wake the dead, so he used a hacksaw blade instead.

The next major obstacle that Sweat found was a brick wall separating C Block from the Industry Building. This time there would be no pipe to crawl through. It was hard work. Using makeshift tools, Sweat managed only to remove two or three bricks a night. Each night, he would replace the bricks to camouflage his work—even though it looked as if no one had been down there in years. He always had a watch on him, so he'd know to be back in his cell by four in the morning.

Sweat did almost all of the work. Matt helped on two nights, but that was it. Matt was impressed with the work Sweat had done and, according to Sweat, said, "I would have given up a long time ago."

The prison's biggest obstacle of all, of course, was the outer wall, the final barrier to freedom. At first, Sweat thought about digging under the wall, but there was so much standing water down there, he couldn't be sure he'd be able to keep his tunnel from filling with water. After the prison turned off the heat during the first week of May, and drained the water from the pipe, Sweat knew it was the key to the escape.

He made a dress rehearsal and tried two manholes as the escape hatch before choosing the second one. One of his reasons was that the second manhole couldn't be seen from CCF's Tower 2. He later learned the point was moot because Tower 2 had not been manned during the overnight shift for more than twenty years.

Sweat admitted that the prison riot that occurred only days before the escape caused both he and Matt a great deal of anxiety. They were certain a lockdown would be declared and their escape hatches discovered. It never occurred to them that Albany would tell Department of Corrections and Community Supervision (DOCCS) deputy commissioner for correctional facilities Joseph Racette to nix a lockdown because of budget concerns.

He said he realized that, at the end of his dress rehearsal for the escape, he could have escaped alone and might have done a better job of it. But he was a man of his word and went back to get Matt. The second time through the escape route, with Matt in tow, was much more difficult. Matt was claustrophobic and still too heavy. At one point, inside the pipe, Sweat had to tie them together with a bed sheet and pull Matt along. When Matt finally made it out of the pipe, his pants came halfway down, prompting Sweat to say, "I didn't know you cared!"

"What was up with the 'Have a Nice Day!' Post-it?"

Sweat said another inmate gave him that a couple of days before the escape. Interrogators wanted to know how Matt and Sweat split up. Sweat explained his frustration with Matt who was old and liked to drink. It was after they were chased out of John Stockwell's cabin that Sweat decided he'd had enough. They knew there were people nearby and moving stealthy was essential, but Matt didn't get the concept. The final straw came when Matt, who'd been drinking heavily, fell loudly and stayed down. Sweat took the opportunity to run away from him and never saw him again. Sweat headed east and north. Matt, Sweat learned, headed west to his demise.

How was it that Matt was armed and Sweat not? Sweat said he had been armed. They each had carried a shotgun for a while. Matt wanted to shoot people with his, but Sweat only wanted his to shoot things they could eat. After a while on his own he decided he didn't need it anymore because he was finding adequate quantities of food in camps along his route.

"What did you do with the gun?"

"I broke it down and threw it into some deep running water."

"Why did you do that?"

"I didn't want any hikers or, you know, children to find it," Sweat said, trying his best to sound angelic.

His interrogators raised an eyebrow of skepticism at that.

As Sweat gabbed, his health rapidly improved. On June 30, doctors announced that his condition had been upgraded to fair. He would not need surgery.

Police said it was doubtful Sweat would be returned to Dannemora, that he would be sent to a maximum-security prison the inner workings with which he was unfamiliar, perhaps Sing Sing.

Obviously, the privileges that he enjoyed at CCF would no longer be available to him. No more Honor Block *ever*. Sweat had proven himself (again) to be a man devoid of honor. He would, police said, most likely be under 24-7 lockdown for the rest of his life.

Among those most happy about Sweat's capture was the family of Kevin Tarsia, which issued a statement thanking Cook for his vigilance. When Cook saw something out of whack he was a total pro and went with his gut.

The Tarsia family thanked the thousands of law enforcement officers who'd worked tirelessly over the past three weeks to catch the killer.

The statement read, "On June 6 (the day of the escape) our lives were once again turned upside down and one of our worst nightmares became reality. We were back to July 4, 2002, reliving Kevin's death all over again.

"To lose a loved one is always difficult, but to have someone you loved be ambushed, shot fifteen times and then run over with a car simply for stopping to check unusual activity in a town park, just doing his job, is a pain that no one can understand if you have not been through it first hand."

On July 4, 2015, Fred LeBrun of the *Albany Times Union* compared the Dannemora story to a really great episode of *Law and Order* with its shifting angles and riveting support cast. And the story was not over, LeBrun pointed out. The public had the penalty phase to look forward to: "the finger pointing, the accounting, multiple recreations by various investigators, some of whom have agendas of their own, looking into who screwed this up and why and how it happened." LeBrun envisioned lengthy and multiple trials before all was said and done. He pointed out that the version of the story that would be respected most, the one most apt to become the historical version, was that of David Sweat himself—perhaps not the best source, he being a convicted murderer with a history of manipulating the people and systems around him. So, what should they believe? Perhaps the actual truth would never be completely known. It appeared, from information leaked out so far, that Sweat planned to inform on only himself, Matt, and Joyce Mitchell. Other than that, he was mum—an understandable silence, being that he would be under the supervision of corrections officers for the rest of his life.

LeBrun noted that great aspects of Sweat's story didn't survive scrutiny. Indeed, he believed that without the cooperation of at least some corrections officers, the escape would have been impossible.

Power tools were necessary to do the job, yet Sweat denied using any. This was extremely unlikely, unless somehow the holes were cut by someone else and had already been there. That was another possibility but one fraught with conspiratorial mystery. Investigators preferred closing doors to opening them.

Sweat said that he and Matt worked seven hours a night in the bowels of the prison's infrastructure, night after night, without anyone realizing it—all because they were good at balling up laundry under the covers to make it look as if they were in their cots. How could this be true? Were bed checks that cursory? Or, a better question, did they exist at all?

LeBrun voiced what many were feeling, that stalwart peace officers had gotten very lucky, bringing these two brutal killers to justice without anyone being injured except the escapees themselves. He called for the FBI to go hard at this case, to seek out the money trail and the unanswered complaints from within the New York State prison system that budget cuts were making it impossible to keep inmates, staff, or for that matter, the public safe.

The police killing of Richard Matt and shooting of David Sweat took place against a backdrop in which the use of undo force (in particular fatal force) by policemen, predominantly against black males, had been heavily criticized, in particular events in Missouri and New York City.

Michael J. Palladino, president of the Detectives' Endowment Association, grabbed at the irony of the situation on July 9: "Politics is amazing. Last week, law enforcement shot and wounded an unarmed prison escapee, David Sweat, and Governor Cuomo labeled the trooper a hero. This week, under the Governor's new policy, had prisoner David Sweat succumbed to his wounds, the same trooper would be stripped of his hero label and introduced to the special prosecutor."

Major Charles Guess, commander of Troop B, made a few concluding remarks from his barracks in Ray Brook: "Everyone would agree, even us in law enforcement, you can't make this stuff up."

He said that he had been a troop leader for about seven months when Matt and Sweat escaped. It was like being thrown into the Super Bowl on day one of your football career. The manhunt was the first big mission of Troop B under his command. He could not be more proud of his team, or of the excellent interagency communication throughout the process. Guess was pleased that Sweat has been cooperative and helpful with his statements, but there was more work to be done. Everything needed to be rechecked in a timely fashion so Troop B could be sure that the information they presented to the district attorney's office was accurate.

He described the escape as a symptom of a "systemic breakdown" at the prison and said that characterizing the escape as involving others unknown on the outside was a stretch, at least "at this time." Of course, he added, all of the people that Mitchell and the escapees had contact with would be carefully investigated.

Rita Hayworth and Shawshank Redemption: Hope Springs Eternal was a novella written by Stephen King as part of his book *Different Seasons*, first published in 1982. Though the method of escape shown in the 1994 movie based on the novella might have been similar to the method used by Matt and Sweat, there was a strong moral difference between this tale and that. In the film, the character Andy Dufresne has been falsely imprisoned, charged with killing his wife and her lover, crimes for which he was innocent. There was nothing false about the imprisonment of Matt and Sweat. They were a cop killer and a torture killer. The other difference between the two tales was time. In the movie it took Dufresne twenty years to burrow his way to freedom. Matt and Sweat dug out of Dannemora in a matter of months.

On June 30, as expected, there was a major shakeup at the Dannemora prison as it reeled over its failure to protect the public from desperate murderers. The superintendent and eleven other staffers were suspended with pay by the state's Department of Corrections and Community Supervision. Suspended were superintendent Steven Racette, first deputy superintendent Donald Quinn, and deputy superintendent for security Stephen Brown. There were others: guards who'd allegedly slept through the escape.

Racette would eventually resign under duress over the escape. On his way out the gate, he told a reporter from the *Adirondack Daily Enterprise* that CCF was a lot like the *Titanic*, a disaster waiting to happen. Officers were regularly out of position. It was the norm. Protocol was ignored. But he'd said enough, and he zipped his lip.

Racette shut himself off to the media, so his wife Cherie appointed herself his public information officer, one determined to let the world know what a raw deal Steven had gotten. He was a scapegoat, pure and simple. She noted that Steven had worked thirty-seven years for New York State, at ten different prisons, and that his style was always to work as a member of a team. Although she understood that huge mega-happenings like the escape and subsequent manhunt would result in heads rolling, that didn't make it fair. He and his family had made many sacrifices for the State of New York. When crunch time came they didn't have his back. Way before all of the facts were gathered, her husband was given an ultimatum: resign or be demoted. It also irked her that the press knew Steven was to be ousted before he did. That was a show of disrespect. Tell a man to his face that's he's got to quit if he knows what's good for him. Steven didn't then or now feel that he'd done anything wrong. He had requested better security systems at CCF, but those requests had been denied in budget-conscious Albany—too expensive.

On the other side of the coin, Cherie was counting her blessings. Steven and she now had more time to spend with their elderly parents. She worked in a doctor's office, and Steven had taken a new low-stress, part-time job at a tractor supply store. Life was good, she concluded.

During the suspensions, the state's assistant commissioner for correctional facilities, James O'Gorman, ran the Dannemora prison.

The CCF workforce held its collective breath. Who would be given the boot? On June 26, insecurity flourished when state officials confirmed that scheduled 2 percent raises for a dozen CCF supervisors were being withheld pending the outcome of the state inspector general's investigation.

The escape was not Dannemora's only problem. The *New York Post*, piling on and loving it, reported on June 29 that the FBI was investigating CCF for drug trafficking—in particular, heroin. According to a source close to the federal investigation, the subject of drug trafficking inside CCF first came up during the state's investigation but was not followed up on. The *Post* reported that in addition to drugs, "other possible criminal activity" was being investigated.

Buffalo TV station WIVB released the grisly photo it had acquired of the body of Richard Matt, taken in situ. The photo showed blood and brain matter protruding from a gaping hole in Matt's head. Other TV news and newspapers published the photo over the next few days, but almost all showed it with the offensive area electronically blurred.

That same day, the New York State Department of Corrections (NYSDOC) announced that there would be a series of changes at the CCF in light of the escape: first and foremost was the elimination of the so-called Honor Block in which maximum security was loosened to reward inmates' good behavior. The perks, such as cooking facilities, telephone usage, and extended recreation had been taken advantage of by the escapees. Two prisoners had abused the privileges, and the entire cellblock had to pay the price.

Every cell in the prison would be checked at least once per week. A senior security staff member would supervise these searches. The existing tunnels in the prison's infrastructure would be blocked with security gates and searched monthly. Previously, searches were biannual.

If private contractors working on the building used power tools, those tools would be kept in a secure trailer where they would be inaccessible to inmates and inspected daily.

A high-ranking corrections officer on the overnight shift would supervise bed checks to make sure they are done properly, that is, "at varying and unpredictable intervals." These checks, it was hoped, would signal an end to nocturnal tunneling.

The number of cells searched daily and randomly for contraband would be tripled, with each cell searched at least once every two months.

Whenever an infamous outlaw is killed, there is hesitance and confusion regarding the disposal of the remains. Lee Harvey Oswald had to be buried in secret, with members of the press as his pallbearers. He had zero friends, and only three relatives attended. The story of Richard Matt's body was equally bleak.

According to Franklin County coroner Brian Langdon, Matt stopped being a ward of the state at the time of his death and became the responsibility of Franklin County. The county's deadline for claiming the body, midday on June 30, passed without action. On Wednesday, July 1, Franklin County officials announced that, because no one from Matt's family had claimed his body, the remains would be buried in an unmarked grave. Another county coroner, Bert Wilcox, said the county didn't have a potter's field and so would have to purchase a plot in a local cemetery.

Wilcox added, "They'll probably go to the least expensive one they can find. The county won't pay for a marker."

Before that could happen, members of Matt's family, Nicholas Harris and his mother, did claim the body. On Thursday, July 2, Langdon released Matt's body to the Heald Funeral Home in the Plattsburgh area. According to owner Jay Heald, the body stayed in Plattsburgh only briefly before it was transferred to an undisclosed funeral parlor in Tonawanda, New York, for private burial.

Harris spoke with Lou Michel, a reporter from the *Buffalo News*. Michel noted that Nicholas Harris was only twenty-three years old but looked younger, dressed for the playground in tee shirt and gym shorts to his knees, the jock look betrayed only by the cigarette he held in his right hand.

Harris said that if he hadn't claimed his old man's body, it would "just be rotting up there." The funeral, he explained, was not going to be public. Certain people who had contacted him would be invited.

They were having this funeral in honor of his biological dad's memory. The only reason he was making a public statement was to thank those who'd helped in defraying the costs. A lady whose husband was a corrections officer and knew his father came by and asked, "Are you Nicholas?" He said yes, and she handed him an envelope with a donation. Another person sent him a money order and signed it "a complete stranger." That was really, really nice. But he wanted it known that he was not going out of his way to seek contributions.

Among those expected at the funeral was a daughter of Matt's that Nicholas would be meeting for the first time.

Harris, always Richard Matt's best public relations man, said that his father's IQ had been 180, well into the genius range, and that high IQs ran in the family. As he spoke he was on his mother's front lawn fixing his off-road bike. He described himself as a student whose life was placed on hold by circumstances beyond his control. He spent his tuition money on transporting and cremating his dad's corpse.

At first Harris had wanted an open casket, but the condition of the remains nixed that. Harris planned to keep some of Matt's ashes. Most of the ashes would be scattered at a secret location, a spot that was special to Richard Matt.

Harris remembered talking to the same reporter a few weeks earlier, when Matt was still on the run and the escape was fresh. Harris said back then that he'd kept in touch with Matt by writing letters, even when he was in prison, which was most of the time. Having his biological father so prominent in the news had been overwhelming, Harris said. The worst of it was when several media outlets chose to publish photos of Matt's corpse at the site of his killing, showing the ruined head. Harris felt ambushed by the image.

"It was not something I would have chosen to see," Harris said.

Harris liked Lou Michel, liked the way the Buffalo paper had treated him, but some of the media had been brutal. He said the media had been on him relentlessly. He'd been *harassed*.

He'd had opportunities to cash in too. Calls came in from lots of film companies who wanted to make movies about the whole thing. He was considering offers, with a strong caveat.

Harris said, "Only if Italian-Americans are portrayed in a favorable light.

My father was proud of his Italian ancestry." Harris was particularly embarrassed by the show *Jersey Shore*, which he felt made Italian Americans look particularly bad.

He admitted that he'd backed off of life for a while, while Matt's daring escape bred a wide variety of distractions, but he planned on getting back on track soon enough. Truth be known, it wasn't just Matt and the prison escape. It was his mother too. She was disabled and needed a lot of attention. She had been physically attacked by Matt, who broke into her house when Nicholas was an infant and they were living in Tonawanda. The game plan was to go back to school in the fall, Harris said, and eventually earn a degree in environmental science and forestry.

Not all of Matt's relatives were as kind as Nicholas to Matt's memory. Matt's brother, Wayne Schimpf, he of the stolen getaway vehicle, said he knew it sounded bad when he said it aloud, but this was the outcome he'd been hoping for. He felt relieved. He could no longer think of his brother as the Rick he knew. All he could think of was the asshole who'd tortured a man to death, who'd threatened him personally with violent death, and who'd escaped and was scaring the crap out of people everywhere.

"He's in hell where he deserves to be," Schimpf said. "I've been living in fear for twenty years that Matt would escape and make good on a threat to kill me for cooperating with North Tonawanda detectives in the Rickerson slaying investigation."

During the manhunt, Schimpf predicted for publication that Matt would not be taken alive. When he learned his prognostication had come true his first thought was "Thank God this can finally end for me and my family." Only then did he think, "That's my brother."

On July 12, 2015, James T. Conway—superintendent of the Attica Correctional Facility, 2002–2010—published in *Newsday* his recommendations for how to improve security problems in Dannemora.

First, he said, a task force should be created to analyze how best to shore up security, thus allowing the newly installed executive team to do their job and run the day-to-day operation of the prison.

Second, "change the culture." There was not just too much fraternization between staff and inmates, but there was staff slacking and ineffectiveness as well. Critical posts should now always be manned.

Last, staff should be moved from place to place in the prison to avoid long-term relationships between the workers and the inmates. Staff should be regularly audited to make sure everyone can and is doing the job they were assigned to do. Labor would be upset, but it needed to be done.

Dannemora became the focal point of deep investigative journalists, whose digging exposed secrets that many wanted kept buried. While the weeks-long manhunt was underway outside CCF, inside there was, according to the *New York Times*, a "campaign of retribution." The prison had been embarrassed, and inmates in Matt and Sweat's block—the Honor Block—were subject to "violence that included beatings while handcuffed, chokings, and head slams." Guards trying to determine where Matt and Sweat went allegedly committed the first beatings. Prisoners were told that, if they didn't spill everything they knew, they would "disappear."

Anyone with extended proximity to the escapees was transferred out of the Honor Block and placed in solitary confinement. Some were transferred to other prisons, despite no evidence of a prisoner conspiracy. As of August 1, sixty inmates had filed grievances to the Prisoners' Legal Services, and the Department of Corrections' Office of Special Investigations (OSI) was also looking into the claims of unjust retributions. Managing attorney at the Prisoners' Legal Services of New York, James Bogin, said prisoners were threatened with waterboarding. Asked about this OSI said it was looking into the allegations, and any guard found breaking the rules would be punished accordingly.

Patrick Alexander lived in a cell adjacent to Matt's. The night after the escape, Alexander said, three guards took him into a broom closet and punched him out. He had a plastic bag placed over his head. Men shouted questions at him even as the beating continued.

One guard, Alexander said, had CIU on his jacket, "Crisis Intervention Unit." That officer jumped up and grabbed him by the throat, lifted his ass right up out of his chair, slammed his head into the pipe along the wall, and repeatedly punched him in the face. Two more officers joined in the fun, and the three beat Alexander in the ribs and stomach.

The *Times* reported that new prisoners at CCF were given a warning: "Cross the guards and bad things can happen."

Prisoners beaten in the face were placed into the secrecy of solitary confinement to give the wounds a chance to heal.

Of course in the world of corrections, one man's abuse is another man's tighter ship. The complaints from prisoners coincided with a "new security policy" put in place by state officials to regain control of a prison that they felt was on the verge of running amok.

Any story that featured the word "retribution" came from the prisoners' side. According to corrections officers, the prison population "went wild" when they heard Matt and Sweat had made it out safely. On the first Monday after the escape, three officers were attacked by the inmates they were attempting to frisk.

One guard told the *Press-Republican*, "We lost a lot of credibility because of this escape, and the inmates are dissing us. We are going to have to fight like hell to get it back."

Looking at a list of incidents in the prison during the spring of 2015, one could interpret CCF as a place working its way up to a major incident. In the six months before the escape, there had been an uptick in assaults and contraband, especially drugs.

It was believed that the great bulk of the drugs inside the prison were smuggled in, either inside of packages or by visitors. Staff members, it was believed, were bringing in only a small percentage of the narcotics.

Not all reporting of the "retribution punishments" was as measured as that from the *Times* or the *Press-Republican*. Most in fact leaned toward the hysterical—nowhere more so than on the "World Socialist Website" where the fact that Governor Cuomo had personally questioned one inmate only hours before he was beaten became the headline, while that same article compared the scene at Dannemora to the "torture chambers" of Abu Ghraib and Guantanamo Bay.

Not that any of this was new. A man who sold real estate in New York City in 2015, but served time in Dannemora for drugs during the late 1970s, recalled for NPR his intro to Little Siberia. When his bus arrived at the prison the guards demonstrated how things were going to be. They arbitrarily pulled one incoming inmate from the bus and beat the shit out of him as the others watched. They held him down and kicked him. It was the most frightening thing the future real estate salesman had ever seen.

He thought to himself, "My God, I'm in another world."

It was, he learned, a world in which the code of silence was absolute.

What was the big deal? After all, prison wasn't supposed to be nice. In answer to that attitude, the *Times* searched the recent past at CCF for incidents that upped the brutality ante. Forty-four-year-old Leonard Strickland—a schizophrenic prisoner off his meds, who claimed to have given birth to a baby, to be God, and to be a billionaire married to Beyoncé—argued with guards in 2010 and "ended up dead." According to inmates interviewed by the *Times*, guards shouted racial slurs and pushed Strickland down a flight of stairs. Strickland's head cracked with a sickening noise on the concrete steps several times on the way down. Guards then ganged up on him at the base of the stairs and beat him until he was immobile. When the incident was investigated, guards said they only used the force necessary to protect themselves from injury. Inmates said guards continued to beat a still Strickland, shouting "Stop resisting" as they did so. Strickland died.

The Strickland deal seemed destined to remain a he-said/she-said case, until definitive proof of hideous abuse emerged, a CCF security video showing Strickland, barely conscious and in handcuffs, being dragged across the floor, followed by the "stop resisting" moment that inmates had reported. A prison nurse stood nearby but made no move to offer aid to the beaten prisoner. The video showed the final forty-five minutes of Strickland's life in real time.

By the time an ambulance arrived at CCF, Strickland was "cold to the touch, covered in cuts and bruises, and bleeding from the ears." On the tape an emergency responder noted the injury to Strickland's head and asked if a blow from an officer caused it. A voice offscreen replied, "Yup, there's an injury to the head. I don't know how it occurred, but there's an injury to the head."

Despite this evidence, police and the district attorney brought no charges.[3]

Going further back, to 2008, fifty-two-year-old CCF prisoner, Bradley Caesar, had a confrontation with guards, was beaten mercilessly, and then placed back in his cell where his pitiful pleas for medical attention went unheeded. Caesar died because his broken ribs wouldn't allow his lungs to inflate and he suffocated. The only punishment in that case was to a prison nurse, fined $500. That nurse still worked at CCF.

The *Times* also noted the strong racial component in CCF's surreptitious methods. There were 950 guards, mostly Dannemora locals who were used to the forested wilderness, and all but a few of them were white. The inmate population was predominantly black, fishes out of water; many of them were former residents of New York City, their wilderness an urbanscape of charred and crumbling brick.

The *Times* said that, during the campaign of retribution, one of the worst offenders was a CCF officer nicknamed "Captain America." The guards who dished out the punishment, inmates said, wore no name badges, but one was distinguishable because of a large American flag tattoo he had on his left arm.[4] While it became common for guards to punch and rough up inmates in areas where there were no surveillance cameras, "Cap" went the extra mile. He was the one who mentioned "waterboarding" and tied a plastic bag over a prisoner's head. Research showed that "Cap" had been sued three times for alleged assault and harassment. Two of those suits were still active. The third terminated when the prisoner in question died.

There *had* been a riot on May 31—two gangs, Bloods versus Muslims, going at it—only a week before Matt and Sweat broke out. Forty inmates brawled in the recreation yard for about a half hour until teargas broke it up. No officers were hurt, but seven inmates sustained injuries, the worst being a broken leg. Dannemora was a powder keg, its walls containing a turf war for the inner-prison drug trade. Matt and Sweat must have been hip to this. It was like a built-in diversion. They lived in a prison that was on high alert for trouble, but that trouble was elsewhere. No one was looking at them.

During the May 31 crisis, Superintendent Steven Racette asked officials in Albany for permission to lockdown and thoroughly search the entire prison. Superintendents, Racette understood, lacked the power to order a lockdown and search of their own prison and must first ask the permission of the deputy commissioner of facility operations, who somewhat emphatically refused the superintendent's request. The DOCCS wasn't impressed with the riot. It couldn't afford the overtime.

And now, weeks later, with his head among those rolling, Racette understood that such a lockdown and search would have discovered the escapees' secret. There was "why none of this is Racette's fault" in a nutshell.

The DOCCS's response was based on budget, of course. Locking down and thoroughly searching cost money, but it would have been a drop in the bucket compared to the money spent in the aftermath of the escape.

The *Times* article received criticism, notably from Richard Steier in the *Chief Leader* (a weekly newspaper for civil employees), and Michael Powers, head of the New York State Correctional Officers and Police Benevolent Association (NYSCOPBA), saying that quoting felons constituted irresponsible reporting.

From outsiders, faith in the NYSDOC was at an all-time low—low enough to provoke federal response. The FBI knew that the Department of Corrections' (DOC) Narcotics Unit and Internal Affairs were already investigating the drug problem in Dannemora, but they launched their own investigation anyway only days after the escape.

Narcotics and Internal Affairs operated out of Albany as part of the Office of Special Investigations. The previous director of operations for that office was arrested in January for sexual harassment. The office has been in disarray since. The new department head had just moved into the job when the escape occurred. His previous background was in "white-collar crimes, not prison operations."

On July 5, Sweat's medical condition had improved to the point where he could be discharged from the Albany Medical Center and moved to the Five Points Correctional Facility in Romulus, New York in Seneca County.

The transfer took place at 3:05 a.m. and was not announced in advance. For security reasons, the Department of Corrections and Community Supervision (DOCCS) wouldn't discuss the details of the transportation. Sweat would spend his first twenty-four hours at Five Points in the infirmary receiving a full medical evaluation, before being moved to a solitary confinement cell equipped with a bed, a writing platform, a toilet, and a facility-controlled shower that would limit movement.

He was put on suicide watch—that is, under constant observation from close enough to intervene should he try to harm himself. He would not be given items that could be used to cut or stab, as well as items that could form an impromptu noose.

Sweat's new home was what was called by prisoners "The Box," a fourteen-by-eight-foot, prefabricated Single Housing Unit (SHU) made of precast concrete five inches thick and reinforced by steel. The SHUs, like everything else at Five Points, were fifteen years old. The units were built elsewhere and carried two at a time by flatbed truck to the prison. At the prison site, the SHUs were bolted together end to end to form a cellblock. This was considered "super-maximum security," or "super-max." Every SHU was perpetually monitored with security cameras. Interaction between Sweat and prison employees was minimized. He would be allowed to leave the SHU only for reasons of severe illness or for visitation with an approved visitor. All activities, including eating and showering, were carefully observed. Sweat would be ordered to face the exterior wall at the back of his cell or lie face down on the bed while a two-inch-thick steel door at the back of the SHU opened for one hour a day. During that hour, Sweat could step out onto a nine-by-seven-foot concrete balcony caged in heavy wire for some "fresh" air, all the time observed by a "console officer" who sat in front of TV screens. In the steel door was a slot, which could only be opened from the outside. Through the slot the prisoner received his meals on a tray. Sweat's new bed was five feet long and thirty-two inches wide, a slab of steel bolted to the wall. His mattress was thin, and he had one small pillow, a pillowcase, and two sheets. Once a week Sweat's prison garb was washed and his linen changed. His stainless-steel toilet had no seat or cover and was flushed by pushing a button on the side of the sink. That sink had no faucet handles, just a push-button spigot. The shower was in the SHU but had no faucet handles or curtain. The console officer controlled the quantity and temperature of the shower water. Sweat, if he chose, could shower as many as three times a week. Showers were each about five minutes long. Sweat would be allowed to use a disposable razor that would be given to him just before he shaved and returned intact immediately after he finished. He would not be allowed to wear a watch or talk on the telephone. He was allowed to write letters. Visitors were allowed once a week, only on Saturdays or Sundays.

To see visitors, guards would lead Sweat to the visiting room in handcuffs and waist chains. During visits, Sweat would sit in a confined cage area, separated from his visitor by wire mesh. Visits were limited to five hours. Sweat was required by the rules to clean his cell three times a week. Come cleaning time, he would be issued a sponge, a toilet brush, mini-broom dusting cloth, and a mop, all of which had to be returned when cleaning was through. After thirty days without disciplinary action, Sweat would be rewarded by being allowed to wear earphones. Another thirty trouble-free days and he would be given library privileges. And a month after that he received sneakers, a pair of shorts, and one additional shower per week.

In the SHU, Sweat's most famous neighbor was serial killer Lemuel Smith, another argument for the death penalty. He was a rapist/murderer who earned historic infamy when he became the first prisoner to kill a female corrections officer.

TEN
BACK TO NORMAL?

With the news of David Sweat's capture came a collective sigh in the village of Dannemora and the surrounding area.[1] The news trucks that had lined Cook Street were gone. Kids were once again allowed to play outside, to ride their bikes up and down the street. Command centers for various law enforcement agencies were dismantled and vanished. Things were back to normal, and Dannemora was back to being just a quiet little town.

One thing the residents knew was the lay of the land, and they loved passing judgment on the presumed route the escapees took. Instead of heading west along Standish Road and Wolf Pond Road before turning north along an old railroad cut, they should have started out heading north.

The return to normalcy was not all good, however. During the three weeks of hubbub, there had been an influx of money from all of those reporters and cops who needed to eat and drink and sleep.

For close to a month the Best Western in Plattsburgh had had to turn on the No Vacancy light. The stores and restaurants had to stay open for longer hours. Coffee sales were through the roof. Plus, prison employees, who constituted a large chunk of the village, raked in the overtime.

With the manhunt over, Clinton Correctional Facility (CCF) prisoners were allowed to return to the yard for exercise. That meant that guards were once again using the external loudspeakers to give instructions. The sound of those announcements, which could be heard well past the prison walls and into the village, were another sign that the crisis was over.

There would be many "Law Enforcement Appreciation" events in the aftermath of the escape. The Malone Rotary Club sponsored one of the first on July 16. Seven men involved in the manhunt were given awards. New York assemblywoman Janet Duprey said, "To those of you who gave so much for so many hours, thank you is not enough."

Sweat-shooter Jay Cook couldn't attend the ceremony because he was still involved in an ongoing investigation. But that didn't mean Cook wasn't a frequent subject of conversation:

"To me, it was a fitting end to this whole nightmare—that a local trooper, born and raised here, worked his entire career here, he was the one who brought this to a very successful conclusion," said Franklin County sheriff Kevin Mulverhill.

The honored officers turned the praise right back on the people of the community. "When it rained," one said, "the people of Clinton County went and bought us a canopy to put over our heads."

Duprey wanted to look ahead, to list the things learned by the escape, and to scheme out ways of fixing the exposed problems: "The focus now is shifting to improving prison safety for corrections officers and inmates," she said, "and that can't be done on a sustaining basis without proper staffing."

A few days earlier, the assemblywoman had received her first tour of CCF since the escape, and she saw the embryonic stages of some of the prison's planned $300,000's worth of improvements and renovations. She said that, from then on, there was also going to be sufficient staffing. Before, there had been guard towers along the wall that were sometimes left unmanned. Now there would be guards up there at all hours—but she was not at liberty to discuss details.[2]

The Malone Rotary Club promised that as soon as the investigation into the shooting and capture of David Sweat was complete, Sergeant Cook would be getting an award too.

The manhunt had generated a vocal nostalgia for the good old days of the electric chair. *Boston Globe* columnist Jeff Jacoby wrote that the Dannemora prison escape demonstrated why, for some prisoners, life without parole was not enough.

The primary argument made by opponents to the death penalty was that life without parole (LWP) was adequate as the ultimate punishment, for it put a person behind bars and kept him or her there until death. Here was a case where LWP had not protected the public from two cold-blooded killers. Only the death penalty, administered swiftly, could do that.

Jacoby concluded, "No living murderer is ever irrevocably incapacitated. Justice may not always require a killer's execution. But when it does, life without parole is an inadequate, and dangerous, substitute."

In mid-July, the corrections system filed formal disciplinary charges against Sweat. If found guilty, a foregone conclusion, he would become a permanent resident at the Single Housing Unit (SHU). These charges were different and separate from any criminal prosecution that might be brought by the Clinton County District Attorney's Office, another foregone conclusion.

DA Andrew Wylie's decisions and ubiquitous TV presence were not without controversy. Many felt the last thing you should do following a case that cost taxpayers a boatload of money was to hold an expensive trial for a guy that everyone already knows is guilty. You couldn't punish him. "What could be gained?" was the question.

The DA, the criticism went, was doing something just to be doing something. But Wylie had a ready though tepid answer for that. He had asked a grand jury to indict Sweat on charges of escaping because he considered it his duty to file charges when a crime has been committed.

Now facing a tough question, the father of five children resorted to an unseemly hypothetical, "Does anyone have children here? Let's say Mr. Sweat got out of jail? OK? He escaped and found your daughter and he raped your daughter. Would you want me to charge him with that? Whether it's escape first degree, whether it's any other charge, he needs to be charged. That's how my office always proceeds."

All of that argument missed the point. You could charge him and you could convict him, but there was no way to *punish* him.

Wylie had at least one supporter in Colin Read, who told the *Wall Street Journal*, "If somebody commits a crime I think you have to go through the motions. It's part of the cost of the judicial system to go through this due process."

Read was a member of Clinton County Legislature, chair of the County Operations Committee, and a member of the Rotary Club from 2005 through 2012. He chaired the finance and economics faculty at State University of New York (SUNY) Plattsburgh and had published a dozen books on local and global finance and economics. He wrote a Sunday column for the *Press-Republican* entitled "Everybody's Business," served on the board of directors of Glens Falls National Bank and Trust Company, and he and his wife Natalie owned North Star Vineyard in Moores, New York.

To this investigation, Read added,

The Dannemora Prison Break cost our county and our state millions of dollars to catch these notorious criminals and displaced thousands of residents for weeks on end. In the end, a ruthless and intoxicated escapee died and another was shot. Numerous families were broken by this terrible experience, and an entire county was frustrated. We are all grateful that, in the end, the escapees were caught, and prison reforms have been initiated.[3] One could argue that it is simply good money after bad to bring the surviving escapee to justice. However, these court costs will likely not be formidable as there are few cases as obvious and as unchallenged as this one. We must insist that those who break the law are properly adjudicated, though. It is true that there is likely little deterrence on a lifer, but the process is not only put in place for those who get caught. It is also to demonstrate to the community, and to other possible future offenders, that we will always pursue justice, even if it is inconvenient. Our district attorney is following the procedures we should all expect.

Chances were good that any resulting trial would be brief and inexpensive. Escape was a pretty easy thing to prove. Besides, even without a prosecution, the escape would be investigated anyway. It was an extraordinary event, and every detail would be picked at. Why not frame that investigation in terms of a prosecution? It was the way the system worked.

Despite this adherence to procedure, it was not a legal given that prison escapees were charged for their escape. Disciplinary actions within the corrections system were sometimes considered sufficient.

In a recent case in Ohio involving two prisoners serving LWP, Allen County prosecutor Juergen Waldick refused to prosecute. This decision spawned criticism as well, but nothing earthshaking. Some pointed out that, should the prisoner's convictions be overturned in an appeal, they could be released, whereas an escaping conviction would function as insurance to keep them behind bars. The argument was valid, but the chances of these guys—one was T. J. Lane who killed three students at Chardon High School—having their convictions overturned were astronomical.

In Iowa on the other hand, escaped inmate Martin Shane Moon was tried for escape, was convicted, and had a superfluous fiver tagged onto the LWP he was already serving.

When a story stayed in the headlines for as long as this one, there was money to be made. This story produced a cottage industry, the sale of Dannemora souvenirs, some of them in questionable taste. At the Clinton County Fair in July, Plattsburgh residents Kenzie and Josh Jerome (with their children Jackson, four, and Abigail, six months) sold an assortment of Matt and Sweat prison-escape tee shirts. Business was brisk. The most popular shirt showed a facsimile of Matt and Sweat's famous farewell note, an offensive Asian version of a smiley face, accompanied by the slogan, "Have a nice day." Also in demand were shirts showing Matt and Sweat's most famous mug shots with the word "KILLED" over Richard Matt's photo and "CAPTURED" over David Sweat's.

For those who didn't feel like wearing their souvenir, there were coffee mugs and posters as well. For out-of-towners, items were available on eBay. Most found the merchandise funny, but there were schoolmarms in every crowd who thought it disgusting that people would try to profit from the situation.

In the aftermath of the great escape and manhunt, the New York State Department of Corrections (NYSDOC) was experiencing anxiety at all levels. The escape and long manhunt had put an unprecedented and unfavorable spotlight on New York State's prison workers. The labor union that represented the state corrections officers, fighting back a collective urge to panic, became completely occupied with damage control. The fear was that, if public opinion was left unchecked, prison guards across the state would suffer for the failures at CCF. On August 8, 2015, the union changed its legal representation. New York State Correctional Officers and Police Benevolent Association (NYSCOPBA) retained the Buffalo-based firm of Lippes Mathias Wexler and Friedman LLP. The previous representation had mostly handled contract negotiations. The new firm was much larger and knew how to lobby. It would, in addition to negotiating contracts, hopefully manage the public relations nightmare and the seemingly inevitable disciplinary hearings. One of the new firm's first statements was to call the escape at Dannemora an "anomaly" yet symptomatic of "a deficiency in the prison" and a "breakdown in the corrections system." The firm explained that this was why the inspector general's office was now focused on what happened, what was wrong, and how to fix it. They concluded on a warm and fuzzy note, that it was the firm's hope that once the analysis of the escape was completed, NYSCOPBA would share a seat at the table when new policies and procedures were drafted.

On Thursday, August 20, David Sweat—in shackles, handcuffs, and a dark green prison jumpsuit—was escorted by six officers in bulletproof vests, with "CERT" written on the flap above the left breast, from the special housing unit at Five Points for five hours to the Plattsburgh courtroom where he was arraigned on new escape charges. One of those officers at all times kept a firm grip on the chain and padlock around Sweat's waist. Sweat was formally charged with two counts of first-degree escape and one count of promoting prison contraband (hacksaw blades), all felonies. Each count could result in an extraneous seven-year prison sentence.

The prisoner was well groomed, his goatee recently trimmed. He wore a splint and brace on his injured arm, which was held in place with a blue sling, and remained silent during the hearing with the exception of acknowledging that his court-appointed attorney, Joe Mucia, was representing him.

Mucia stood. Sweat remained seated. Mucia said to the court, "We would like to waive the reading of the indictment."

Judge Patrick R. McGill said, "Does the defendant wish to enter a plea at this time?"

"Not at this time, your honor."

"I will enter a plea of not guilty for the defendant," the judge said.

And that was it—over in less than a minute. Sweat was escorted out of the courtroom by a guard who held him at the back of his belt with his right hand and by his left sleeve near the shoulder with his left hand. He was led in this fashion back to a waiting corrections department van for the five-hour trip back to Five Points.

The debate continued. Taxpayers said it was a waste of time and money. DA Wylie defended, "They committed a crime of escape in the first degree, and it's my job as prosecutor in this county to prosecute the people that commit crimes in this county. And that's the bottom line: He committed a crime in this county and I am prosecuting him for that crime."

Sweat's appearance in court had been a bit of a surprise. Because of security concerns, Sweat was expected to appear for his arraignment via videoconference.

Joe Mucia told reporters that Sweat appeared calm and in a good mood because he was. Mucia, citing attorney-client confidentiality, refused to convey what Sweat had said to him during the hearing, or discuss any future legal strategy. He did however comment that he found Sweat's personality to be far more subdued than he had thought it would be and that the arraignment hearing had come to the prisoner as a surprise, that he'd been "whisked out of bed" that morning, unaware that he was going for a ride.

On August 22, an appreciation event for those who participated in the manhunt was held at the Dannemora Community Center. Those who attended saw, upon entering, a large sign reading "Thank You" above a blue ribbon. The community center had sold "Clinton Strong" tee shirts at Jim's Sports, with proceeds to pay for the appreciation.

Organized by Kristi Cranford and her mother Paulette Ambrosio, the event featured entertainment by 98.9 WOKO radio, a bouncy house, outdoor games, lots and lots of food, and an appearance by Pipsqueak the clown.

Ambrosio said it was just supposed to be fun, a payback for the sacrifices that those involved in the manhunt endured—sacrifices such as missing the birth of their children, weddings, and graduations. There were a lot of dads out there in the woods who couldn't be home for Father's Day.

Celebrants were arriving by the van-full and then taken back when their shift came up. In attendance were veterans of the great manhunt in a variety of uniforms, local, county, state, and federal; Corrections Emergency Response Team (CERT) teams; and CCF staffers.

One attendee was Keegan Eick, a firefighter trainee when the escape occurred. He was used in the manhunt during the first day of the search—manning roadblocks mostly—until he was replaced by a horde of qualified law enforcement that came flooding into the area.

Even then Eick was on standby, ready to be called out any instant if the need occurred. "I was glad it ended when it did," Eick told WCAX-TV. He'd expected the search to last longer because Matt and Sweat were so smart. Now, he was "just happy it was over."

There was a theme, and the Clinton Strong shirts represented it well. Dannemora had a big nasty prison in it, but the village was a small and nice place to live, a place where people came together in crisis.

"Stuff happens," Eick said. Sure, people came from all over to check out the prison. It didn't change their neighborhood.

Near the end of August, investigators released to the public a video, shot with a GoPro camera mounted to a helmet and showing the full route the inmates took during the escape, from the method they used to exit their cells to the moment they popped up out of the manhole on the other side of the wall.

For the first time the public realized how complex the escape route was, involving climbing down ladders—wading in standing water filled with cigarette butts and other items discarded by guards, or by prisoners through their air vents—navigating catwalks, squeezing through tight openings, and shimmying through the steam pipe. The trip from cell to fresh air in the Village of Dannemora, the video revealed, took twenty minutes.

An itemized accounting of state spending during the manhunt by the New York State Comptroller's Office revealed that the Department of Corrections and Community Supervision (DOCCS) spent $12.6 million to protect the public and hunt down the escapees. The bulk of that money went toward paying prison personnel overtime. The state doled out more than $1 million for meals, travel, and related costs. These numbers were made public only after a Freedom of Information Law request from the Gannett chain of newspapers.

Politicians refused to look at the number as controversial. One was dead, one was back behind bars, and no civilians or law enforcement were injured. That was a very happy ending and worth every penny—and they were certain taxpayers would agree.

But, of course, this wasn't the entire bottom line. State troopers accrued plenty of overtime. The itemized accounting also didn't include federal expenses, in FBI and U.S. Border Patrol and Customs overtime. Even the bean count from the prison system was probably a partial, as there was still a strong chance that "additional invoices may be received at a later date," according to Danielle Barone, the corrections department's associate counsel.

In September 2015 the New York State comptroller Tom DiNapoli announced that overtime costs alone for the approximate 250,000 state employees was headed for a record high, somewhere in the neighborhood of

$700 million. DiNapoli said that the numbers were partially but not entirely due to the unexpected costs of the June prison break.

Ah, troubles inside the Dannemora prison were not over. On August 31, just when the news of the escape and its aftermath was dying down to a daily trickle, the CCF thrust itself back into the headlines. Prison officials confirmed to WPTZ news that the prison was again in lockdown. Why? They didn't want to talk about it. Their statement was as much tap-dancing as information: The prison had taken proactive steps to ensure the safety of staff and others. The facility is expected to return to normal sometime next week.

It was up to the *Press-Republican* to dig out the reason: there had been two brawls in the prison yard on August 27 and 28. The fights resulted in what is called a "facility-wide frisk," at which time a cache of weapons and drugs were uncovered.

CCF officials must've felt they'd seen this movie before. There had been a prison riot just before the escape as well. Was something larger brewing this time as well? The news was particularly unsettling to the traumatized citizens who lived near the prison and had just managed to feel safe again.

One Dannemora resident Beverly Clark told WPTZ, "It's very scary because you never know if they [the prisoners] will take over, jump the guards or get out." Authorities continued to keep mum on the state of the prison but did say during the first week in September that the lockdown was being "eased." Assemblywoman Janet Duprey offered further details. She said the reason for the CCF lockdown was gang-related violence, the most serious of which involved more than sixty inmates and tear gas. Prison gang fights had been a problem across the state. When fights broke out, it was the corrections officers who were responsible for ending them. Her concern was that, if they couldn't get the situation under control, there would be corrections officers getting hurt.

On Tuesday, September 1, 2015, Central New York corrections officers returned to Chateaugay Central School to give back to the community for the hospitality they demonstrated during the manhunt. The CERT team from Rome, New York, brought school supplies and a $500 check. The NYSCOPBA and the prison guards' union donated soft-sided book sacks to hold the supplies. The visiting officers—Sergeant Bob Backus, Sergeant Larry

Greenway, Tom Achen, Scott Pratt, Greg Chrysler, Barry Van Dreason, and Lieutenant Todd Worden—received a standing ovation from the assembly. Janet Duprey was on hand to laud the visiting officers, Franklin County sheriff Kevin Mulverhill, and the state police. Job well done.

During the late spring and early summer excitement, local photographer Damian Battinelli had taken artistic portraits of police, families living near the prison, and the terrain. He fashioned these images into a series called "The Escape," which was on display at the Strand Center for the Arts in Plattsburgh from September 22 until October 2.

About his show, the photographer said that he wanted to capture a different point of view than what folks saw on television. He went for more of a behind-the-scenes-type feel to it. "The days were dreary and raining all the time, so I was just trying to capture that dreariness from the inmates' point of view. Interesting thoughts come when you look at the terrain and think about them running," Battinelli said.

On September 14 and 18, NBC aired Matt Lauer's interview with Joyce Mitchell. While authorities were still trying to figure out how Matt and Sweat got their power tools—Sweat said he and Matt had no power tools; all of the power had been manpower—Mitchell told Matt Lauer that there was a time when Matt admitted to there being power tools and that they fell into the escapees' hands serendipitously. Mitchell said, "Matt actually had told me at one point in one spot they had found a toolbox. And Mr. Sweat picked the lock and they found power tools in it."

During the manhunt, she "prayed and prayed" that there would be no violence. She couldn't explain how much she wanted the men to be recaptured without anyone getting hurt. During that time she of course had been terrified that getting rid of Lyle was still part of the plan, so she kept her husband on a short leash.

"I didn't let my husband out of my sight," she said.[4]

Regarding Lyle's behavior during the aftermath of the escape, she couldn't praise him strongly enough.

"He is a very amazing man," she said. "And he is a blessing from God for me. He's a terrific husband. A very, very loving father."

NBC News did not allow its audience to take Mitchell's explanation of events at face value. She had misbehaved in a shockingly reckless way, and some dissembling was to be expected. To get the critical, psychological perspective on Mitchell's tale, NBC went to Dr. Phil McGraw of the *Dr. Phil* show. He said not only was there dissembling but also he "took exception" to her story.

It wasn't that he didn't believe potentially sociopathic maximum-security prisoners were capable of the type of manipulation, con artistry, and violence that Mitchell described. He simply didn't believe that this was what happened to her. Mitchell, he said, demonstrated a psychological tactic called "talking yourself out of a situation that you behaved yourself into." Mitchell wasn't describing a spur-of-the-moment decision that she later regretted. She was rather trying to explain away a "pattern of behavior over a period of time."

Mitchell wanted us to believe that her troubles were such that she had no one to turn to. Dr. Phil didn't buy it. She was presenting herself as easy prey. He said it was rare for people not to have "safety zones" where they could reach out for help and not feel isolated (although Mitchell did face a difficult problem, having misbehaved in a way that could lose her both her job and her husband). He suspected that, had she wanted to, she could have prevented the hopelessness of isolation.

Dr. Phil said, "The number-one tool of the abuser, the manipulator, is isolation. They cut you off from family, friends, church, and resources. But she was not cut off from any of those things."

Matt Lauer was more willing than Dr. Phil to take Mitchell's statements at face value. In an interview with WPTZ's Stephanie Gorin, Lauer said that he agreed with Mitchell's characterization that she had painted herself into a corner.

"She is in a situation right now that I'm sure she never dreamed she'd be in, but it is because of her own actions that she's there," Lauer said.

She did have a friendship with the escapees, and she admitted that she was wrong. She became too close with them, crossed the lines, and crossed the boundaries. It started small, the smuggling of cookies and brownies, and escalated. She talked about seeing the warning signs, realizing that she was crossing the line, but she was, for whatever reason, unable to do what she should have done to end it. The plan, she said, was for her to show up in her Jeep and park by the manhole cover with a change of clothing, a tent, a shotgun, and fishing poles in the car. She would pretend that she was on the phone as they popped up like gophers from the manhole. They were supposed to get changed into clean clothes and then head back to Mitchell's house where they would find Lyle, already unconscious from the pills she'd given him, and kill him. But there was no way she was going to take part in any of that. She certainly didn't want her husband killed, and allowing the escapees use of her Jeep was tantamount to suicide. So, even though her actions may have helped the men get out of the prison, her inactions did much to keep the escape from being successful.

Did she feel remorse?

"Very much so. If you can believe her," Lauer said.

Asked what surprised him most about Mitchell, Lauer guessed it was that—despite the training civilian employees were supposed to get when they went to work in a prison and although they'd seen a video warning them of the games inmates played when manipulating others—this seemingly normal woman allowed herself to get into this situation and didn't see the many opportunities she'd had along the road to get out of it. Was Mitchell fully to blame for this? No. Was she completely innocent? "Absolutely not," Lauer said.

Mitchell had insisted that the interview air before her sentencing, in the hopes that her performance would kindle such warm forgiveness that her punishment would be lightened. It didn't work out that way.

Sheriff David Favro said that he didn't know anyone who bought into Joyce Mitchell's act. He theorized that, if there were people out there who believed her, they weren't from the North Country. In that neck of the woods there was always someone you could talk to, always a sympathetic ear and shoulder. She said she didn't have anyone she could tell. Nobody bought that.

Joyce Mitchell had her hands cuffed in front of her and was wearing her white-and-black-striped prison outfit as guards led her into the Plattsburgh courtroom on September 28 for her sentencing. In the gallery was husband Lyle Mitchell, his face hanging, apparently under the weight of his mustache. There was a dullness in his eyes, and his face hung as if weighted down by the gravity of his situation.

Judge Ryan found himself face-to-face with a crumbling Joyce Mitchell. She looked about to dissolve. He gave her an opportunity to plead for mercy, and her already brimming emotions quickly got the best of her, so she blubbered as she read her two-page statement:

"Please let me start by saying how sorry I am, how much remorse I have." She paused and looked back at Lyle, mouthing the words, "I'm sorry."

Again facing Judge Ryan, she continued: "If I could take it all back I would. I can't begin to explain how sorry I am for all of this. I am fifty-one years old, and this is by far the worst mistake I have made in my life. I know I should have told someone. I live with regret every day and will for the rest of my life. I've never been so disappointed in myself. I've not only let myself down, but my family. I am seeking mental help and counseling. I acknowledge my actions and am still trying to understand why I made the choices I did. I realize I need to be responsible for my actions." She begged the court not to send her to prison, offering to gladly wear an ankle bracelet.

DA Wylie said Mitchell had cooperated with investigators and had given up her teaching certificate as per the terms of her plea deal. He also noted that New York State was seeking restitution against Mitchell.

Mitchell's attorney reminded the court that the escapees used power tools to make their escape, which his client did not supply, so they must have come from elsewhere. Just sayin'.

Judge Kevin Ryan was like Dr. Phil. He didn't believe a word of what Mitchell said. Her story had changed so often; now it seemed more of a concoction than truth.

"Ms. Mitchell," Judge Ryan said. "I just don't find your explanation credible. Your husband's life would not have been more in danger by exposing the plot to escape."

Her statement, he said, had been filled with contradictions. She said she wanted to be responsible for her actions but then offered a laundry list of excuses. She said she didn't know why she helped the prisoners and then said it was because she feared for the lives of her family. She knew that killing her husband was part of the plan, yet she admitted to having sexual contact with Matt and giving Sweat dirty pictures. She wanted to protect her husband and yet helped his potential murderers to freedom. She wasn't a newbie, unfamiliar with the psychology of a maximum-security prison. She was a veteran, a supervisor, and had been trained in the very psychological techniques that the escapees had used on her.

The impact, the judge said, of Mitchell's actions on the community was difficult to measure. Terrorized residents lived in fear or left their homes. Millions of dollars of taxpayer money was spent on overtime costs for law enforcement, corrections, and public information officers.

"You did terrible things," he concluded. "At any time you could have stopped the escape from happening." Judge Ryan then sentenced Mitchell to two and a third years to seven years in prison for first-degree promoting prison contraband, and one year to run concurrently for criminal facilitation. In addition, she was fined $6,000. A "restitution hearing" was scheduled for November 6.

Mitchell was led from the courtroom, beginning her transition period from jail to prison. She had a head start on many convicts. She knew the ins and outs of the state corrections system. As she departed, the star of the show, she turned and mouthed the words "I love you" to her husband, who looked gloomier than ever.

Afterward, the district attorney told reporters he had hoped the penalty would be even worse. Mitchell's actions were an insult to the families of murder victims William Rickerson and Kevin Tarsia.[5]

Asked what he thought of Mitchell's performance, he noted that once again she was making excuses, still doling out truth as if it were a precious commodity. When she did tell the truth it was only begrudgingly, when she was presented with certain details she couldn't circumvent with lies. After each interview, she'd said that she had provided the whole truth, and "every time she later admitted to leaving out details."

The DA would have liked additional charges—enhanced charges, because of her criminal culpability. He complained that his hands were tied by what "the state allowed us to prosecute her with." The DA would have liked to have prosecuted Mitchell for conspiracy to commit murder (regarding the plot on her husband) and sexual abuse of an inmate (regarding sexual activity with Matt, since an inmate cannot give consent) but did not think he would be able to prove those charges beyond a reasonable doubt.

He felt he had an ethical obligation to not prosecute on charges he didn't think he could prove. "If you want to talk about wasting money, that would have been a complete waste of money." Therefore, his best bet was to offer Mitchell a deal, one that she accepted. Justice had been accomplished swiftly and economically.

Inspector general Catherine Leahy Scott agreed, stating that her office's investigation—conducted by more than a dozen investigators with "state and national experience," including county, state, and federal police; certified fraud examiners; and computer forensic specialists—would make it clear that Mitchell was not a victim but a convicted felon. The eventual report on that probe would, she promised, detail how Mitchell spent months assisting two cold-blooded killers. With criminal intent, Scott concluded, Mitchell used her position to abuse and manipulate systemic prison security lapses.

The DA was asked how long Mitchell would actually spend behind bars. He replied that she would be eligible for merit release after serving five-sixths of her minimum sentence and eligible for parole after completing the minimum sentence.

Reporters scoured the area looking to civilians for comment. How did the person on the street feel about Mitchell's sentencing? Opinions, predictably, widely varied.

One lady was sympathetic to Mitchell. "I've made mistakes in my life. Nothing of that caliber, of course. I hope her life isn't ruined only because she's a fellow human being."

Another woman said, "I believe she feels sorry and she regrets what she did—but she did it."

A third saw Mitchell as a phony: "Her apology, the tears, that was all just a play role, just like she did getting them out."

A local man thought in terms of the psychological damage done because of Mitchell's actions—or lack of actions: "A large portion of the local population was terrorized," he said. Others agreed. They'd all been victims. Folks locked themselves in, feeling vulnerable, afraid—especially at night.

Another villager said that the real problem was that, once the threat was over, the fear didn't go away. Posttraumatic stress was involved: "My two kids are still scared. They can't stop thinking about killers on the loose. They don't want to be alone in their room. They're sleeping on the floor of my room."

The *Adirondack Daily Enterprise* editorialized that Mitchell's plea for mercy fell apart in a couple of key ways. Mitchell claimed her fear for her own safety and the safety of her family drove her to do what she did—except that was the revised version of the story. She'd already admitted to interrogators that she started her relationship with the escapees because she was lonesome and starved for attention. In her first statement to police, she told a story in which she was a willing coconspirator with Matt and Sweat, until the very last moment when she decided she couldn't go through with it and stood up the escapees at the manhole. Back then she had described Matt and Sweat as something akin to sideline boyfriends. There wasn't a single mention of coercion. If she was afraid of the escapees, she failed to mention it. She hadn't mentioned fear. She was scared of punishment perhaps but not scared of Matt and Sweat. She promised them not only that she would help them escape but also that she would run away with them to Mexico. She was a bored and horny woman who'd let things get out of hand.

That version of the story was long gone by the time she sobbed at her sentencing. Her revised edition didn't make sense. She knew the rules. She knew what would have happened had she reported the escape plan. Matt and Sweat would have been placed in solitary confinement, and it was doubtful they had the juice outside the facility to put a hit on someone who ratted them out.

"We don't believe Ms. Mitchell was a victim in this case. We think she enjoyed flirting with danger," the editorial read. Even though things did not turn out as Mitchell had planned, she still did the things she did with criminal intent.

Yes, terror, sometimes traumatizing terror, was Joyce Mitchell's product, and she should never walk free again. And that was from locals where you'd figure Mitchell would be most apt to catch a break.

Many were glad the court business was through. It was all they showed on TV, and people were getting sick of her face. Boo hoo hoo. The next day, Mitchell was committed to the Bedford Hills Correctional Facility, an all-female, maximum-security state prison in Westchester County, just north of and adjacent to New York City.

Soon after Mitchell's sentencing the DA Wylie was addressing the Plattsburgh Noon Rotary Club and was asked if here wasn't a large portion of the puzzle still missing, that the escapees had to have had a lot more help than was known in order to escape: How could they know which manhole to come up out of? They must've had a blueprint of the prison and a detailed map of the area surrounding the prison."

Wylie discouraged that kind of talk. He said that there was of course a *possibility* that Matt and Sweat had help that authorities know nothing about. The

DA said that actual drawn blueprints were not prerequisites for the escape. A clever observer, he said, who spent a lot of time inside the Dannemora walls, might find visual aboveground clues as to how the internal infrastructure was designed. Much could be seen from the third floor-tailor shops, which had windows higher than the prison's outer wall. The escapees could look over the wall and see the outside world. Plus, they had probably noticed the "bump in the courtyard" and correctly assumed that it was where the steam pipe traveled from the prison blocks to the tailor shop and out through the wall. Wylie concluded, "So after years of being there, they could identify that as the source of exit from the facility."

There really had been a lot of construction going on in the prison's inner workings, and the story that the prisoners found power tools laying around or abandoned down there was not implausible, nor was the notion that they might have found blueprints or maps down there as well, left behind by a working crew.

Still, he conceded, those were maybes and could've beens. The bottom line is that it was an impressive and completely unlikely thing that Matt and Sweat had pulled off: "It's amazing to me that they were able to do that," Wylie said.

Wylie was asked about the cost and who was going to pay it. He started by applauding the law enforcement officers, corrections officers, and family members who collaborated to bring this story to a happy ending, and then noted that the governor's office would pick up the bill.

Down in Elmira, at the site of another maximum-security prison, one only a few miles from the New York/Pennsylvania border, training sessions were using the escape in Dannemora as a teaching point for future corrections officers.

A recent corrections-school graduate said the CCF escape taught him a big lesson, not to let his guard down. He had learned to take his job seriously—every day, every minute. Because you never knew. Anything could happen at any time. Never get lax. Do your inspections properly. Be firm, fair, and consistent at all times.

Shane Hobel was one of the nation's five most elite trackers, an expert in both wilderness and urban survival skills, and ran the Mountain Scout Survival School in the Hudson Valley.

Hobel was raised by his mother and his grandfather to be a tracker. He studied under a Native elder and attended Tom Brown Jr.'s tracker school. He didn't understand why law enforcement agencies, when pursuing outlaws, didn't employ forensic trackers. He told this investigation that, if he had been deputized to participate in the hunt, he could have captured Matt and Sweat on day nine.

It was time for law enforcement to be rid of the bureaucracy and the ego, time for them to admit that as trackers even the most skilled detectives were amateurs. Hobel would have been glad to help, and he wasn't concerned with making a name for himself. He didn't want credit. They could take the credit. He just wanted to get it done.[6]

The key reason Matt and Sweat were brought to justice was that the escapees were amateurs as well. They may have had the sense of direction to get out of the prison, but once out their internal compass failed them.

Matt and Sweat's plan was spoiled from the get-go. They came out the manhole, the getaway car wasn't there, and they had no plan B. It was just, "Oh shit, into the woods."

If they had survival skills, they could have built tools and made clothes; they could have gone deep, deep into the woods, and they might never have been found. Instead, *they needed to rely on civilization*, they required modern utilities, and so they had to cling to the edges of the wilderness, seek out cabins and homes to break into.

Hobel pointed out that as long as they needed civilization to survive, they needed to risk encounters with their pursuers, which made their eventual capture inevitable.

And the Adirondacks were no joke. The area was massive, formidable, and grueling. In the winter, the Arctic weather in that area could be worse than in Alaska. They were drinking water out of streams and ponds, and that gave them dysentery—evidence of which was found in discarded underwear.

Hobel hoped that the next time something like this happened, well-trained trackers might join (i.e., lead) the search. The police today over-relied on K-9 teams, which were not as reliable as they would have you believe. The dogs could only follow one scent at a time, and it was always the latest scent they've been told to follow. A man who was a professional tracker, on the other hand, could do more than follow footprints or sniff out a scent. He could *think* like those he was tracking. He could itemize and prioritize the escapee's wants and needs. The man he was hunting would need shelter (or fire for warmth if no shelter was available), a source of drinking water, and food.

CCF historian Walter "Pete" Light said that a number of things had to come together for Matt and Sweat to get under the wall. "They took their time," Light said.[7] "They were sharp." Plus, New York State wanted to save money. The notion that getting over (or under) the wall was impossible led to complacency, and an austerity budget. Staff during the overnight hours was skeletal. The thinking was that additional personnel weren't necessary.

Light had been a prison guard for more than thirty years but noted that, during his stint, there was no Honor Block. Honor Block was a reward for in-prison behavior and not affected by what the prisoners did to be sent to Dannemora in the first place.

You could kill a cop, you could torture a man to death during the commission of a robbery, or you could have a history of escape attempts, but if you obeyed rules in CCF, you would be rewarded for your compliance.

Clearly, in retrospect, Light commented, there were those who shouldn't be rewarded with new freedoms no matter how compliant they were after their arrival in Little Siberia.

A pretrial hearing for Sweat scheduled for September 29 was postponed. Reason: Mucia and Wylie were dealing. Mucia said it was his hope that they could settle without an expensive trial.

If there was any uncertainty as to whether Matt and Sweat had exceeded their fifteen minutes of fame and had become a lasting part of popular culture, it was erased on Tuesday, October 6, when the following clue appeared on the nightly TV game show *Jeopardy*:

"THE ESCAPE OF 2 PRISONERS FROM THE CCF IN THIS STATE
LED TO A LONG 2015 MANHUNT."

Answer: "What is New York?"

The category was "STATE OF EMERGENCY."

Political cartoonists were lampooning the more absurd aspects of the case as well. In one example, Dana Summers of the Tribune Content Agency drew a surprisingly forgiving caricature of Joyce Mitchell. Wearing a yellow apron over her black-and-white-striped prison suit, she was on a TV set, like the French Chef or the Frugal Gourmet, and standing in front of a sign that read "JOYCE MITCHELL'S COOKING FOR INMATES SHOW." In the red polka-dotted oven mitts that covered her hands she held a tray of something fresh from the oven, and she was saying, "And voila! You have my famous bribery baked goods! . . . Next we'll be making my mouth-watering beef burgundy a la hacksaw!"

ELEVEN
AUTUMN
AND
WINTER

By October 2015, there were three separate investigations underway regarding the escape, but none of them were cooperating with the media. The inspector general, the Department of Corrections, and the FBI were all probing away.

They didn't get much cooperation so they didn't give any. Prison employees will tell you: what happens in prison stays in prison. So good luck to investigators trying to get employees to squeal. Sure, stuff happens "off the book." It was nobody's business, nobody on the outside. Prisoners will talk, sure, but who could believe them? Who *should* believe them?

In was frustrating for investigators. But they forged on into the autumn—how could they give up? There was such a disconnect between what happened and the known facts that it drove them nuts.

Also in October, a Texas-based psychic sued New York State for the $100,000 reward money.[1] The psychic, Eric Drake, said in the suit that he called the governor's office back in June and provided him with information that led to the apprehension of Matt and Sweat.

The suit read in part: "Plaintiff foresaw the following concerning David Sweat and Richard Matt: 1) The two inmates separated for some reason. 2) That the police were walking right by or over them when they were hiding. 3) That Joyce Mitchell had more information than had appeared, and that the police should play 'bad cop' 'bad cop' to get more information. 4) That one of them was heading for mountains and clear rivers."

These predictions, Drake claimed, were "right on point." The lawsuit went on to say, "The odds of someone without the gifts of the Spirit of God, guessing on the information that the Plaintiff provided to the authorities is probably less than one out of twenty-five billion."

Drake claimed that when he later called to claim the reward money he found that no one would tell him how to file for payment. Drake said he planned to use the reward money to publish a book of prophecies "regarding the United States of America, which are a thousand times greater than the suffering of the Great Depression."

Apparently addicted to prognostication, Drake couldn't get through the lawsuit without throwing in a few unrelated predictions, that no one named Clinton, Trump, or Biden would become president in 2016 and that the Obama family would soon face deep sorrow.

A quick look into Drake's resume revealed that he once claimed to have successfully predicted the death of elderly people, such as President Obama's grandmother, and claimed to have cured cancer patients through prayer.

A judge waived the fees normally attached to filing a lawsuit because Drake only had $80 in the bank.

In November, all three of those charged in connection with the escape appeared individually in a Clinton County courtroom.

On November 4, at his arraignment, Gene Palmer waived his right to have a grand jury hear his case, and though Palmer was seated next to him, his lawyer entered a plea of not guilty on his behalf to three charges.[2] Palmer was next scheduled to appear in court on January 8, 2016, for a pretrial conference. Following the hearing, attorney William Dreyer said that he and district attorney Andrew Wylie were negotiating a deal but gave no details. (The January 8 court hearing was held without any progress in the case. At that hearing Wylie announced that he was "ready to go to trial" if necessary.[3])

Joyce Mitchell appeared a few days later for a restitution hearing that lasted less than ten minutes.[4] Judge Kevin K. Ryan ordered Mitchell to repay New York State $79,841, plus a 10 percent surcharge.[5] The amount was based on the cost of repairing the cells formerly occupied by Richard Matt and David Sweat, damage to the steam pipes, and a brick wall. The restitution had nothing to do with the cost of the manhunt, which was estimated to be in the neighborhood of $23 million. That was because the law said restitution could only compensate for damages made during the commission of a crime, not in its aftermath.

On November 12, the Franklin County District Attorney's Office made it official: the use of force in the killing of Richard Matt and the capture of David Sweat was justified.[6] Both escapees were given an opportunity to surrender before they were shot.

The next day, Sweat pleaded guilty to two felony counts of first-degree escape and a felony count of promoting prison contraband for possessing hacksaw blades. He was scheduled to be sentenced on February 3, a mere formality.

Simultaneous to the hearing, the inspector general released a statement noting that Sweat had taken his time to "manipulate and extort" the Clinton Correctional Facility's (CCF) "profound lapses in security" and for the umpteenth time promised to quickly complete that office's investigation, which would not only detail how the escape was accomplished but also propose reforms that would prevent a repeat of this episode.

As the surviving known players in the escape worked their way through the judicial system, frustrated New York State lawmakers proposed changes in the law that might discourage future escape attempts. Two bills in particular drew attention.[7]

The first was the "Prisoner Privilege Limitation Law," proposed by Assemblyman James Tedisco, the House Democratic whip. The bill proposed that prisoners considered the worst of the worst, a category into which Matt and Sweat comfortably fit, would no longer have access to street clothes.

It also called for an across-the-board elimination of anything resembling "Honor Block" privileges for violent prisoners. If you have been convicted of a violent crime, the bill said, no amount of in-prison good behavior could earn prisoners additional freedoms such as being allowed to cook their own food.

Discussing his bill, Tedisco noted that "Matt and Sweat only behaved well in Dannemora so they could escape from Dannemora."

The third part of the bill would require trained corrections officers to supervise all contact between inmates and civilian employees. Tedisco was not against incentives for inmates and encouraging good behavior, only against those incentives for the most dangerous prisoners who were apt to manipulate the system with their earned privileges.

The other bill, authored by state senator Betty Little, would increase prison terms for those who helped inmates escape. Maximum penalties would increase to twenty-five years in prison.

As the foliage became painted with a variety of autumnal hues, frustration grew on a number of fronts. It had now been *five months* since the governor ordered an inspector general (IG) report on the escape, and there was still no report, no release date. The only comment from Catherine Leahy Scott's office was that they were working on an "expedient and thorough" report based upon an "extensive and multifaceted" investigation. (On December 21, Scott finally got around to interviewing Gene Palmer, who remained the only prison guard to face charges in connection with the escape. There was still no indication when the report would be finished and ready to be issued.[8])

James Tedisco likened waiting for the IG report to waiting for Halley's Comet. It was frustrating. No real reforms could be put in place until after the report was released with its anticipated recommendations. He noted the proximity between the IG's and governor's offices ("down the hall") and hoped that it didn't signal collusion.[9]

James Miller, a spokesperson for the prison guards' union, the New York State Correctional Officers and Police Benevolent Association (NYSCOPBA), said he was concerned about employee safety in light of future reforms. Too many corrections officers, he said, were suffering injuries such as broken jaws and multiple concussions. From 2011 to 2015 the number of prisoners in the state system had stayed the same, but the number of violent prisoners had gone up by 6 percent—with a corresponding rise in attacks on corrections officers and inmate-on-inmate crime. Miller hoped the controversy over the escape would stimulate much needed changes, and he was aware that to get the government to make changes all too often "something drastic" had to happen as a catalyst, which of course it had.[10]

On November 19, the National Law Enforcement Officers Memorial Fund named Sergeant Jay Cook as their "Officer of the Month" for the month of November. Craig Floyd, chairman and CEO of the memorial fund, said, "Sergeant Cook's recognition and his quick response in apprehending the suspect were integral to capturing a cop killer and securing a community that had been on high alert."[11]

In December the New York State Assembly Correction Committee and committee chairman Daniel O'Donnell, a Democrat representing Manhattan, launched a probe of New York's prison system, designed to examine prison system operations and recent instances of inmate abuse.[12]

Karen Murtagh, executive director of Prisoners' Legal Services of New York, testified regarding the many letters she had received following the prison escape from inmates remaining in CCF's Honor Block, complaining that they had been taken by interrogators to rooms without cameras to be beaten and threatened. Some were transferred to other prisons or placed in solitary confinement. Murtagh suggested that there be a change in policy regarding how violent incidents were handled. She said reforms should include "training on de-escalation techniques, annual psychological screening of corrections staff, replacement of upper-level staff in institutions with high levels of brutality, and mandating severe consequences for abusive staff."[13]

Professor Michael Mushli of Pace Law School, cochair of the American Bar Association Subcommittee on Prison Oversight, was asked to rate New York's prison oversight on a scale of one to ten and gave it a "zero point five." He pointed out what most understood instinctively, that because prisons are a "closed-off" part of society, without "transparency and public accountability" there were bound to be "horrible things" happening.[14]

Also testifying was a lawyer representing the family of a thirty-year-old Fishkill Correctional Facility inmate who was beaten to death by guards in April 2015.

The prison guards' union refused to participate in the hearing, and testimony regarding shoring up security at New York's prisoners was postponed until after the release of the inspector general's report. No one held their breath.

By years end, the inspector general's office told the *Press-Republican* that "hundreds of interviews with staff and inmates" at CCF had been completed, but they were still "piecing together" what happened.[15]

Some changes had already taken place at the prison, of course. The guard towers were now manned at all times, and there had been added to the schedule thirty eight-hour shifts, mostly during the afternoon and at night. At CCF anyway, Honor Block was a distant memory.

On December 7, Sergeant Cook told the *Today* show that he was extremely thankful to the people from all over the United States and Canada who'd written him cards and letters of thanks and praise. The manhunt, he recalled, was the most "stressful and tiring" detail of his career. He thanked everyone involved in the manhunt, everyone who worked tirelessly and put his or her own safety at risk on a daily basis. He talked about how miserable the manhunt would have been if it weren't for the members of the local communities who offered food, drink, and supplies, and the fire departments who never failed to provide shelter when it rained. He didn't understand why he was the one who'd encountered Sweat, but he was glad that his training helped him do the right thing and that the whole detail came to such a satisfactory conclusion. He didn't feel special, as anyone with his training and his position would have done the same thing under the same circumstances. He didn't think the events on that fateful day had changed him. He still enjoyed his job as much as ever and hadn't given any thought to retirement. His two daughters had college plans, and he and his wife wanted to support that effort the best they could. People presumed he was traumatized to a degree by what happened, but he didn't think so. He slept fine. He didn't even think much anymore about the manhunt unless someone brought it up—and of course, people were still frequently bringing it up.

He ended his statement with a bit of philosophy, a look at the big picture: "I hope our nation can come together to fight our enemies and not fight ourselves. We face pure evil, and law enforcement needs help, not distraction."[16]

A motif of the escape's aftermath was "Thank goodness that no one was hurt." The feared carnage hadn't come to pass. The only injuries were to the escapees themselves. This slogan ignored the death of thirty-five-year-old Plattsburgh man James Kohl, who was shot accidentally with a gun that was kept "loaded and handy" because of the fear caused by the escape. The incident also occurred during the early morning hours of July 5, after a solid night of Fourth of July drinking—so the escape happily shared the blame.[17] It was lucky that more incidents like this hadn't occurred. The area was "locked and loaded," and there were frequent tales of families taking turns with armed-guard duty.[18]

On December 8, District Attorney Wylie sent letters to some Clinton County residents saying, "Please take notice that Eavesdropping Warrants authorizing the interception of telephone communications were issued by Honorable John Lahtinen on June 7, 2015, with extensions were granted on several dates, as required by law. All interceptions of telephone communications terminated on June 13, 2015. During the period of authorized interceptions, your conversations were intercepted." The letter concluded by asking the recipient to please *not* respond.

Say what?

In explanation, Wylie told WPTZ-TV19 that the phone taps were put in place to listen in on the phone calls to and from David Sweat, Richard Matt, Joyce Mitchell, and Gene Palmer, and their family members. The DA refused further comment on the eavesdropping.

That story didn't wash with Cathy Phillips, a Malone woman who received one of the letters. She told WPTZ that she'd never broken the law, knew none of the principals in the escape, and yet her phone was tapped. "I'm just so angry," she said. "You tell me why they did, why they started tapping my line the very next day [after the escape]. I feel violated that they can do this."

Under state law, the district attorney had to inform Phillips of the tap within ninety days. Phillips's letter was dated December 8, 2015, but did not arrive until January 5, 2016.

In December, the state assembly passed a law requiring all prison guards and other staff members with direct inmate contact to sit through eight hours of training annually in how to recognize signs of poor mental health. The previous rule required eight hours of training in the subject when employees were brand new to the job, and that was it. Now there would be a yearly refresher course. Governor Andrew Cuomo, signing the bill into law, said it was important because mental illness was a trigger in many incidents of prison violence, whether that violence is to the self, a fellow inmate, or a corrections officer.[20]

With the New Year came more troubling news regarding both CCF and the entire state prison system. Although the inspector general's report was still nowhere to be seen, information was coming out because of a trial being held in Albany City Court in which a former Department of Corrections and Community Supervision (DOCCS) director of operations was charged with official misconduct. The trial, plus interviews conducted by the local press, indicated that the internal affairs unit was bogged down by nepotism, cover-ups, and "unbridled sexual harassment."[21]

This was pertinent to our story because internal affairs investigators were said to have privately criticized members of their own department who looked into charges that Joyce Mitchell had behaved inappropriately with a prisoner (David Sweat) and yet allowed her to keep her job. If Mitchell had been fired for taking photographs of her own private parts and giving them to Sweat in 2014, she obviously would not have been in a position to aid the escapees the way she did in 2015.

On January 9 and 10, 2016, the Titus Mountain Ski Center, the Upper Lodge of which was used as a headquarters by manhunters following the escape, held a "Law Enforcement Appreciation Weekend," during which all cops with active-duty badges and their immediate families were allowed free skiing and riding. During the weekend there was also a dedication ceremony in the Upper Lodge to the new "The Great Escape" history installment.[22]

While Clinton County was determined to go through the legal motions regarding the surviving escapee, Franklin County, which could have charged Sweat for breaking and entering various camps in the county, wanted nothing of meaningless court activity. On January 26, county manager Donna Kissane announced that the county would "not pursue additional charges."[23]

To many, Governor Cuomo's State of the State address on January 13 was about as exciting as an oral rendering of a grocery store shopping list, but everyone perked up and the applause became enthusiastic when Cuomo introduced Sergeant Jay Cook.[24]

Cuomo said, "The climax of the event was a truly heroic event, where a single trooper confronted one of the escapees. It was just that trooper and that escapee a stone's throw from the Canadian border."

Cook rose, and the audience joined him on their feet.

And the beat went on. On January 22, three violent California inmates— Jonathan Tieu, Bac Duong, and Hossein Nayeri—escaped from the Men's Central Jail in Santa Ana, California, by sawing through a metal grate and half-inch-thick steel bars.[25] Instead of climbing down as Matt and Sweat had, these escapees climbed up through plumbing tunnels to the roof, where they rappelled down five stories with a rope of tied bed sheets. The men were awaiting trial for kidnapping, torture, murder, and assault with a deadly weapon. Authorities said that it was impossible for the men to have escaped without help from inside the jail. Six days later, a female civilian employed at the jail was arrested. She was an English teacher at the local community college who for the previous six months had taught English as a second language at the jail, and had developed "some type of relationship" with one of the escapees. Among the items she had allegedly supplied to the men were maps.

In a week all three were captured and back behind bars, but shit, it all sounded so *familiar*.

During the first week of February 2016, Sweat appeared in Clinton County court regarding his escape from Dannemora. Shackled and surrounded by guards, Sweat said, "I would like to apologize to the community and the people who felt fear, and felt it was necessary to leave their homes or their community because of the escape. That was never my intent and I deeply apologize for that."[26]

In response, Judge Patrick McGill said, "I don't know what you were thinking. According to a report by the Seneca County Probation Department you tried to escape to show the shortcomings of the correctional system, or as a protest for treatment received from correction officers. Did you do anything to bring about a change in the facility by organizing, complaining, or lodging complaints with regard to treatment or decisions made in the correctional facility? Maybe if you had expended the energy you expended in escaping to reform the program and conditions in the prison, it might have changed the outcome."

Judge McGill sentenced Sweat to a range of seven to fourteen years in prison, a penalty to be added to his existing life sentence. Sweat was also ordered to pay $79,841 in restitution. District Attorney Wylie explained that, should Sweat be paid for an interview or otherwise come into money, the state would claim that money.[27]

At the end of February, it was Gene Palmer's turn to learn his fate. He pleaded guilty to the charges against him and was sentenced to six months in prison and $5,375 in fines and court surcharges. Palmer also agreed to resign from his job. Palmer's attorney, William Dreyer, said it was unlikely that Palmer would serve the entire six months. Dreyer said, "His state of mind is that he's happy that it's over with. He's unhappy that he did what he did. He's remorseful about what he did. He ruined a twenty-eight-year career. He's looking forward to getting this behind him."[28]

Although Catherine Leahy Scott released statements following the sentencing of both Sweat and Palmer, and her office let slip that her report on the escape was due to be released "any day," the weeks continued to roll by without any report being released.

In the middle of March, assemblywoman Janet Duprey honored Corrections Emergency Response Team (CERT) leaders in Albany for their heroic efforts during the manhunt. She discussed the long hours they put in and the difficult conditions they endured, and then read their names one by one while members of the state assembly stood and gave them thunderous applause.[29] On April 1, District Attorney Wylie announced that, instead of running for a judge's position in the fall, he would instead seek reelection as DA.[30]

Exposed for all to see by the troubling events of 2015 at CCF was the mismatch between the prison guards union—the New York State Correctional Officers and Police Benevolent Association, twenty thousand strong—and the state corrections department's internal affairs unit, recently boosted to 150 strong. The *New York Times* pointed out in April 2016 that prison guards operate under the assumption that they can do whatever they want to because there are little or no consequences. "A guard could be found guilty of brutalizing an inmate and not be fired," the *Times* reported.[31] It was embarrassing and frustrating for those assigned to keep guards on the straight and narrow.

That month, the corrections department announced that it was fed up and determined to be more effective when battling the guards' union. But it wasn't going to be easy. There were parts of the state, like Clinton County, where prisons were the largest employers. Elected officials in those areas were loath to cross the union, resulting in protection for the union from the state legislature.

The *Times* pointed out that Governor Cuomo, who oversaw a supposed strengthening of internal affairs, also has a chief of staff who (1) formerly worked for the guards' union, and (2) is the daughter of an Albany lobbyist whose firm pocketed more than $500,000 from the union.

Under current rules, the guards have it made. They do not have to answer questions from outside law enforcement agencies; all disciplinary actions against guards, when they do occur, are kept secret from the public. Investigators have been refused entrance to facilities and, on at least one occasion at CCF, an investigator was attacked by a corrections officer and had his jaw broken.

The result, the *Times* says, is brutality. The brutes go unpunished while whistleblowers suffer.

In March 2016 the governor's office introduced a bill to make it easier to fire bad guards (lowering the threshold for termination from a felony to a misdemeanor) but couldn't find a legislator to sponsor it.

In May CCF again made the news in an unpleasant fashion, when it was reported that a twenty-five-year-old inmate named Terry Cooper had died. He had been serving a twelve-year sentence for assault and attempted robbery. The Clinton County coroner refused to say how the inmate died, adding that no information would be made public until the official report was issued and that could take up to four months.[32] This did nothing to squelch feelings that bad things were happening inside those Dannemora walls.

On May 25 the New York State Police honored, among others, Major Charles Guess, citing his leadership, and Sergeant Jay Cook, for his capture of Sweat. The men received the Superintendent's Commendation Awards.[33]

In June 2016, just past the one-year anniversary of the escape, the inspector general's report was released, blaming the escape on "longstanding, systemic failures in management and oversight by DOCCS."[34] CCF at the time of the escape exhibited "a culture of complacency," "a culture of carelessness," and "a deviation from acceptable correctional practices." The culture was such that, when asked about sticking to regulations, many CCF employees admitted that they didn't know the regulations. At one time, inspections of CCF's tunnel infrastructure had been frequent, but not since 1995. Weekly inspections of cell integrity, one of which would have busted Matt and Sweat, had been discontinued so long ago that there were corrections officers who didn't know what they were. Despite this, DOCCS self-assessments always reported that the facility was in "full compliance with required standards." When new statewide security measures were put in place following an escape in Elmira, there is no evidence that they were ever instituted at CCF. The February 2015 Office of Special Investigations examination into alleged improprieties between Joyce Mitchell and David Sweat simply went through the motions and erroneously declared the allegations baseless.

The inspector general reported that Allan Trombley was the correction officer who should have stopped Mitchell's misconduct in the tailor shop but who was instead reading at his desk.

The report didn't request that new security measures be put in place as much as require that regulations currently in place be followed to the letter. It questioned the wisdom of allowing the DOCCS to oversee itself. Perhaps surveillance cameras could be put in place to verify that employees were doing their job.

The inspector general announced that she was creating a unit designed to audit and monitor DOCCS. She complained that the investigation was made more lengthy and difficult than it needed to be by the lack of cooperation from CCF staff, which as a group either lied or suffered from selective amnesia. Like Sergeant Shultz, the portly guard on the TV show *Hogan's Heroes*, they knew *nothing*.

The report contained some impressive statistics. Sweat, it said, exited his cell through the back door eighty-five times and returned all but once. That meant that there were an estimated four hundred required cell checks that would have caught him but didn't.

The report revealed that Joyce Mitchell smuggled more than seventy containers of pepper into the prison and gave them to Matt. (Following the May 31 prison riot and the fear of an imminent lockdown, Matt and Sweat got rid of this pepper. This turned out to be a mistake as no lockdown came.)

Sweat told the inspector general's investigators that his original escape plan was to go over the wall rather than under. He would use a "vulnerability" in his cell door's locking mechanism to exit his cell and a rope and hook to scale the wall while guards were "watching a movie or something." The plan was abandoned when Matt became involved. No way "Fatso" could scale a wall.

One of the key items the prisoners acquired while planning their escape was a tape measure. Using it, Sweat could measure the openings he was cutting and Matt could measure his girth, so they could be sure Matt wouldn't get stuck somewhere along the line. Mitchell supplied it, putting it in a drawer in the tailor shop where Matt picked it up.

The long, orange extension cord that Sweat used to provide himself with an electric fan and light during his work had been found near the site where contractors had recently installed a new boiler. In addition to tools, the box held rechargeable battery packs and disposable breathing masks. The gang box was removed by contractors on April 27, 2015, and, despite Sweat's sticky fingers, no missing tools were reported.

According to prison records, security staff conducted an unannounced search of the cells in Honor Block—but how thorough could the searches have been? The officer who conducted the search said it was "not his practice" to inspect the cell walls. Sweat later told investigators that he doubted this search ever took place.

The report brought forth some new and slightly gruesome details when it came to the sexual relationship between Matt and Mitchell. After one trip into a private area with Mitchell, Matt returned and thrust his fingers under a fellow inmate's nose, saying, "Here, smell this."

Mitchell's coworkers noticed a change in her during the two months before the escape. She was wearing makeup. An extra button on her shirt would be unbuttoned. She'd lost weight. She was trying to look more beautiful, sexier, while on the job.

For obvious reasons, maps are prohibited in prison. But Mitchell smuggled a whole atlas into her tailor shop so Matt could familiarize himself with the roads leading away from Dannemora. When she still thought she was "escaping" with the prisoners, Mitchell went so far as to call cabins for rent in Vermont, inquiring about rates.

Only days before the escape, Mitchell's husband Lyle became worried about the frequency at which Joyce was bringing contraband into the prison. He worried that she was being extorted and talked to Matt and Sweat about it. They told him that it was supposed to be a surprise, but they were making a birthday present—or anniversary present, they weren't sure—for Lyle from Joyce. That relieved Lyle's worry and ended the questioning. According to Sweat, Joyce really did have a surprise in store for Lyle, once allegedly saying, "Pop my husband, he's worth more to me dead than alive." Joyce admitted to the words but claimed she was just being a "smart aleck."

According to the investigator general, Sweat timed the escape so it would coincide with the shift of correction officer Ronald Blair, because Sweat didn't like the guy, didn't like the way he conducted body counts, whacking prisoners on the feet with his flashlight. Sweat hoped that Blair would face disciplinary charges after the escape. The plan worked; Blair was suspended in the escape's aftermath.

Sweat said the escape did not go off without a hitch. As intended, they left behind a tote bag full of tools that they would no longer need, but they also left behind the New York State road map that Mitchell had smuggled into the tailor shop for Matt.

The report thoroughly itemized the proper procedures at CCF, supporting their central thesis that new regulations do not need to be put in place as much as old regulations need to be followed. The "culture of carelessness" at CCF needed to stop.

The problem wasn't new. One guard told the investigation that he was a thirty-three-year vet of CCF, and during all of that time it was routine for guards to sign forms stating searches and counts had been performed when, in fact, they had not. It was common practice to fill out forms in advance, stating that everyone was in their cell and all was well.

Common belief was that escape was impossible, so keeping everyone happy and nonviolent was the goal. Prison brass, of course, said it was shocked that security at their maximum-security facility was so lax.

Up until 1990 there had been monthly searches of the prison's inner tunnel system, a search that took a full day to complete. These searches were discontinued not because of budget cuts but rather out of concern about asbestos. An asbestos abatement project was completed in 1995, and when tunnel inspections resumed, they were done only annually.

The inspector general's conclusions were, in a nutshell, to (1) train staff better; (2) increase camera surveillance; (3) stringently follow regulations already in place: prisoner counts, cell inspections, perhaps using thermal imaging sensors to distinguish prisoners from dummies, gate security, metal detectors, random frisking of employees, and so forth; (4) inspect the catwalk and tunnel system more than once a year, hopefully monthly; (5) supply oversight of DOCCS to "ensure the integrity of the system"; (6) use canines to detect contraband; (7) keep a closer eye on tools left behind by contractors and maintenance people; (8) better oversee tailor shops; (9) revamp the "honor" system; and (10) more severely discipline and effectively counsel officers and civilian employees who break the rules.

The inspector general's report received immediate criticism. Franklin County sheriff Kevin Mulverhill said that the report seemed to indict all CCF employees as abusive, lazy, and bumbling when he knew this not to be so. "I absolutely believe that the majority of officers do an outstanding job," he said. "I think you're dealing with a very small percentage of officers."[35]

One person who agreed with Sheriff Mulverhill was Assemblywoman Janet Duprey, who said, "These corrections officers work very difficult jobs under really tough circumstances every day. I don't agree with a lot of the things that are in that report." She felt the report downplayed the blame the state should have received, such as when it refused to declare a lockdown following the May 2015 riot, a lockdown that would have certainly discovered the holes in Matt and Sweat's cells.[36]

Preceding the IG report by a few days was another report, this one issued by the prisoner advocacy group known as Correctional Association of New York, which, using mostly anonymous statements from inmates, stated that there had been "an uptick" in abusive behavior by CCF employees in the aftermath of the escape.[37] The charges included beatings, excessive use of solitary confinement, and "rampant racism."

A few months earlier, during April, in a cell at the Bedford Hills Correctional Facility, Joyce Mitchell quietly penned a sad letter to Department of Corrections acting commissioner Anthony J. Annucci. She wrote,

> I was wondering if there was anything you could do to help me to possibly getting clemency. I realize what I did was very wrong. No one will ever know the remorse I feel for everything that happened due to my part in the Clinton escape. I turned myself in. . . . I tried to help with any information I could to try and bring these men back to prison. They threatened to kill my husband, Lyle, as well as my son and mother. I could not let them harm my family. I love my family very much and they mean everything to me. No one knows how scared I was. I now [sic] I did wrong. I tried to help and no one knows there was a person on the outside that was going to kill my husband. I am really not a bad person. I made bad choices. My family is my life and I could not let anything happen to them. I mentally beat myself every day. I am so sorry for all the fear the community, officers and all others involved in the search for these men. I am very sorry for the fear everyone was dealing with while these men were on the loose. I will never be able to forget what part I had in this terrible ordeal. I know I really don't have the right to ask for clemency. I am in hopes that you can help me and see your way in helping me be granted clemency. I have admitted to everything I did. I have lost so much. I have lost my freedom, my dignity, my job, my friends. Luckily, I still have what is most important to me, my husband and family. Please understand the person I was at the time was someone very scared for their family. Unfortunately, I got in

over my head and I didn't know what to do. I am 52 years old. I was 51 when this happened. I have never been in trouble with the law. I cry for all the pain my family is going through. This will never go away.[38]

In response, district attorney Andrew Wylie noted that the recipient of Mitchell's letter would not be able to grant clemency; that could only be done by the governor. Wylie, for his part, said he would strongly urge that Mitchell's letter be disregarded.

Annucci was not nearly as surprised that Mitchell was begging for freedom as he was that he himself still had a job. Despite the deluge of fallout following the escape, Annucci remained dutifully employed. He said, "Ultimately the commissioner is accountable for everything in the system. I serve at the pleasure of the governor. Any time he wants to make a change, it is up to him."[39]

In the long run, it became clear that the story of the escaping prisoners was so popular because we could so easily identify with the escapees. Along with our fear that, while Matt and Sweat were out, innocent people would be victimized, there was an undeniable sense of *envy*. We are all prisoners, men and women who have, like Joyce Mitchell long before she was locked up, forged our own chains and bars, and perpetually seek release.

AC-KNOWL-EDG-MENTS

I wish to thank the following persons and organizations without whose help the writing of this book would have been impossible: Jim and Jenny Baleno of Brushton, New York, my mom Rita Benson who had friends in the right places (Up North); Rod Bigelow; Barbara Briggs; William Chase, supervisor, Town of Dannemora; Patricia Desmond; Frank Dimatteo, author of *President Street Boys*; Beau Duffy, public information officer, New York State Police; Michael P. Dunn, chief deputy, Office of the Sheriff, County of Niagara; my literary agents Jake Elwell and Elise Erickson of Harold Ober Associates; Clinton County sheriff David N. Favro; Captain Fredric Foels, City of Tonawanda Police Department; retired North Tonawanda chief of detectives Glenn D. Gardner; editor Mary Garrett; Keith Gorgas; Katy Grabill; Chief William R. Hall, North Tonawanda Police Department; Tom Haushalter; Rich Henning; Mary Ellen Heyman; editor Stephen P. Hull; the North Tonawanda History Museum; Journey Home; Joshua Lamitie; Clinton Correctional Facility historian Walter "Pete" Light; Brian Monette; Clinton County legislator Colin Read; Joan Rocco, records access officer, Niagara County Sheriff's Office; Dene Savage, director, Business Development, Titus Mountain Family Ski Center, LLC; Edward Schintzius; Philip Semrau; Sherri L. Strickland; Susan Sylvia; Donna Taylor, treasurer-clerk, Village of Dannemora; Private Investigator Donald A. Tubman; and Kathy Vahue.

NOTES

INTRODUCTION

1. New York State Adirondack Park Agency, "History of the Adirondack Park," accessed May 29, 2016, http://apa.ny.gov/About_Park/history.htm.

2. Rod Bigelow and Walter "Pete" Light, *Images of America: Dannemora* (Charleston, SC: Arcadia, 2015), 7–8.

3. Walter "Pete" Light, Clinton Correctional Facility's historian, interview by author, November 3, 2015.

4. Cara Chapman, "DA Shares Impact of Manhunt," *Press-Republican*, August 1, 2015.

5. David Favro, interview by author, December 17, 2015.

6. Glenn Gardner, interview by author, December 11, 2015.

7. Ibid.

8. Louis Haremski, interview by author, January 14, 2016.

9. Brian Mann, "Adirondack Life Looks at Aftershocks of the Dannemora Manhunt," NCPR, October 27, 2015, accessed October 27, 2015, http://www .northcountrypublicradio.org.

10. Megan Kuharich and Jeff Truesdell, "'Devastated' Father of Cop Shot by Escaped N.Y. Prisoner Relives Painful Memories with Son's Killer on the Loose," *People*, June 17, 2015, accessed September 10, 2015, http://www.people.com.

ONE   LITTLE SIBERIA

1. Unless otherwise noted, the information in this chapter is based on the research of the Clinton Correctional Facility's historian, Walter "Pete" Light, interviewed by me November 3, 2015, and from his book *Images of America: Dannemora*, written with Rod Bigelow.

2. The first two were Newgate in New York City (1797) and Auburn (1817). Auburn prisoners, starting in 1825, built Ossining prison (Sing Sing).

3. Lyon Mountain, in addition to being a mountain, is the name of its surrounding area as well, a hamlet within the Town of Dannemora, population 423 at the 2010 census. The actual mountain peaks at 3,820 feet above sea level. It

was named after Nathaniel Lyons, an early nineteenth-century settler. At the top is the Lyons Mountain Fire Observation Station, a popular hiking destination. The northeast slopes of Lyon Mountain drain into Chazy Lake, within the watershed of the Saint Lawrence River.

4. Michael Schwirtz and Michael Winerip, "Tunnels, Disguises and Sewers: Clinton Prison's Inmates Have Found Many Ways to Flee," *New York Times*, June 10, 2015, A20.

5. Ibid.

6. Ibid.

7. Ibid.

8. Paul Grondahl, "Dozens Escaped Dannemora Prison before Richard Matt and David Sweat," *Timesunion*, July 10, 2015, accessed September 18, 2015, http://www.timesunion.com.

9. Escape from Alcatraz had been tried in 1937 and 1962, all escapees disappeared without a trace and presumed dead. The most famous attempt, by Frank Morris and the Anglin Brothers, occurred on June 11, 1962. The Anglins' nephews, however, claimed that they had proof that the men survived, including Christmas cards that the family received in December 1962.

10. The *easiest time* in the state was spent at the legendarily kind Lake Pleasant jailhouse in Lake Pleasant, New York. It was a town that earned its name, population 781, the seat of Hamilton County, surrounded by vast forest, and 128 miles southwest of Dannemora. In the jailhouse there, the primary defense against escape was simple: no one particularly wanted to leave. It was a facility that could have existed in the fictional town of Mayberry on *The Andy Griffith Show*. The meals were home-cooked; the cells, well heated; the beds, soft; and discipline, light. The old joke went that prisoners who misbehaved had to go without dessert.

11. Frank Dimatteo, interview by author, December 30, 2015.

12. Dan Heath, "Dannemora Barber Marks 50 Years in Business," *Press-Republican*, December 6, 2015, accessed December 6, 2015, http://www.pressrepublican.com.

13. Lockstep is marching in very close single file, with legs moving in synch with the inmate in front so that the legs stay close to one another at all times, a style that can be accomplished even when inmates are shackled together at the ankles, which in this case they no doubt were.

14. "Joseph Wood Sizzles," *Topeka State Journal*, August 2, 1892, 1.

15. "Delivery Plot Is Unearthed in Jail," *Warren Tribune*, November 10, 1927, 1.

16. Bigelow and Light, *Images of America*, 95.

17. Mastro was born in New York City, was unmarried, and had a seventh-grade education. He joined the Army, was stationed at Fort Slocum, and deserted

on June 5, 1926. Before coming to Dannemora, he had escaped from Auburn but was recaptured by a local police officer. He was transferred from Auburn to Dannemora on December 15, 1926.

18. The year 1929 was a big one for prison riots. There were two uprisings at Auburn State Prison in New York, at the Colorado State Penitentiary in Canon City (now called the Colorado Territorial Correctional Facility), and at the federal penitentiary in Leavenworth, Kansas.

19. On June 28, 1987, one inmate was shot and "at least four" stabbed. The shot inmate was hit by a sharpshooting guard in a tower. The incident was sparked by a fight between inmates at 7:21 p.m. during the after-dinner recreation period. No guards were hurt. By late evening the incident was over.

20. "Population Demographics for Dannemora Village, New York, in 2015 and 2015," Suburban Stats, accessed May 30, 2016, http://suburbanstats.org.

21. Ross Douthat, "The Dannemora Dilemma," *New York Times*, June 13, 2015, accessed September 20, 2015, http://www.nytimes.com.

22. Kirk Semple, "Manhunt Over and Patrols Gone, Calm and Quiet Return to Dannemora," *New York Times*, July 5, 2015, accessed September 20, 2015, http://www.nytimes.com.

23. Ibid.

24. The incident held the U.S. record for largest mass murder, a record it held until September 11, 2001.

25. In a 2012 jailhouse interview with TV's "Dr. Phil," Pelosi claimed he was innocent, that Generosa (who died in 2004 of cancer) and another friend committed the crime to collect an estimated $97 million inheritance.

26. In a bizarre coincidence, the obstetrician who temporarily lost his license to practice medicine because of his involvement with this "adoption" also delivered both of my children. Oo-wee-oo.

27. Steinberg was paroled in 2004 and lives in New York City.

28. That's Rick Matt's stomping grounds, along the southern edge of Lake Erie between Erie, Pennsylvania, and Buffalo, New York.

29. In 1978 I did something I'd never done before or since. I surreptitiously followed a person, shadowed him. That person was Gregory Corso, and I followed him across the East Village of New York into a branch of the New York City library where he went directly to the reference section, pulled down a copy of *The Baseball Encyclopedia*, and looked up the career batting statistics for hall-of-fame Pittsburgh shortstop Honus Wagner. They are awesome.

30. Niki Kourofsky, *Adirondack Outlaws: Bad Boys and Lawless Ladies* (Helena, MT: Farcountry Press, 2015).

31. Ibid.

1. Lois Clermont and Joe LoTemplio, "Prison Escape Probe Focuses on Contractors," *Buffalo News*, June 8, 2015, accessed June 20, 2016, http://www .buffalonews.com.

2. According to PBS, Colditz was a castle prison atop a cliff overlooking the Rive Mulde and the town of Colditz, near Leipzig, Germany. Hitler's bright idea had been to take all of the prisoner-of-war officers with a history of escape and put them in a truly formidable prison. The plan, as was true of many of Hitler's plans, did not work. By putting the escape-savvy officers all in one place, he managed to create a think tank, an escape super-team, and before the war was over sixteen officers did successfully make it out. One successful effort was led by Lieutenant Commander William Stephens. With socks covering their shoes, he and three others crawled through windows, slithered over roofs, scaled down a wall using knotted sheets, and fled to Switzerland disguised as French workman, getting past checkpoints with forged documents, including a leave pass with swastika stamp in the name of an actual French electrician employed by the Germans, and a service pass with photo and stamps. Perhaps the most interesting aspect of the escape plan was the involvement of the prison band, which deviated from the score they were playing to signal the escapees that the sentries on parole were at opposite ends of the courtyard. Peter Tyson, "Escaping Colditz," NOVA Online, updated January 2001, accessed June 20, 2016, http://www.pbs.org.

3. If there were such a thing as the Prison Escape Hall of Fame, Hinds would be a charter member. The Brit, Alfred George "Alfie" Hinds, became during the 1950s the only man to escape from *three* high-security prisons.

4. William K. Rashbaum, "New York Prisoner's Keys to Escape: Lapsed Rules, Tools, and Luck," *New York Times*, July 20, 2015, accessed October 4, 2015, http:// www.nytimes.com.

5. To a tabloid newspaper reporter, "getting the wood" is slang for having one's story run on the front page.

6. Paul Grondahl and Keshia Clukey, "Dannemora's Old Guard 'Flabbergasted' by Prison Break," *Timesunion*, June 10, 2015, accessed September 18, 2015, http:// www.timesunion.com.

7. Anne Neville, "'Anything Is Possible' with Richard Matt, Says Cop Who Helped Imprison Violent Escapee 'for Life,'" *Buffalo News*, June 8, 2015, accessed April 15, 2016, http://www.buffalonews.com.

8. Corky Siemaszko, "Son of Escaped Prisoner Says Richard Matt Is Genius Career Criminal: 'I Can't Believe They Let This Happen'—Report," *(New York) Daily News*, June 11, 2015, accessed April 15, 2016, http://www.nydailynews.com.

9. Eric DuVall, "Richard Matt's Troubles Began Early in Life," *Rochester Democrat and Chronicle*, June 10, 2015, A3.

10. "Escaped NY Prisoners May Have Had Help from Staff—Governor," Reuters, June 8, 2015, accessed June 17, 2016, http://www.reuters.com.

11. New York State, Governor Andrew M. Cuomo, "Governor Cuomo Announces $100,000 Reward for Information Leading to the Arrest of Escaped Inmates," June 7, 2015, accessed September 4, 2015, http://www.governor.ny.gov.

12. Sarah Caspari, "New Details of David Sweat Escape: Were Prison Guards Asleep on the Job?" *Christian Science Monitor*, July 21, 2015, accessed September 16, 2015, http://www.csmonitor.com.

13. Ray Sanchez, Evan Perez, and Ben Brumfied, "Prison Escapee Richard Matt Wrote to Daughter, Vowed to See Her, Report Says," CNN, July 3, 2015, accessed September 20, 2015, http://www.cnn.com.

14. Dialogue fashioned from Lou Michel, "'See You on the Outside,' Matt Said in Letter Delivered to Daughter in Buffalo Suburb," *Buffalo News*, July 3, 2015, accessed October 10, 2015, http://www.buffalonews.com.

15. Ashley Fantz, "Drugs, Money, Love, and Cell Phones: How Prison Guards Go Bad," CNN, June 27, 2015, accessed April 15, 2016, http://www.cnn.com.

THREE   DAVID SWEAT

1. Patricia Desmond, interview by author, November 3, 2015.

2. Megan Brockett, "Convict's Mother: 'I Couldn't Believe He Did It,'" *USA Today*, June 23, 2015, accessed September 25, 2015, http://www.usatoday.com.

3. Pamela Sweat's credibility is questionable, as aspects of her story cannot be verified. She says, for example, that David attended Calvin Coolidge Elementary School, but that school has no record of him. Neighboring schools had no record of him either.

4. N. R. Kleinfield, "Broken Boys, Thieves, Killers, and Now Escapees," *New York Times*, June 12, 2015, accessed July 9, 2015, http://www.nytimes.com.

5. Ibid.

6. "David Sweat's Brutal Path to Prison," *Pressconnects*, June 13, 2015, accessed October 21, 2015, http://www.pressconnects.com (based on court documents unsealed in 2003).

7. APC stood for American Power Conversion, a manufacturer of "uninterruptible power supplies, electronics peripherals and data center products."

8. This and remainder of the chapter sourced from "David Sweat's Brutal Path."

9. Adam Chick, "Deputy Kevin Tarsia Remembered," *12 WBNG Action News*, July 3, 2012, accessed September 10, 2015, http://www.wbng.com.

1. Kleinfield, "Broken Boys."

2. Lou Michel, "Escaped Killer's Son Shares Memories of His Notorious Father," *Buffalo News*, September 2, 2015, accessed September 27, 2015, http://www.buffalonews.com.

3. "Matt, Hoak Honored," *Tonawanda News*, January 18, 1977, 16.

4. Kleinfield, "Broken Boys."

5. Michel, "Escaped Killer's Son."

6. Eric DuVall, "Richard Matt's Troubles Began Early in Life," *Rochester Democrat and Chronicle*, June 10, 2015, A3.

7. Ibid.

8. Bentley material from Dan Herbeck, "People Who Knew Richard Matt Describe His Jekyll-and-Hyde Past, Including Two Suicide Attempts," *Buffalo News*, June 21, 2015, accessed October 17, 2015, http://www.buffalonews.com.

9. Ibid.

10. Kleinfield, "Broken Boys."

11. Herbeck, "People Who Knew."

12. "People Record for Richard W Matts," Advanced Background Checks, accessed April 18, 2016, http://www.advancedbackgroundchecks.com.

13. Kleinfield, "Broken Boys."

14. Sasha Goldstein, "Escaped Prisoner Richard Matt Appears in 1997 Home Movie: 'This Is the Face of a Maniac!'" *(New York) Daily News*, June 23, 2015, accessed July 9, 2015, http://www.nydailynews.com.

15. Dan Herbeck, "Suspect in Grisly '97 Slaying Faces Trial, Officers Bring Matt Back after His Release from Mexican Prison," *Buffalo News*, January 25, 2007, accessed April 18, 2016, http://www.buffalonews.com; see also Gardner, interview.

16. The remainder of this depiction of William Rickerson's murder and its aftermath, unless otherwise noted, is derived from Gardner, interview; Edward C. Schintzius, interview by author, November 2, 2015; Haremski, interview; Rick Pfeiffer, "County Court: Letter Linked to Matt," *Niagara Gazette*, April 7, 2008, accessed September 8, 2005, http://www.niagara-gazette.com; and North Tonawanda police reports contemporary to the events they portray.

17. A chemical that exhibits chemiluminescence, with a blue glow, when mixed with an appropriate oxidizing agent—such as blood.

18. Erika Brason, "North Tonawanda Man Heavily Guarded in Murder Trial," WGRZ.com, April 7, 2008, accessed September 8, 2015, http://www.wgrz.com.

1. Haremski, interview.

2. Ibid.

3. Ibid.

4. Thomas J. Prohaska, "Matt Tortured Rickerson before Death, Driver Says: Accomplice Gives Details of 27-Hour Car Ride," *Buffalo News*, March 15, 2008, accessed September 7, 2015.

5. This quote and the following courtroom dialogue is fashioned from Rick Pfeiffer, "Matt Trial: Murder Defendant Is Subject of Powerful Security Effort," *Niagara Gazette*, April 7, 2008, accessed September 8, 2015, http://www.niagara -gazette.com.

6. Detective Edward Schintzius retired as a cop in 2001; spent two years working security in a federal court for the U.S. Marshals; did handwriting analysis for the district attorney for six years; retired for the last time in 2009; and as of 2016 lives in Silver Creek, New York (coincidentally about a quarter of a mile from the spot where Richard Matt killed William Rickerson), where he loves to fish on Lake Erie.

7. Dan Pye, "Matt Trial: Richard Matt Found Guilty," *Niagara Gazette*, April 15, 2008, accessed September 8, 2015, http://www.niagara-gazette.com.

8. Ibid.

9. Ibid.

10. Rick Pfeiffer, "County Court: Max for Richard Matt," *Niagara Gazette*, May 31, 2008, A1.

11. Ibid.

12. Kirstan Conley, "Escaped Killer Has a History of Breaking Out of Prison," *New York Post*, June 8, 2015.

13. Ibid.

14. Gardner had planned on staying a top cop until he was sixty-two years old at least. But when he was just fifty-five his wife came down with lung cancer. Doctors gave her three years. Gardner asked his wife what she wanted to do, and she said she wanted to live her remaining years in Las Vegas, so he retired and they moved. Three years later, plus a few bonus months, his wife died and he returned to North Tonawanda where he became a part-time bus driver—not a real bus driver but the guy in charge of getting his grandkids to and from school. In the small-world department comes this tidbit: Gardner and his girlfriend went to a wedding; the bride, a good friend of his girlfriend's daughter, turned out to be Richard Matt's daughter—and "she couldn't have been nicer," Gardner said.

15. Today, Lou Haremski is the proprietor of Loose Lumber (http://looselumber

.com). With his son who has a degree in furniture design, he designs and builds unique pieces of furniture for, as he says, "everywhere from the bedroom to the boardroom," using exotic woods such as Ipe, Wenge, Sycamore Fiddleback, Paduak Purpleheart, and Makore. Each piece they build is one of a kind and cannot be found in a store.

16. Mordino passed away on December 6, 2013, at the age of seventy. He worked for the Erie County DA's office for thirty-eight years and put an estimated 250 murderers behind bars, one of the longest-serving prosecutors in county history.

17. Matt's habeas corpus case, usually a last resort for prisoners whose appeals have run out, was still pending before U.S. Magistrate judge Leslie G. Foschio when Matt escaped from CCF.

SIX   THE BLONDE AND THE BURGER

1. The information is this chapter relies on the reporting of *People* magazine, CNN, the *Watertown Daily Times*, WPTV, WPTZ, *NBC News*, *ABC News*, *The Today Show*, Syracuse.com, the *Press Examiner*, the *Press-Republican*, the *Times Union*, and the *New York Daily News*. Articles are contemporary to the events they depict. See bibliography for details.

2. Prior to being elected as Clinton County surrogate court judge, Ryan was for twenty-one years a practicing attorney, concentrating in criminal, matrimonial, and real estate law. He'd earned his BA at College of the Holy Cross in 1971 and his JD at Albany Law School in 1974. He was appointed to be a city court judge in Plattsburgh in 1990 and had been an elected judge in Clinton County since 1996. In addition to serving as surrogate judge, he was also an acting county court judge presiding over half of the county's criminal cases.

3. According to New York State law, no prisoner is considered capable of sexual consent with a prison employee, regardless of age and gender.

SEVEN   THE HUNT

1. Except where otherwise noted, the information in this chapter relies on the reporting of the following news outlets: *Rochester Democrat and Chronicle*, *New York Daily News*, *Press-Republican*, *Christian Science Monitor*, *Watertown Daily Times*, *Albany Times-Union*, CNN, *NBC News*, *ABC News*, *New York Times*, *Fox News*, *Newsday*, *Buffalo News*, WPTZ, WNYT, WCAX, *New York Post*, Syracuse.com, NCPR, *Toronto Sun*, and MyChamplainValley.com. Articles are contemporary to the events they depict.

2. Joshua Lamitie, interview by author, November 16, 2015.

3. Desmond, interview.

4. Brockett, "Convict's Mother."

5. David Sweat was actually thirty-five years old at the time of this interview. His mother apparently had forgotten his recent birthday.

EIGHT   ONE DOWN

1. Except where otherwise noted, the information in this chapter relies on the reporting of the following news outlets: *Press-Republican*, *New York Daily News*, *New York Post*, *Watertown Daily Times*, *Albany Times Union*, WPTZ, WCAX, MyChamplainValley.com, *Buffalo News*, *NBC News*, *ABC News*, CNN, Syracuse. com, and *Ledger Gazette*. Articles are contemporary to the events they depict.

2. The Gokeys later hired an "Albany lawyer" to help them win a portion of the $100,000 reward that Governor Andrew Cuomo had offered for information leading to the capture. They were encouraged by the fact that Cuomo mentioned them, although not by name, when speaking to the press about the violent outcome of the search for Matt.

3. Franklin County was billed $700 by the funeral home that took Matt's body to Albany.

NINE   THE CAPTURE OF SWEAT

1. Except where otherwise noted, the information in this chapter relies on the reporting of the following news outlets: *Time*, *Rochester Democrat and Chronicle*, *New York Daily News*, *Press-Republican*, *Christian Science Monitor*, *Watertown Daily Times*, *Albany Times-Union*, CNN, *NBS News*, *ABC News*, *New York Times*, *Fox News*, *Newsday*, *Buffalo News*, WAMC, WPTZ, WNYT, WCAX, *New York Post*, Syracuse.com, NCPR, *Toronto Sun*, and MyChamplainValley.com. Articles are contemporary to the events they depict.

2. According to other witnesses in the tailor shop, this was a lie. Before Sweat was fired from the tailor shop for improper behavior, he and Mitchell were engaging in sexual activity on a daily basis. And there was no psychological expertise involved when it came to figuring out Mitchell's sexual neediness. She complained about her libido for all to hear, and in the most vulgar terms. "I'm horny as fuck," was one of her memorable expressions.

3. Members of Strickland's family have filed a wrongful death suit.

4. On October 1, the same paper identified Captain America by name, adding that he was a former steward in the state corrections officers union and a gang intelligence officer.

1. Except where otherwise noted, the information in this chapter relies on the reporting of the following news outlets: *Rochester Democrat and Chronicle*, *New York Daily News*, *Christian Science Monitor*, *Watertown Daily Times*, *Albany Times-Union*, CNN, *NBC News*, *ABC News*, *New York Times*, *Fox News*, *Newsday*, *Buffalo News*, WNYT, *New York Post*, Syracuse.com, NCPR, *Toronto Sun*, and MyChamplainValley.com. Articles are contemporary to the events they depict.

2. Jarred Hill, "NY Community Honors Law Enforcement: 'Thank You Is Not Enough,'" WPTZ.com, July 17, 2015, accessed October 4, 2015, http://www.wptz .com.

3. These included the elimination of "Honor Block" and its privileges, better bed checks that required a verification that a prisoner was in his cell, and changes within the building's catwalk system to make it more difficult for prisoners to escape via that route.

4. David Sweat told investigators that killing Lyle was Joyce's idea, so the truth may never be known.

5. Each year, in the name of Kevin Tarsia, the New York State Deputies Association Scholarship Committee gave a $500 award to a graduating high school senior living in Broome County who would be attending a college or university in the fall to study criminal justice.

6. Shane Hobel, interview by author, October 7, 2015.

7. Light, interview.

ELEVEN   AUTUMN AND WINTER

1. Casey Tolan, "A Psychic Is Suing New York State Because He Didn't Get the $100,000 Reward for Catching Two Escaped Inmates," Fusion, October 25, 2015, accessed April 25, 2016, http://fusion.net.

2. "Guard Accused of Helping 2 Killers Escape Prison Pleads Not Guilty," *New York Times*, November 4, 2015, accessed November 5, 2015, http://www.nytimes .com.

3. Brad Evans and Liz Strzepa, "No Resolution Yet in Gene Palmer's Case," WPTZ.com, January 10, 2016, accessed January 8, 2016, http://www.wptz.com.

4. Assistant district attorney Nicholas Evanovich represented the people at the hearing.

5. Joe LoTemplio and Suzanne Moore, "Judge Ordered Higher Restitution for Mitchell than Set by Law," *Press-Republican*, November 6, 2015, accessed November 6, 2015.

6. Joe Gullo, "Report: Use of Force Justified in Killing Richard Matt, Capturing David Sweat," MyChamplainValley.com, November 12, 2015, accessed November 12, 2015, http://www.mychamplainvalley.com.

7. Jim Tedisco, "The 'Prisoner Privileges Limitation Law' to Protect Public from 'Dannemora-Duo-Like' Prison Breaks, Violence," *Timesunion*, June 16, 2015, accessed April 25, 2016, http://www.timesunion.com; Dave Lucas, "Legislators Push 'Prisoner Privilege Limitation Law,'" WAMC, June 16, 2015, accessed April 25, 2016, http://www.wamc.org.

8. Pat Bradley, "Inspector General Meets with Guard Charged in Wake of Prison Escape," WAMC, December 21, 2015, accessed December 21, 2015, http://www.wamc.org.

9. Vanessa Misciagna, "Union, Lawmakers Hope IG Prison Escape Report Brings Change," WPTZ.com, November 17, 2015, accessed November 28, 2015, http://www.wptz.com.

10. Ibid.

11. Robert Harding, "Sgt. Jay Cook, Trooper Who Captured NY Prison Escapee, Wins National Award," Auburnpub.com, November 20, 2015, accessed November 20, 2015, http://www.auburnpub.com.

12. Michael Virtanen, "Mothers, Experts Plead for Oversight of NY Prison System," *Pressconnects*, December 2, 2015, accessed December 2, 2015, http://www.pressconnects.com.

13. Brian Mann, "In Clinton Dannemora Prison, Violence, an Inmate Death and New Scrutiny," NCPR, December 22, 2015, accessed June 22, 2016, http://www.northcountrypublicradio.org.

14. Virtanen, "Mothers, Experts."

15. One possible issue causing the delay was a persistent rumor that the hole in the steam pipe was not originally cut by the escapees with a hacksaw, or with power tools for that matter, but had been cut by NYS maintenance crews from the Office of General Services working on the pipe and then inadequately patched when the work was completed.

16. Jay D. Cook, "Sgt. Jay Cook, Officer Who Shot NY Prison Escapee David Sweat, Opens Up About Ordeal," *Today*, December 7, 2015, accessed December 7, 2015, http://www.today.com.

17. Plattsburgh Police Chief Desmond Racicot said Kohl and his friend Derrick Young were getting hammered in Young's apartment when Kohl picked up Young's handgun. Young told him to put it down and reached for the gun, the gun went off, and Kohl was fatally wounded. It sounded a bit like something that could have happened on any Fourth of July anywhere in the United States.

18. Suzanne Moore, "Police: Accidental Shooting Kills Plattsburgh Man," *Press-*

Republican, July 6, 2015, accessed April 22, 2016, http://www.pressrepublican
.com.

19. Liz Strzepa, "Phone Tapping during the Manhunt: Malone Woman Speaks Out," WPTZ.com, January 13, 2016, accessed January 13, 2016, http://www.wptz
.com.

20. "NY to Increase Mental Health Training for Prison Staff," *Lockport (NY) Union-Sun and Journal*, December 28, 2016, accessed December 28, 2016, http://www.lockportjournal.com.

21. Brendan J. Lyons, "Abuses Detailed in N.Y. State Prison Internal Affairs Unit," *Timesunion*, January 8, 2016, accessed January 8, 2016, http://www
.timesunion.com.

22. Dene Savage, director, business development, Titus Mountain Family Ski Center, LLC, e-mail to author, January 11, 2016.

23. Brad Evans, "David Sweat Won't Face Additional Charges in Franklin County," WPTZ.com, January 26, 2016, accessed January 26, 2016, http://www
.wptz.com.

24. "Gov. Cuomo on the State of New York," *New York Times*, January 13, 2016, A26.

25. "English Teacher at California Jail Arrested in Connection to Escape of Three Inmates," *Fox News*, January 28, 2016, accessed January 28, 2016, http://www.foxnews.com; Molly Jackson, "California Inmates' Escape Likely an Inside Job, Experts Say," *Christian Science Monitor*, January 26, 2016, accessed January 26, 2016, http://www.csmonitor.com.

26. Heath, "Dannemora Barber."

27. "Inmate Sentenced in Prison Breakout," *New York Times*, February 4, 2016, A20.

28. Zach Hirsch, "Veteran Corrections Officer Gene Palmer Sentenced to Six Months in Jail," *WSKG News*, February 29, 2016, accessed February 29, 2016, http://wskgnews.org.

29. Joe LoTemplio, "Corrections Team Honored in Albany for Manhunt," *Press-Republican*, March 15, 2016, accessed March 15, 2016, http://www.pressrepublican.com.

30. Pat Bradley, "Clinton County DA Rejects Campaign for Judge, Opts to Run for Reelection," WAMC, April 1, 2016, accessed April 1, 2016, http://www.wamc.org.

31. Michael Winerip, Michael Schwirtz, and Tom Robbins, "New York State Corrections Dept. Takes On Guards' Union Over Brutality," *New York Times*, April 12, 2016, A1.

32. Brian Mann, "Inmate Dies at Clinton Correctional Facility in Dannemora," NCPR, May 24, 2016, accessed May 24, 2016, http://www.northcountrypublic radio.org.

33. "New York State Police Honor Troopers in Annual Ceremony," *Timesunion*, May 26, 2016, accessed May 26, 2016, http://www.timesunion.com.

34. Unless otherwise noticed, the remainder of this section is from Catherine Leahy Scott, inspector general, *Investigation of the June 5, 2015 Escape of Inmates David Sweat and Richard Matt from Clinton Correctional Facility* (Albany, NY: State of New York Office of the Inspector General, June 2016).

35. Liz Strzepa, "Sheriff Mulverhill: IG Report Only Reflects Small Percentage of Officers at Clinton Correctional Facility," WPTZ.com, June 9, 2016, accessed June 9, 2016, http://www.wptz.com.

36. Liz Strzepa, "Assemblywoman Janet Duprey: I Don't Agree with Some of the Inspector General's Findings," WPTZ.com, June 10, 2016, accessed June 10, 2016, http://www.wptz.com.

37. Matthew Hamilton, "Advocates' Report Details Alleged Abuses after Dannemora Escape," *Timesunion*, June 9, 2016, accessed June 9, 2016, http://www. timesunion.com.

38. Joe LoTemplio, "Mitchell Seeks Clemency from Prison Sentence," *Press-Republican*, June 12, 2016, accessed June 12, 2016, http://www.pressrepublican.com.

39. Brian Mann, "NY Corrections Commissioner Hangs On, Despite Dannemora Escape, Scandals," NCPR, June 9, 2016, accessed June 9, 2016, http://www.northcountrypublicradio.org.

BIBLI-OGRA-PHY

Adams, Char. "'I Just Got in Over My Head': Joyce Mitchell Blames Depression for Helping Murderers Escape New York Prison in Jailhouse Interview." *People*, September 11, 2015. Accessed September 13, 2015. http://www.people.com.

Advanced Background Checks. "People Record for Richard W Matts." Accessed April 18, 2016. http://www.advancedbackgroundchecks.com.

Ahmed, Saeed. "Source: Employee Questioned in New York Prison Escape." CNN, June 9, 2015. Accessed August 31, 2015. http://www.cnn.com.

Auburn Citizen. "Former Convict Here Killed at Clinton." October 4, 1929, 5.

Axelson, Ben. "Upstate NY Prison Escape Makes 'Jeopardy' Clue." Syracuse.com. Accessed October 7, 2015. http://www.syracuse.com.

———. "NY Prison Escape: Psychic Wants $100K for Helping Find Richard Matt, David Sweat." Syracuse.com. Accessed October 26, 2015. http://www.syracuse.com.

Balsamo, Michael. "Troopers Hunting Escapees Scrambled to Save Sweat." *Rochester Democrat and Chronicle*, June 29, 2015, A1.

Basu, Tanya. "Prison Escape Prompted Inmate Beatings." *Time*, August 11, 2015. Accessed September 9, 2015. http://www.time.com.

Belcher, Mark. "Corrections Officer Fires Back at Claims of Prisoner Abuse." WIVB.com, August 13, 2015. Accessed October 6, 2015. http://www.wivb.com.

Benitez, Gio, and Shahriar Rahmanzadeh. "'Lucky to Be Alive,' Says Man Who Claimed to See Murderers after New York Prison Break." 12 News, June 9, 2015. Accessed January 22, 2016. http://www.12newsnow.com.

Biek, Katherine. "Lyle Mitchell 'Today' Show Interview: Joyce Mitchell's Husband Breaks Silence in NBC Interview." WPTV, June 23, 2015. Accessed September 13, 2015. http://www.wptv.com.

Bigelow, Rod, and Walter "Pete" Light. *Images of America: Dannemora*. Charleston, SC: Arcadia, 2015.

Blain, Glenn. "NY Lawmakers to Probe Prisons after Escape of Two Convicted Murderers." *Los Angeles Daily News*, Accessed November 29, 2015. http://www.dailynews.com.

Blau, Reuven. "Escaped N.Y. Convicts Bickered Over Whether They'd Camp Out in Cabin or Keep Moving." *(New York) Daily News*, July 23, 2015. Accessed October 5, 2015. http://www.nydailynews.com.

Blau, Reuven, Meg Wagner, and Corky Siemaszko. "They Have No Honor! Privileged Block Gone at Prison." *New York Daily News*, July 2, 2015, 8.

Bradley, Pat. "Clinton County DA Rejects Campaign for Judge, Opts to Run for Reelection." WAMC, April 1, 2016. Accessed April 1, 2016. http://www.wamc.org.

——— . "Inspector General Meets with Guard Charged in Wake of Prison Escape." WAMC, December 21, 2015. Accessed December 21, 2015. http://www.wamc.org.

——— . "Legal Proceedings Continue in Wake of Prison Escape." WAMC, July 29, 2015. Accessed October 7, 2015. http://www.wamc.com.

Brasley, Steven. "New York Prison Break Suspects to Appear in Court Next Week." MyChamplainValley.com, October 28, 2015. Accessed October 29, 2015. http://www.mychamplainvalley.com.

Brason, Erika. "North Tonawanda Man Heavily Guarded in Murder Trial." WGRZ.com, April 7, 2008. Accessed September 8, 2015. http://www.wgrz.com.

Brockett, Megan. "Convict's Mother: 'I Couldn't Believe He Did It.'" *USA Today*, June 23, 2015. Accessed September 25, 2015. http://www.usatoday.com.

Buffalo News. "Joseph M. Mordino, Longtime Erie County Prosecutor." December 7, 2013. Accessed September 10, 2015. http://www.buffalonews.com.

——— . "Prison Disciplinary Process against David Sweat Begins." July 15, 2015. Accessed September 5, 2015. http://www.buffalonews.com.

——— . "$216,900 Payment Ordered for Trial: Attorneys Prosecuted Matt Murder Case." September 17, 2008. Accessed September 17, 2008. http://www.buffalonews.com.

Campbell, Jon. "Dannemora Escape: Joyce Mitchell Sent to Bedford Hills Prison." *Lohud*. Accessed September 30, 2015. http://www.lohud.com.

——— . "Escapee Charged with 3 Felonies, Already Serving Life Prison Term." *Rochester Democrat and Chronicle*, August 21, 2015, 10A.

——— . "Meals, Supplies Added $1M to Prison-Break Search." *Rochester Democrat and Chronicle*, August 31, 2015. Accessed September 2, 2015. http://www.democratandchronicle.com.

——— . "Woman Pleads Guilty to Role in Prison Break." *Rochester Democrat and Chronicle*, July 28, 2015. Accessed October 5, 2015. http://www.democratandchronicle.com,

Capelouto, Susanna, and Alexandra Field. "Husband of Alleged Prison Break Helper Joyce Mitchell Feels Betrayed." CNN, June 19, 2015. Accessed October 2, 2015. http://www.cnn.com.

Carlin, Christopher J. *Protecting Niagara: A History of the Niagara County Sheriff's Office*. Tulsa, OK: AEGIS, 1995.

Caspari, Sarah. "New Details of David Sweat Escape: Were Prison Guards Asleep on the Job?" *Christian Science Monitor*, July 21, 2015. Accessed September 16, 2015. http://www.csmonitor.com.

CBS New York. "L.I. Woman Thinks She Got Knock on Door from Escaped Prisoners at Upstate Home." June 29, 2015. Accessed June 29, 2015. http://newyork.cbslocal.com.

Chapman, Cara. "Camper on Matt: 'He Was Trying to Kill Someone.'" *Press-Republican*. Accessed November 12, 2015. http://www.pressrepublican.com.

———. "DA Shares Impact of Manhunt." *Press-Republican*, August 1, 2015.

———. "Locals Say 'Thank You' with Law Enforcement Appreciation Fun Day." CorrectionsOne.com, August 23, 2015. Accessed October 3, 2015. http://www.correctionsone.com.

Chick, Adam. "Deputy Kevin Tarsia Remembered." *12 WBNG Action News*, July 3, 2012. Accessed September 10, 2015. http://www.wbng.com.

Chicago Tribune. "Convict Killed as He Tries to Flee Dannemora." October 4, 1929, 2.

Chung, Jen. "Prison Worker Helped Inmates Because of the Fantasy and the Sex." Gothamist, July 29, 2015. Accessed October 6, 2015. http://www.gothamist.com.

Clermont, Lois. "Coroner Was on Guard over Matt's Body." *Press-Republican*, June 29, 2015. Accessed September 1, 2015. http://www.pressrepublican.com.

Clermont, Lois, and Joe LoTemplio. "Prison Escape Probe Focuses on Contractors." *Buffalo News*, June 8, 2015. Accessed June 20, 2016. http://www.buffalonews.com.

Clermont, Lois, Nathan Ovalle, and Rob Fountain, eds. *Prison Break: The Story That Captivated a Nation*. Plattsburgh, NY: Press-Republican, 2015.

Clinton Prison at Dannemora. Plattsburgh, NY: Clinton County Historical Museum, 1987.

Clukey, Keshia. "During Search for New York Prison Escapees Richard Matt and David Sweat, Camp Owner Describes Close Call." *Timesunion*, June 27, 2015. Accessed July 2, 2015. http://www.timesunion.com.

———. "Strategy, Luck Key in Hunt for Richard Matt, David Sweat." *Timesunion*, July 12, 2015. Accessed October 3, 2015. http://www.timesunion.com.

Cohen, Shawn. "12 Prison Staffers Suspended after Convicted Killers Escape." *New York Post*, June 30, 2015. Accessed July 1, 2015. http://www.nypost.com.

Conley, Kirstan. "Escaped Killer Has a History of Breaking Out of Prison." *New York Post*, June 8, 2015.

Conlon, Kevin, and Mark Morgenstein. "Manhunt: Escaped Killers 'Could Literally Be Anywhere.'" CNN. Accessed September 4, 2015. http://www.cnn.com.

Connor, Tracy. "David Sweat Says Prison Guard Gene Palmer Not Involved in Escape: Prosecutor." *NBC News*, June 30, 2015. Accessed July 3, 2015. http://www.nbcnews.com.

———. "Joyce Mitchell on Night of Prison Escape: 'I Had No Intention of Ever Showing Up.'" *Today*. Accessed September 18, 2015. http://www.today.com.

———. "Joyce Mitchell on Role in Prison Escape: 'I Was Only Trying to Save My Family.'" *Today*. Accessed September 14, 2015. http://www.today.com.

Conway, James T. "3 Ways to Improve Clinton Prison." *Newsday*, July 12, 2015. Accessed September 11, 2015. http://www.newsday.com.

Cook, Jay D. "Sgt. Jay Cook, Officer Who Shot NY Prison Escapee David Sweat, Opens Up About Ordeal." *Today*, December 7, 2015. Accessed December 7, 2015. http://www.today.com.

Craig, Susanne, William K. Rashbaum, and Benjamin Mueller. "New York Prison Escapee Traded Art for Favors from a Guard." *New York Times*, June 25, 2015. Accessed July 3, 2015. http://www.nytimes.com.

Crilly, Rob. "Hunt Closes on Escaped Murderer in US after DNA Find." *Telegraph*, June 28, 2015. Accessed September 1, 2015. http://www.telegraph.co.uk.

DaSilva, Staci. "Dickinson Center Residents React to Mitchell's Arrest." MyChamplainValley.com, June 13, 2015. Accessed October 19, 2015. http://www.mychamplainvalley.com.

———. "Protecting America: The Responsibilities of U.S. Customs and Border Protection." MyChamplainValley.com, November 17, 2015. Accessed November 28, 2015. http://www.mychamplainvalley.com.

Dedam, Kim Smith. "In the Line of Fire." *Press-Republican*, July 29, 2015. Accessed October 7, 2015. http://www.pressrepublican.com.

Diaz-Balart, Jose. "Lyle Mitchell: 'I Don't Know What to Think.'" MSNBC, June 23, 2015. Accessed September 13, 2015. http://www.msnbc.com.

Dillon, Nancy. "Kin of Deputy Killed by David Sweat Relieved after Escaped Convict's Capture: 'One of Our Worst Nightmares Became Reality.'" *(New York) Daily News*, June 29, 2015. Accessed July 2, 2015. http://www.nydailynews.com.

Douthat, Ross. "The Dannemora Dilemma." *New York Times*, June 13, 2015. Accessed September 20, 2015. http://www.nytimes.com.

Dunleavy, Patrick. "How State Officials Enabled the 'Shaw-Skank' Prison Escape." *New York Post*, August 18, 2015. Accessed September 20, 2015. http://www.nypost.com.

DuVall, Eric. "Richard Matt's Troubles Began Early in Life." *Rochester Democrat and Chronicle*, June 10, 2015, A3.

Eckert, W. T. "Cuomo: The 'Nightmare' Is Over." *Watertown (New York) Daily Times*, June 29, 2015. Accessed November 9, 2015. http://www.watertowndaily times.com.

Engel, Pamela. "Prison Worker Tells 'Today Show' What Was Going through Her Mind When She Helped 2 Inmates Escape." *Business Insider*, September 11, 2015. Accessed October 3, 2015. http://www.businessinsider.com.

Engle, Lesley. "Defense, Clinton County DA Negotiating David Sweat Plea Deal." MyChamplainValley.com. Accessed September 23, 2015. http://www.mycham plainvalley.com.

Espinosa, J. Noel. "American Charged in Matamoros Murder." *Brownsville (TX) Herald*, February 24, 1998.

Evans, Brad. "David Sweat Won't Face Additional Charges in Franklin County." WPTZ.com, January 26, 2016. Accessed January 26, 2016. http://www.wptz.com.

———. "Joyce Mitchell to Be Sentenced for Role in Prisoner Escape." WPTZ.com. Accessed September 28, 2015. http://www.wptz.com.

———. "Lyle Mitchell's Attorney: Client Has No Intention of Leaving Wife." WPTZ.com, July 8, 2015. Accessed September 13, 2015. http://www.wptz.com.

———. "Matt Lauer on Joyce Mitchell: She Feels Remorse for Prisoner Escape." WPTZ.com. Accessed September 14, 2015. http://www.wptz.com.

———. "North County Residents Notified of Phone Taps during Prison Escape." WPTZ.com. Accessed January 8, 2016. http://www.wptz.com.

———. "Richard Matt Was Drunk at Time of Death, Autopsy Says." WPTZ.com, August 5, 2015. Accessed October 6, 2015. http://www.wptz.com.

Evans, Brad, and Liz Strzepa. "No Resolution Yet in Gene Palmer's Case." WPTZ. com, January 10, 2016. Accessed January 8, 2016. http://www.wptz.com.

Fantz, Ashley. "Drugs, Money, Love, and Cell Phones: How Prison Guards Go Bad." CNN, June 27, 2015. Accessed April 15, 2016. http://www.cnn.com.

———. "Ex-Prison Worker, Joyce Mitchell's Confession: Sex, a Painting and a Plan." CNN, July 29, 2015. Accessed September 9, 2015. http://www.cnn.com.

Filler, Lane. "The Fascination with the Dannemora Escapees." *Newsday*, June 16, 2015. Accessed September 20, 2015. http://www.newsday.com.

Fowler, Tara. "'I Was Doing Him a Favor': Five Things to Know About Gene Palmer, the Second Prison Worker Accused of Helping Convicts Escape." *People*, June 26, 2015. Accessed October 19, 2015. http://www.people.com.

———. "Joyce Mitchell's Husband Lyle: 'In My Heart I Know She Would Not Have Hurt Me.'" *People*, June 23, 2015. Accessed October 2, 2015. http://www.people.com.

———. "Tearful Joyce Mitchell Claims She Was Sexually Assaulted by Convict Richard Matt: 'There Was Never Any Consensual Sex.'" *People*. Accessed September 14, 2015. http://www.people.com.

Fox News. "English Teacher at California Jail Arrested in Connection to Escape of Three Inmates." January 28, 2016. Accessed January 28, 2016. http://www.fox news.com.

Fraser, Douglas F. "Letter: Sweat Deserves Humane Treatment." *Timesunion*, August 4, 2015. Accessed October 7, 2015. http://www.timesunion.com.

Frater, Jamie. "Top 10 Amazing Prison Escapes." ListVerse, August 27, 2008. Accessed September 13, 2015. http://www.listverse.com.

Genis, Daniel. "New York State's Scariest Person." Vice, June 10, 2015. Accessed August 31, 2015. http://www.vice.com.

Golding, Bruce. "Family 'Ditches' Slain Escapee's Corpse." *New York Post*, July 2, 2015, 10.

Goldstein, Sasha. "Escaped Prisoner Richard Matt Appears in 1997 Home Movie: 'This Is the Face of a Maniac!'" *(New York) Daily News*, June 23, 2015. Accessed July 9, 2015. http://www.nydailynews.com.

Gooley, Lawrence P. *Lyon Mountain: The Tragedy of a Mining Town*. Peru, NY: Bloated Toe Enterprises, 2004.

Gorin, Stephanie. "Legislators Want Tougher Laws for Those Who Help Prisoners Escape." WPTZ.com. Accessed November 17, 2015. http://www.wptz.com.

Gould, Martin. "Exclusive: It's a Family Affair—Prison Worker Who Helped Shawshank Murderers Dramatic Escape Had Grandfather Who Was Inmate at the Same Jail." *Daily Mail*, July 29, 2015. Accessed September 16, 2015. http://www.dailymail.co.uk.

Green, Alexa. "Family: David Sweat's Trouble Began at Early Age, Brought Butcher Knives to School." *Time Warner Cable News*, June 10, 2015. Accessed October 21, 2015. http://www.twcnews.com.

Grondahl, Paul. "Dozens Escaped Dannemora Prison before Richard Matt and David Sweat." *Timesunion*, July 10, 2015. Accessed September 18, 2015. http://www.timesunion.com.

———. "Prison Escapee David Sweat Severely Isolated, Controlled in 'The Box.'" *Timesunion*, July 23, 2015. Accessed October 5, 2015. http://www.timesunion.com.

Grondahl, Paul, and Keshia Clukey. "Dannemora's Old Guard 'Flabbergasted' by Prison Break." *Timesunion*, June 10, 2015. Accessed September 18, 2015. http://www.timesunion.com.

Guardian. "New York Prison Break: Escapees May Be Headed to Vermont." June 10, 2015. Accessed August 31, 2015. http://www.theguardian.com.

Gullo, Joe. "Report: Use of Force Justified in Killing Richard Matt, Capturing David Sweat." MyChamplainValley.com, November 12, 2015. Accessed November 12, 2015. http://www.mychamplainvalley.com.

Hamilton, Matthew. "Advocates' Report Details Alleged Abuses after Dannemora Escape." *Timesunion*, June 9, 2016. Accessed June 9, 2016. http://www.times union.com.

Hammer, Mike. "Crooked Prison Worker's Sex behind Bars." *National Enquirer*, August 5, 2015. Accessed October 2, 2015. http://www.nationalenquirer.com.

Harding, Robert. "Sgt. Jay Cook, Trooper Who Captured NY Prison Escapee, Wins National Award." Auburnpub.com, November 20, 2015. Accessed November 20, 2015. http://www.auburnpub.com.

Healy, Allie. "Watch: New Video Shows Escape Route Taken by Richard Matt, David Sweat." Syracuse.com, August 24, 2015. Accessed October 7, 2015. http://www.syracuse.com.

Hearn, Daniel Allen. *Legal Executions in New York State: A Comprehensive Reference, 1639–1963*. Jefferson, NC: McFarland, 1997.

Heath, Dan. "Dannemora Barber Marks 50 Years in Business." *Press-Republican*, December 6, 2015. Accessed December 6, 2015. http://www.pressrepublican .com.

Helsel, Phil. "Captured Prison Escapee Moved from Infirmary, Will Face Hearing." *NBC News*, July 15, 2015. Accessed October 4, 2015. http://www.nbcnews.com.

———. "We're Coming for You." *NBC News*, June 13, 2015. Accessed September 4, 2015. http://www.nbcnews.com.

Herbeck, Dan. "People Who Knew Richard Matt Describe His Jekyll-and-Hyde Past, Including Two Suicide Attempts." *Buffalo News*, June 21, 2015. Accessed October 17, 2015. http://www.buffalonews.com.

———. "Richard Matt Claimed He Was Beaten, Tortured in Mexican Prison." *Buffalo News*, June 26, 2015. Accessed August 31, 2015. http://www.buffalonews .com.

———. "Suspect in Grisly '97 Slaying Faces Trial, Officers Bring Matt Back after His Release from Mexican Prison." *Buffalo News*, January 25, 2007. Accessed April 18, 2016. http://www.buffalonews.com.

———. "Suspect in Rickerson Slaying May Have Fled the Country." *Buffalo News*, February 11, 1998. Accessed September 25, 2015. http://www.buffalonews.com.

Herbert, Geoff. "Lyle Mitchell Says Prison Escapees, Wife Planned to Drug Him: 'She Was in Too Deep.'" Syracuse.com, June 23, 2015. Accessed September 13, 2015. http://www.syracuse.com.

———. "Upstate NY Prison Worker's Ex-Husband: 'She's a Cheater,' Likely Assisted Escape." Syracuse.com, June 11, 2015. Accessed September 10, 2015. http://www.syracuse.com.

Hill, Jarred. "Law Enforcement Honored after Dannemora Manhunt." WPTZ.com, July 17, 2015. Accessed October 3, 2015. http://www.wptz.com.

———. "NY Community Honors Law Enforcement: 'Thank You Is Not Enough.'" WPTZ.com, July 17, 2015. Accessed October 4, 2015. http://www.wptz.com.

———. "State Lawmakers against Joyce Mitchell Keeping Pension." WPTZ.com, August 1, 2015. Accessed September 17, 2015. http://www.wptz.com.

Hill, Michael. "Lyle Mitchell's Attorney Says Client 'Blown Away' by Wife's Role in Prison Break." *Saratogian*, June 18, 2015. Accessed September 13, 2015. http://www.saratogian.com.

———. "Police: Prison Escapee Still Cooperating a Month after His Capture as Investigation Continues." *U.S. News and World Report*, July 29, 2015. Accessed October 7, 2015. http://www.usnews.com.

Hines, Ree. "Dr. Phil on Joyce Mitchell's Prison Escape Story: 'I Don't Buy What She's Saying.'" *Today*. Accessed September 14, 2015. http://www.today.com.

Hirsch, Zach. "'The Escape' Photography Series Zooms In on the Manhunt." NCPR. Accessed September 22, 2015. http://www.northcountrypublicradio.org.

———. "Intense Emotions at Joyce Mitchell's Sentencing." WRVO Public Media. Accessed September 29, 2015. http://www.wrvo.org.

———. "Veteran Corrections Officer Gene Palmer Sentenced to Six Months in Jail." *WSKG News*, February 29, 2016. Accessed February 29, 2016. http://wskgnews.org.

Holt, Lester, Michelle Melnick, and Tracy Connor. "The Inside Story of the Take-down of Prison Escapee Richard Matt." *NBC News*, August 27, 2015. Accessed September 14, 2015. http://www.nbcnews.com.

Jackson, Molly. "California Inmates' Escape Likely an Inside Job, Experts Say." *Christian Science Monitor*, January 26, 2016. Accessed January 26, 2016. http://www.csmonitor.com.

Jackson, Peter. "Colditz Escape: Tale of First British 'Home Run' Revealed." BBC, March 27, 2012. Accessed October 19, 2015. http://www.bbc.com.

Jacoby, Jeff. "Prison Escapes Show Why Life without Parole Is Not Enough." *Boston Globe*, July 16, 2015. Accessed October 5, 2015. http://www.bostonglobe.com.

Jarchow, Matt. "Graduating Officers Take Dannemora Lessons to Local Jails." *Time Warner Cable News*, August 25, 2015. Accessed September 20, 2015. http://www.twcnews.com.

Jaworowski, Matt. "Joyce Mitchell's Husband Breaks His Silence in Interview with Matt Lauer." *ABC 27 News*, June 23, 2015. Accessed October 2, 2015. http://www.abc27.com.

Jolly, Anna. "Prison Wall Getting Face Lift: Dannemora Barrier a Witness to History." *Press-Republican*, November 14, 2004. Accessed September 27, 2015. http://www.pressrepublican.com.

———. "Prison's Dairy Barn Burns: Clinton Correctional Was Primary Milk Operation for Upstate Prisons." *Press-Republican*, June 25, 2002. Accessed September 28, 2015. http://www.pressrepublican.com.

Kaplan, Don, Meg Wagner, and Corky Siemaszko. "Joyce Mitchell's Husband: Wife Swears She Didn't Have Sex with Prison Escapees—But 'Showed a Little Affection' to One." *(New York) Daily News*, June 23, 2015. Accessed October 2, 2015. http://www.nydailynews.com.

Kaplan, Sarah. "Richard Matt, the Dangerously Charismatic Escapee at the Center of the N.Y. Manhunt." *Washington Post*, June 12, 2015. Accessed September 27, 2015. http://www.washingtonpost.com.

Karcz, Rachel. "Clinton Correctional on Lockdown." WPTZ.com, August 31, 2015. Accessed September 5, 2015. http://www.wptz.com.

Karlin, Rick. "State Overtime Costs Are Going Up." *Albany Times-Union*, September 9, 2015, A1.

Kelly, Keith J. "Daily News Refuses to Correct Story Misidentifying 'Escapees.'" *New York Post*, August 13, 2015. Accessed October 6, 2015. http://www.nypost.com.

Keneally, Meghan. "Sexual Relationships between Inmates and Prison Employees Fairly Common, Statistics Show." *ABC News*, June 30, 2015. Accessed September 9, 2015. http://abcnews.go.com.

Khalid, Jerome. "Joyce Mitchell Pleads Guilty to Helping New York Inmates Escape." *Press Examiner*, August 9, 2015. Accessed September 20, 2015. http://www.pressexaminer.com.

King, Kate. "District Attorney's Plan to Prosecute Upstate Prison Escapee David Sweat Draws Criticism." *Wall Street Journal*, July 15, 2015. Accessed September 5, 2015. http://www.wsj.com.

———. "Joyce Mitchell's Husband Shocked by New York Prison Break." *Wall Street Journal*, June 23, 2015. Accessed October 2, 2015. http://www.wsj.com.

Kleinfield, N. R. "Broken Boys, Thieves, Killers, and Now Escapees." *New York Times*, June 12, 2015. Accessed July 9, 2015. http://www.nytimes.com.

Kourofsky, Niki. *Adirondack Outlaws: Bad Boys and Lawless Ladies*. Helena, MT: Farcountry Press, 2015.

KRGV.com. "Family of Man NY Escapee Killed Reacts to Death." June 26, 2015. Accessed August 31, 2015. http://www.krgv.com.

Krikorian, Greg. "Hollywood's Heiress's Marriage Turns to Dark Tale of Theft, Murder Plots." *Los Angeles Times*, January 28, 1992.

Kuharich, Megan, and Jeff Truesdell. "'Devastated' Father of Cop Shot by Escaped N.Y. Prisoner Relives Painful Memories with Son's Killer on the Loose." *People*, June 17, 2015. Accessed September 10, 2015. http://www.people.com.

Larimer, Sarah. "Woman Who Aided N.Y. Prison Escape: 'I'm Not the Monster That Everybody Thinks I Am.'" *Washington Post*, September 14, 2015. Accessed September 14, 2015. http://www.washingtonpost.com.

Layton, Jessica. "In Depth Preview: Matt and Sweat on the Inside, a Former Inmate Tells All." WNYT.com, July 23, 2015. Accessed October 5, 2015. http://www.wnyt.com.

Leahy, Michael Patrick. "Correction Officer Unwittingly Delivered Tools inside Frozen Meat to Convicts One Week before Escape." Breitbart, June 24, 2015. Accessed September 24, 2015. http://www.breitbart.com.

———. "Dateline NBC Provides Clue that Joyce Mitchell's Dannemora Story Does Not Add Up." Breitbart, September 21, 2015. Accessed September 21, 2015. http://www.breitbart.com.

———. "Lyle Mitchell's Almost-Last Supper." Breitbart, August 2, 2015. Accessed September 13, 2015. http://www.breitbart.com.

LeBrun, Fred. "Prison Escape Fallout." *Timesunion*, July 4, 2015. Accessed September 19, 2015. http://www.timesunion.com.

Levinson, Sean. "Prison Worker Who Helped 'Shawshank' Prisoners Escape Finally Speaks Out." *Elite Daily*, September 18, 2015. Accessed June 22, 2016. http://elitedaily.com.

LocalSYR.com. "Former Prison Worker Joyce Mitchell Interviewed as Part of State Investigation: Cooperation with Investigation Is Part of Mitchell's Plea Agreement." Accessed September 25, 2015. http://www.localsyr.com.

Lockport (NY) Union-Sun and Journal. "NY to Increase Mental Health Training for Prison Staff." December 28, 2016. Accessed December 28, 2016. http://www.lockportjournal.com.

Loman, Christine. "Border Agent Who Killed NY Prison Escapee Richard Matt: I Had No Choice." Syracuse.com, August 28, 2015. http://www.syracuse.com.

London, Eric. "New York Governor Implicated in Torture by State Prison Officials." World Socialist Website, August 12, 2015. Accessed November 30, 2015. http://www.wsws.org.

LoTemplio, Joe. "Corrections Team Honored in Albany for Manhunt." *Press-Republican*, March 15, 2016. Accessed March 15, 2016. http://www.pressrepublican.com.

———. "Mitchell Seeks Clemency from Prison Sentence." *Press-Republican*, June 12, 2016. Accessed June 12, 2016. http://www.pressrepublican.com.

———. "State Senate and Assembly to Hold Hearings on Prison Escape." *Press-Republican*, August 1, 2015. Accessed October 6, 2015. http://www.pressrepublican.com.

LoTemplio, Joe, and Suzanne Moore. "Judge Ordered Higher Restitution for

Mitchell than Set by Law." *Press-Republican*, November 6, 2015. Accessed November 6, 2015. http://www.pressrepublican.com.

LoTemplio, Joe, and Justin Trombly. "Story of the Year: Prison Escape." *Press-Republican*, January 1, 2016. Accessed January 1, 2016. http://www.pressrepublican.com.

Lucas, Dave. "Legislators Push 'Prisoner Privilege Limitation Law.'" WAMC, June 16, 2015. Accessed April 25, 2016. http://www.wamc.org.

Lyons, Brendan J. "Abuses Detailed in N.Y. State Prison Internal Affairs Unit." *Timesunion*, January 8, 2016. Accessed January 8, 2016. http://www.timesunion.com.

——. "Dannemora Prison Supervisors' Raises on Hold." *Timesunion*, June 26, 2015. Accessed July 2, 2015. http://www.timesunion.com.

Lyons, Brendan J., and Keshia Clukey. "Guards Raised Concerns About Lax Security at Dannemora Prison before Escape." *Timesunion*, July 2, 2015. Accessed July 2, 2015. http://www.timesunion.com.

Mallet, George. "Exclusive: NY Family Recounts Day Camper Shot by Richard Matt." WPTZ.com, September 11, 2015. Accessed September 13, 2015. http://www.wptz.com.

Mann, Brian. "Adirondack Life Looks at Aftershocks of the Dannemora Manhunt." NCPR, October 27, 2015. Accessed October 27, 2015. http://www.northcountrypublicradio.org.

——. "After Prison Break in New York, Viral Video Raises Questions." NPR, June 22, 2015. Accessed December 23, 2015. http://www.npr.org.

——. "Crossed Lines, Cut Corners and Cozy Relationships: Dannemora's Big Prison Break." NCPR. Accessed November 5, 2015. http://www.northcountrypublicradio.org.

——. "In Clinton Dannemora Prison, Violence, an Inmate Death and New Scrutiny." NCPR, December 22, 2015. Accessed June 22, 2016. http://www.northcountrypublicradio.org.

——. "In Dannemora Prison, an Inmate Death and New Scrutiny." NCPR. Accessed December 22, 2015. http://www.northcountrypublicradio.org.

——. "Inmate Dies at Clinton Correctional Facility in Dannemora." NCPR, May 24, 2016. Accessed May 24, 2016. http://www.northcountrypublicradio.org.

——. "NY Corrections Commissioner Hangs On, Despite Dannemora Escape, Scandals." NCPR, June 9, 2016. Accessed June 9, 2016. http://www.northcountrypublicradio.org.

——. "Shake-up Continues at Clinton Dannemora Prison." NCPR, July 2, 2015. Accessed October 18, 2015. http://www.northcountrypublicradio.org.

Mann, Brian, and Mark Kurtz. "Life behind the Walls of Dannemora." NCPR, June

15, 2015. Accessed September 20, 2015. http://www.northcountrypublicradio
.org.

Margolin, Josh, Aaron Katersky, and Emily Shapiro. "Escaped New York Inmate
Richard Matt Shot and Killed by Police." *ABC News*, June 26, 2015. Accessed
August 31, 2015. http://www.abcnews.go.com.

McKinstry, Lohr. "Prosecutor: Matt Swore He Wouldn't Be Taken Alive." *Press-
Republican*, June 27, 2015. Accessed January 4, 2016. http://www.press
republican.com.

McShane, Larry. "Upstate New York Cabin Where Escaped Inmates Richard Matt,
David Sweat Hid Out Provided Bare Necessities." *(New York) Daily News*, June
27, 2015. Accessed July 2, 2015. http://www.nydailynews.com.

Mendelsohn, Michael, Cat Rakowski, and Alexa Valiente. "The Complicated Relationship of NY Prison Escapees Richard Matt and David Sweat." *ABC News*,
July 24, 2015. Accessed October 5, 2015. http://www.abcnews.go.com.

Michel, Lou. "Escaped Killer's Son Shares Memories of His Notorious Father."
Buffalo News, September 2, 2015. Accessed September 27, 2015. http://www
.buffalonews.com.

———. "Funeral for Escapee Richard Matt to Be at Undisclosed Site." *Buffalo
News*, July 7, 2015. Accessed September 27, 2015. http://www.buffalonews.com.

———. "'See You on the Outside,' Matt Said in Letter Delivered to Daughter in
Buffalo Suburb." *Buffalo News*, July 3, 2015. Accessed October 10, 2015. http://
www.buffalonews.com.

Misciagna, Vanessa. "Frustration Abounds at Lack of IG Report of Prison Escape."
WPTZ.com. Accessed November 17, 2015. http://www.wptz.com.

———. "Troop Leader Reflects on Manhunt." WPTZ.com, July 29, 2015. Accessed
October 6, 2015. http://www.wptz.com.

———. "Union, Lawmakers Hope IG Prison Escape Report Brings Change."
WPTZ.com, November 17, 2015. Accessed November 28, 2015. http://www.wptz
.com.

Mohr, Ian. "Club Kid Killer Reveals Prison's Secret Sex Spots." *Page Six*, June 16,
2015. Accessed September 9, 2015. http://www.pagesix.com.

Molongoski, Brian. "Mitchell May Keep Pension Despite Conviction." *Watertown
(New York) Daily Times*, July 31, 2015. Accessed November 30, 2015. http://www
.watertowndailytimes.com.

Moore, Suzanne. "New Court Date Set for Gene Palmer." *Press-Republican*, October 16, 2015. Accessed October 16, 2015. http://www.pressrepublican.com.

———. "Police: Accidental Shooting Kills Plattsburgh Man." *Press-Republican*, July
6, 2015. Accessed April 22, 2016. http://www.pressrepublican.com.

Moore, Suzanne, and Lois Clermont. "Mitchell Statements to Police Conflict with

Claims in Court." *Press-Republican*, September 29, 2015. Accessed September 29, 2015. http://www.pressrepublican.com.

Mueller, Benjamin. "Size of Manhunt Area for 2nd Prison Escapee Significantly Expanded." *New York Times*, June 28, 2015, 22.

Mullen, Jethro, and Dan Simon. "New York Prison Escape Puts Staff-Inmate Relationships in the Spotlight." CNN, June 15, 2015. Accessed October 4, 2015. http://www.cnn.com.

Nadi, Aliza. "Sources Say Inmates Groom Staff at Breakout Prison." *NBC News*, June 12, 2015. Accessed September 4, 2015. http://www.nbcnews.com.

NBC News. "Prison Worker Joyce Mitchell Being Questioned in Connection with Brazen Escape." June 11, 2015. Accessed August 31, 2015. http://www.nbcnews .com.

Neville, Anne. "'Anything Is Possible' with Richard Matt, Says Cop Who Helped Imprison Violent Escapee 'for Life.'" *Buffalo News*, June 8, 2015. Accessed April 15, 2016. http://www.buffalonews.com.

Newberg, Rich. "Matt, Sweat Both Were in Trouble with the Law from an Early Age." WIVB.com, July 28, 2015. Accessed October 5, 2015. http://www.wivb .com.

Newsday. "Former Employee Who Helped Prisoners Says She Was Depressed, Trying to Protect Her Family." Accessed September 14, 2015. http://www.news day.com.

News 10. "NY to Increase Mental Health Training for Prison Staff." Accessed December 27, 2015. http://www.news10.com

New York Correction History Society. "The Evolution of the New York Prison System." Accessed September 27, 2015. http://www.correctionhistory.org.

New York Post. "Escaped Murderer Richard Matt Shot and Killed by Police." June 11, 2015. Accessed August 31, 2015. http://www.nypost.com.

New York State Adirondack Park Agency. "The Adirondack Park." Accessed October 17, 2015. http://apa.ny.gov/about_park/.

———. "History of the Adirondack Park." Accessed May 29, 2016. http://apa.ny .gov/About_Park/history.htm.

New York State, Governor Andrew M. Cuomo. "Governor Cuomo Announces $100,000 Reward for Information Leading to the Arrest of Escaped Inmates." June 7, 2015. Accessed September 4, 2015. http://www.governor.ny.gov.

New York Times. "Gov. Cuomo on the State of New York." January 13, 2016, A26.

———. "Guard Accused of Helping 2 Killers Escape Prison Pleads Not Guilty." November 4, 2015. Accessed November 5, 2015. http://www.nytimes.com.

———. "History of Prisoner Riots." September 14, 1971.

———. "Inmate Sentenced in Prison Breakout." February 4, 2016, A20.

———. "New York Prison Escapee Traded Art for Favors From a Guard." June 25, 2015. Accessed August 31, 2015. http://www.nytimes.com.

———. "With Power Tools and a Ruse, 2 Killers Flee New York Prison." June 7, 2015. Accessed August 31, 2015. http://www.nytimes.com.

Niagara County Sheriff's Office. "The History of the Niagara County Jail." Accessed September 10, 2015. http://www.niagarasheriff.com.

Oneida Daily Dispatch. "Police: NY Man Accidentally Killed by Friend's Handgun." July 7, 2015. Accessed December 9, 2015. http://www.oneidadispatch.com.

Ortiz, Erik. "Escaped New York Prison Convicts Are 'Going to Get Desperate.'" *NBC News*, June 12, 2015. Accessed September 4, 2015. http://www.nbcnews.com.

O'Shaughnessy, Patrice. "Jealous Ex-Boyfriend's Fury Killed 87 in Happy Land Fire 20 Years Ago." *(New York) Daily News*, March 24, 2010. Accessed October 2, 2015. http://www.nydailynews.com.

Palmer, Thomas. "Mystery Solved in N.Y. Daily News' Misidentification of Two Men as Dannemora Escapees Richard Matt and David Sweat in Leaked Cam Photo." *Timesunion*, August 2, 2015. Accessed October 6, 2015. http://www.timesunion.com.

Perkins, Jill. "Brother of Escaped Prisoner Richard Matt Shares Chilling Insight into the Mind of the Killer." WPTV, June 27, 2015. Accessed November 30, 2015. http://www.wptv.com.

Pfeiffer, Rick. "County Court: Letter Linked to Matt." *Niagara Gazette*, April 7, 2008. Accessed September 8, 2005. http://www.niagara-gazette.com.

———. "County Court: Max for Richard Matt," *Niagara Gazette*, May 31, 2008, A1.

———. "Courts: Bates Admits Lying to North Tonawanda Detectives in Matt Murder Trial." *Niagara Gazette*, March 17, 2008. Accessed September 7, 2015. http://www.niagara-gazette.com.

———. "Matt Stonewalled Cops, Detective Says" (regarding the testimony of former detective Glenn D. Gardner). *Tonawanda News*, April 10, 2008. Accessed September 8, 2015. http://www.tonawanda-news.com.

———. "Matt Trial: Murder Defendant Is Subject of Powerful Security Effort." *Niagara Gazette*, April 7, 2008. Accessed September 8, 2015. http://www.niagara-gazette.com.

———. "Matt Trial: Prosecution Rests." *Niagara Gazette*, April 11, 2008. Accessed September 8, 2015. http://www.niagara-gazette.com.

———. "Matt Trial: Step-Brother Links Matt to Murder." *Niagara Gazette*, March 27, 2008. Accessed September 8, 2015.

———. "North Tonawanda: Matt Trial Opens." *Tonawanda News*, March 14, 2008. Accessed September 6, 2015. http://www.tonawanda-news.com.

Pinedo-Burns, Aristides, and Lauren Effron. "Why Female Prison Employees May Risk Having Sexual Relationships with Inmates." *ABC News*, July 2, 2015. Accessed September 9, 2015. http://www.abcnews.go.com.

Pleasance, Chris. "Inside the Route 'Shawshank' Prisoners Used to Escape from Jail as Officials Claim It Took Them 20 Minutes to Get from Their Cells to the Outside World." *Daily Mail*, August 24, 2015. Accessed October 2, 2015. http://www.dailymail.co.uk.

———. "Trooper Who Shot Dead One of the 'Shawshank' Escapees Describes the Terrifying Moment the Cold-Blooded Killer Aimed a Shotgun at Him." *Daily Mail*, August 27, 2015. Accessed October 2, 2015. http://www.dailymail.co.uk.

Preval, Jeff. "Source: Richard Matt Had Escape Plan during '08 Murder Trial." *ABC News*, June 8, 2015. Accessed August 31, 2015. http://www.abcnews.go.com.

Pressconnects. "David Sweat's Brutal Path to Prison." June 13, 2015. Accessed October 21, 2015. http://www.pressconnects.com.

Press-Republican. "Editorial: No Sympathy, No Excuses." Accessed September 30, 2015. http://www.pressrepublican.com.

Prohaska, Thomas J. "Defense in Matt Murder Trial Centers on Inconsistencies." *Buffalo News*, April 11, 2015. Accessed September 8, 2015. http://www.buffalo news.com.

———. "Matt Tortured Rickerson before Death, Driver Says: Accomplice Gives Details of 27-Hour Car Ride." *Buffalo News*, March 15, 2008. Accessed September 7, 2015. http://www.buffalonews.com.

Pye, Dan. "Matt Trial: Richard Matt Found Guilty." *Niagara Gazette*, April 15, 2008. Accessed September 8, 2015. http://www.niagara-gazette.com.

Ramirez, Frank. "Cops: NY Prison Escapees Clashed on Cabin Stay before Splitting Up." *Ledger Gazette*, July 27, 2015. Accessed November 30, 2015. http://www.ledgergazette.com.

Rashbaum, William K. "New York Prisoner's Keys to Escape: Lapsed Rules, Tools, and Luck." *New York Times*, July 20, 2015. Accessed October 4, 2015. http://www.nytimes.com.

Rath, Ted. "Escaped Prisoner Heading to Canada? Good Luck with That." *Toronto Sun*, June 27, 2015. Accessed October 12, 2015. http://www.torontosun.com.

Raymo, Denise A. "CERT Team Returns with Gifts for Area Schools." *Press-Republican*, September 1, 2015. Accessed September 27, 2015. http://www.pressrepublican.com.

———. "Franklin County Fair to Honor Prison-Escape Searchers." *Press-Republican*, August 11, 2015. Accessed October 7, 2015. http://www.pressrepublican.com.

———. "Matt Autopsy Trip Costs County $700." *Press-Republican*, January 25, 2016. Accessed January 25, 2016. http://www.pressrepublican.com.

———. "Relative Defends Joyce Mitchell." *Press-Republican*, June 10, 2015. Accessed June 10, 2015. http://www.pressrepublican.com.

Reuters. "Escaped NY Prisoners May Have Had Help from Staff—Governor." June 8, 2015. Accessed June 17, 2016. http://www.reuters.com.

Rhee, Joseph, Eamon McNiff, Tom Berman, Cat Rakowski, and Lauren Effron, "NY Prison Break: The Final Hours before Escapees Richard Matt and David Sweat Were Captured." *ABC News*, July 23, 2015. Accessed October 5, 2015. http://www.abcnews.go.com.

Rojas, Rick. "Murderer's Escape Alarms Investigators from His Past." *New York Times*, June 8, 2015, A16.

———. "Search for Prison Escapees in Northern New York Became Boon for Region's Economy." *New York Times*, July 2, 2015. Accessed July 3, 2015. http://www.nytimes.com.

Rojas, Rick, and Winnie Hu. "David Sweat, New York Prison Escapee, Is Arraigned." *New York Times*, August 20, 2015. Accessed January 26, 2016. http://www.nytimes.com.

Rowe, Ben. "Prison Escape T-Shirts Are a Hot Item at New York County Fair." *(Sharon, PA) Herald*, July 30, 2015. Accessed October 6, 2015. http://www.sharon herald.com.

Sanchez, Ray, Evan Perez, and Ben Brumfied. "Prison Escapee Richard Matt Wrote to Daughter, Vowed to See Her, Report Says." CNN, July 3, 2015. Accessed September 20, 2015. http://www.cnn.com.

Sandoval, Edgar, Nancy Dillon, and Corky Siemaszko. "'She's a Cheater': Ex-Husband of Woman Suspected of Helping 2 Prisoners Escape Says She Was Unfaithful" (interview with Tobey Premo). *(New York) Daily News*, June 11, 2015. Accessed October 18 2015. http://www.nydailynews.com.

Schenectady Gazette. "Five Injured in Dannemora Prison Riot." June 29, 1987.

Schneider, Avery. "Buffalo-Based Law Firm Takes On Corrections Officers' Union as Client." WBFO, August 8, 2015. Accessed September 20, 2015. http://news .wbfo.org.

Schram, Jamie. "FBI Probing Escaped Killers' Prison for Drug-Smuggling Ring." *New York Post*, June 29, 2015. Accessed July 1, 2015. http://www.nypost.com.

Schram, Jamie, Bruce Golding, Kevin Fasick, and Larry Celona. "Escaped Killers Planned to Flee to Mexico." *New York Post*, June 29, 2015. Accessed July 1, 2015. http://www.nypost.com.

———. "Escaped Killer Tells All, Throws Shaw-Skank under the Bus." *New York Post*, June 30, 2015. Accessed July 1, 2015. http://www.nypost.com.

Schuppe, Jon. "New York Prison Break Exposes Risk of Inmate Con Games." *NBC News*, June 11, 2015. Accessed September 4, 2015. http://www.nbcnews.com.

Schwirtz, Michael. "Prison Escapee Was Killed after He Aimed Gun at Agent, Officials Say." *New York Times*, July 2, 2015. Accessed July 3, 2015. http://www.nytimes.com.

———. "Prison Inmates Put a Name to a Feared Guard Known as Captain America." *New York Times*, October 1, 2015. Accessed October 1, 2015. http://www.nytimes.com.

Schwirtz, Michael, and Michael Winerip. "Tunnels, Disguises and Sewers: Clinton Prison's Inmates Have Found Many Ways to Flee." *New York Times*, June 10, 2015, A20.

Scott, Catherine Leahy, inspector general. *Investigation of the June 5, 2015 Escape of Inmates David Sweat and Richard Matt from Clinton Correctional Facility*. Albany, NY: State of New York Office of the Inspector General, June 2016.

Semple, Kirk. "Manhunt Over and Patrols Gone, Calm and Quiet Return to Dannemora." *New York Times*, July 5, 2015. Accessed September 20, 2015. http://www.nytimes.com.

Serrano, Richard A. "Scheme to Kill Sheinbaum Alleged." *Los Angeles Times*, January 8, 1992.

Shapiro, Emily. "Prison Worker Joyce Mitchell Cries at Sentencing: 'If I Could Take It All Back I Would.'" *ABC News*. Accessed September 28, 2015. http://www.abcnews.go.com.

Shapiro, Emily, and Meghan Keneally. "NY Prison Break and How It Compares to 'Shawshank Redemption.'" *ABC News*, June 8, 2015. Accessed August 31, 2015. http://abcncws.go.com/.

Siemaszko, Corky. "David Sweat Was Almost Caught Twice during His 23 Days on the Lam: Report." *(New York) Daily News*, June 30, 2015. Accessed July 2, 2015. http://www.nydailynews.com.

———. "Son of Escaped Prisoner Says Richard Matt Is Genius Career Criminal: 'I Can't Believe They Let This Happen'—Report." *(New York) Daily News*, June 11, 2015. Accessed April 15, 2016. http://www.nydailynews.com.

16 WNDU. "New Video Maps Out Route of New York's CCF's Escaped Convicts." August 25, 2015. Accessed October 2, 2015. http://www.wndu.com.

Souders, Christine, and Megan Carpenter. "Dannemora Community Members Concerned About Safety." MyChamplainValley.com, June 6, 2015. http://www.mychamplainvalley.com.

Spector, Joseph. "Judge Unmoved by Prison Worker's Jail Break Tale." *Poughkeepsie Journal*, September 28, 2015. Accessed September 28, 2015. http://www.poughkeepsiejournal.com.

———. "Prison Escapees' Aide Sentenced." *Rochester Democrat and Chronicle*, September 29, 2015, 5A.

Spillman, Rose. "Reported Sighting Sends Search Crews to Titus Mountain." WCAX.com, June 23, 2015. Accessed December 5, 2015. http://www.wcax.com.

———. "Saying Thanks to Law Enforcement after Prison Escape Manhunt." WCAX.com, August 24, 2015. Accessed October 6, 2015. http://www.wcax.com.

Stanforth, Lauren. "Escapee David Sweat's Condition Improves, No Need for Surgery." *Timesunion*, June 30, 2015. http://www.timesunion.com.

Steier, Richard. "Editorial: NYSCOPBA's Dilemma." *Chief*, October 9, 2015. Accessed October 9, 2015. http://thechiefleader.com.

Stewart, Ali. "David Sweat Shares Dramatic Story on Escape." *News 10*, July 1, 2015. Accessed October 19, 2015. http://www.news10.com.

———. "Sweat Pleads Guilty in June Escape." *News 10*, November 13, 2015. Accessed November 13, 2015. http://www.news10.com.

Strzepa, Liz. "Assemblywoman Janet Duprey: I Don't Agree with Some of the Inspector General's Findings." WPTZ.com, June 10, 2016. Accessed June 10, 2016. http://www.wptz.com.

———. "Investigators Re-trace Path David Sweat and Richard Matt Used to Escape." WPTZ.com, August 26, 2015. Accessed September 14, 2015. http://www.wptz.com.

———. "North Country Residents React to David Sweat's Plea." WPTZ.com, November 13, 2015. Accessed November 13, 2015. http://www.wptz.com.

———. "Officials Confirm Gang-Related Fights at CCF." WPTZ.com, September 14, 2015. Accessed September 15, 2015. http://www.wptz.com.

———. "Phone Tapping during the Manhunt: Malone Woman Speaks Out." WPTZ.com, January 13, 2016. Accessed January 13, 2016. http://www.wptz.com.

———. "Residents React to Joyce Mitchell's Sentencing." WPTZ.com, September 28, 2015. Accessed September 28, 2015. http://www.wptz.com.

———. "Sheriff Mulverhill: IG Report Only Reflects Small Percentage of Officers at Clinton Correctional Facility." WPTZ.com, June 9, 2016. Accessed June 9, 2016. http://www.wptz.com.

Suburban Stats. "Population Demographics for Dannemora Village, New York, in 2015 and 2015." Accessed May 30, 2016. http://suburbanstats.org.

Suffield Times. "Federal Agent Who Fatally Shot Inmate Who Escaped from NY Prison Says He Had 'No Other Option.'" August 29, 2015. Accessed September 13, 2015. http://www.suffieldtimes.com.

Sykes' Regulars. "The History of the 20th Infantry." Accessed September 27, 2015. http://www.1-20infantry.org.

Tan, Avianne. "Joyce Mitchell's Husband Details Night of Escape." *ABC News*, June 18, 2015. Accessed October 2, 2015. http://www.abcnews.go.com.

Taylor, Kate. "Escapees' Helper Says She Was Driven by Fear and Depression." *New York Times*, September 14, 2015. Accessed September 14, 2015. http://www .nytimes.com.

Tedisco, Jim. "The 'Prisoner Privileges Limitation Law' to Protect Public from 'Dannemora-Duo-Like' Prison Breaks, Violence." Timesunion, June 16, 2015. Accessed April 25, 2016. http://www.timesunion.com.

Terrie, Philip G. *Contested Terrain: A New History of Nature and People in the Adirondacks*. Syracuse, NY: Syracuse University Press, 1997.

Thomas, Ellie S. "The House That Crime Built." Preservation Foundation, 2011. Accessed October 17, 2015. http://www.storyhouse.org.

Timesunion. "Escapee Richard Matt's Body Moved to Buffalo Area: Television Report Says Two Family Members Claimed Matt's Remains." July 3, 2015. Accessed September 1, 2015. http://www.timesunion.com.

———. "New York State Police Honor Troopers in Annual Ceremony." *Timesunion*, May 26, 2016. Accessed May 26, 2016. http://www.timesunion.com.

———. "Notable Inmates of Dannemora." June 9, 2015. Accessed September 20, 2015. http://www.timesunion.com.

Today. "Joyce Mitchell: Prisoner Richard Matt Gave Me Pills to Drug My Husband." Accessed September 18, 2015. http://www.today.com.

Todd, Nancy L. *National Register of Historic Places Registration: Church of St. Dismas, the Good Thief*. Albany: New York State Office of Parks, Recreation and Historic Preservation, September 1991.

Tolan, Casey. "A Psychic Is Suing New York State Because He Didn't Get the $100,000 Reward for Catching Two Escaped Inmates." Fusion, October 25, 2015. Accessed April 25, 2016. http://fusion.net.

Tonawanda News. "Matt, Hoak Honored." January 18, 1977, 16.

Toor, Mark. "Detective Union Head: Resisting Arrest Is at Heart of Problem." *Chief*, July 13, 2015. Accessed September 11, 2015. http://thechiefleader.com.

———. "Ex-Prison Worker Who Aided Escape Gets 2-7." *Chief*, October 5, 2015. Accessed October 5, 2015. http://thechiefleader.com.

Topeka State Journal. "Joseph Wood Sizzles." August 2, 1892, 1.

Virtanen, Michael. "David Sweat, Convicted Killer Who Escaped N.Y. Prison, Arraigned." *(Toronto) Star*, August 20, 2015. Accessed October 3, 2015. http:// www.thestar.com.

———. "Mothers, Experts Plead for Oversight of NY Prison System." *Pressconnects*, December 2, 2015. Accessed December 2, 2015. http://www.pressconnects .com.

———. "Overtime Report Suggests Costs of Hunt for Escaped Killers in New York

Topped $1 Million a Day." *London (ON) Free Press*, August 14, 2015. Accessed October 6, 2015. http://www.lfpress.com.

———. "Some Prisoners Say They Were Beaten after Murderers Richard Matt, David Sweat Escaped." 4 New York, August 11, 2015. Accessed September 17, 2015. http://www.nbcnewyork.com.

Wagner, Meg. "First Pic of Dead Killer." *(New York) Daily News*, July 2, 2015, 8.

———. "Joyce Mitchell Admits She Lied to Police About Prison Escape, Came Clean Because She Feared for Her Husband's Life." *(New York) Daily News*, September 18, 2015. Accessed September 18, 2015. http://www.nydailynews.com.

———. "Joyce Mitchell Says Inmate Richard Matt Forced Her to Perform Oral Sex: 'There Was Never Any Love between Myself and Mr. Matt.'" *(New York) Daily News*, September 14, 2015. Accessed September 14, 2015. http://www.nydailynews.com.

———. "SEE IT: Investigators Reenact Richard Matt and David Sweat's Escape, Say Crawl to Freedom Took 20 Minutes." *(New York) Daily News*, August 24, 2015. Accessed October 3, 2015. http://www.nydailynews.com.

———. "SEE IT: Lookalike for Escaped Killer David Sweat Says He Was Repeatedly Stopped during Manhunt." *(New York) Daily News*, June 29, 2015. Accessed July 2, 2015. http://www.nydailynews.com.

———. "Teens Say They Almost Picked Up Escaped Prisoner David Sweat, Who Asked for Ride Hours before Capture." *(New York) Daily News*, June 29, 2015. Accessed July 2, 2015. http://www.nydailynews.com.

Walden, Justin, and Rachel Coker. "Three Men Charged in NY Deputy's July 4th Killing." PoliceOne.com, July 8, 2002. Accessed September 10, 2015. http://www.policeone.com.

Walker, Tim. "Dannemora Prison Break: Inmates David Sweat and Richard Matt Joked Their Elaborate Escape Would Be 'Just Like The Shawshank Redemption.'" *Independent*, July 21, 2015. Accessed October 5, 2015. http://www.independent.co.uk.

Warren Tribune. "Delivery Plot Is Unearthed in Jail." November 10, 1927, 1.

Washington Post. "How to Escape a Maximum Security Prison." June 8, 2015. Accessed September 17, 2015. http://www.washingtonpost.com.

Washington Times. "Editorials from around New York." Accessed September 30, 2015. http://www.washingtontimes.com.

Watertown (New York) Daily Times. "Assemblywoman Balks at Plea Deal for Joyce Mitchell." July 31, 2015. Accessed October 6, 2015. http://www.watertowndailytimes.com.

———. "Clinton County DA Reflects on Aftermath of Dannemora Prison Break." August 3, 2015. Accessed September 20, 2015. http://www.watertowndailytimes.com.

———. "Escapee Matt's Death under Legal Review by Franklin DA." July 19, 2015. Accessed September 17, 2015. http://www.watertowndailytimes.com.

WBNS 10TV. "Escaped Killer in Good Physical Shape When Shot." June 28, 2015. Accessed September 1, 2015. http://www.10tv.com.

Weaver, Teri. "Report: The Inside Story of How David Sweat, Richard Matt Escaped from NY Prison." Syracuse.com, July 20, 2015. Accessed October 5, 2015. http://www.syracuse.com.

Weinstein, Matt. "Guardians of the Adirondacks." *Rochester Democrat and Chronicle*, November 22, 2015, 23A.

WICZ-TV. "Family and Friends Remember Slain Deputy Kevin Tarsia." July 4, 2015. Accessed September 10, 2015. http://www.wicz.com.

Winerip, Michael, and Michael Schwirtz. "An Inmate Dies and No One Is Punished." *New York Times*, December 13, 2015. http://www.nytimes.com.

Winerip, Michael, Michael Schwirtz, and Tom Robbins. "New York State Corrections Dept. Takes On Guards' Union Over Brutality." *New York Times*, April 12, 2016, A1.

Winter, Tom, and Tracy Connor. "Clinton County Prosecutor Open to Prison Breakout Trial for David Sweat." *NBC News*, August 20, 2015. Accessed October 5, 2015. http://www.nbcnews.com.

———. "Prison Seamstress Joyce Mitchell Pleads Guilty in Escape." *NBC News*, July 28, 2015. Accessed September 16, 2015. http://www.nbcnews.com.

WNYT.com. "Family Talks About Leading Police to Escaped Dannemora Prisoner." September 11, 2015. Accessed September 13, 2015. http://www.wnyt.com.

WPTZ.com. "Wife of 'Ousted' Prison Superintendent Speaks About Escape." Accessed November 18, 2015. http://www.wptz.com.

Yakas, Ben. "Woman Who Allegedly Helped Prisoners Escape Was Just Their Plan B, Sheriff Says." Gothamist, June 17, 2015. Accessed September 9, 2015. http://www.gothamist.com.

Yan, Holly, and Rob Frehse. "Report: New York Prison Escapee Spent Months Carving, Finding His Way Out." CNN, July 21, 2015. Accessed October 5, 2015. http://www.cnn.com.

Yan, Holly, Ray Sanchez, and Evan Perez. "David Sweat: Breakout Bud Matt Was out of Shape, Getting Drunk." CNN, July 1, 2015. Accessed September 1, 2015. http://www.cnn.com.

INDEX